Financial Management Theory in the Public Sector

Financial Management Theory in the Public Sector

Edited by Aman Khan and W. Bartley Hildreth

Westport, Connecticut
London

Library of Congress Cataloging-in-Publication Data

Financial management theory in the public sector / edited by Aman Khan and W. Bartley Hildreth.
    p.   cm.
Includes bibliographical references and index.
ISBN 1–56720–625–5 (alk. paper)
1. Finance, Public. I. Khan, Aman.
HJ141.F56   2004
352.4′01–dc22   2004014665

British Library Cataloguing in Publication Data is available.

Library of Congress Catalog Card Number: 2004014665
ISBN: 1–56720–625–5

First published in 2004

Praeger Publishers, 88 Post Road West, Westport, CT 06881
An imprint of Greenwood Publishing Group, Inc.
www.praeger.com

Printed in the United States of America

∞™

The paper used in this book complies with the
Permanent Paper Standard issued by the National
Information Standards Organization (Z39.48–1984).

10   9   8   7   6   5   4   3   2   1

To

Our Students

Contents

Preface

Public financial management lacks a coherent framework. To an extent, this is not at all unexpected given the diverse interests governments serve. Financial management decisions are needed in government to promote efficiency (such as lowest cost, highest return, positive net present value, etc.), as they do in the private sector. Achieving an efficiency goal, however, can be at variance or even in conflict with other policy goals, such as conducting affairs within a budget consensus, avoiding unnecessary risks, and complying with control systems and debt covenants.

Finance decisions also rest on human behavior, but choices are often colored by personal and institutional biases and imperfections. Furthermore, resources are limited, although the claims on those resources are endless. Yet, decisions must be made to preserve prescribed schedules.

Because the central premise for for-profit organizations is to increase owners' wealth, corporate financial management is more unified. Normative and predictive theories predominate. Corporate finance textbooks are thematically consistent. That is not to say that there are no competing theories and debates in that field. For public organizations, it is the latter, at least for now, that remains the principal focus.

This book contains 11 chapters, each focusing on a different theoretical approach to public financial management and each drawing heavily from recent developments in economics, business, and political science in order to provide a more contemporary view of the field and its theoretical underpinnings.

The first set of articles examines financial management from the ideals of human rationality and the explanation of deviations from the predictive model of expected utility maximization.

Information and certainty result in lower transaction costs and more efficient financial behavior. Building on the reality of financial transactions as the building blocks of financial management, John R. Bartle and Jun Ma find value in focusing on the contractual relationships involved in transactions, and the resulting theory of transaction cost economics, as a model of public financial management. As the authors note, however, governance structures and management capacity permit opportunistic behavior.

Rational choice analysis assumes both sides of a transaction have symmetric access to full and complete information. Information asymmetry is the absence of this fundamental condition, as when information is known to a buyer but not the seller, or a borrower but not the lender. Among the results is strategic uncertainty. Brian K. Collins and Aman Khan examine information asymmetry as a theoretical focus on public investment management. They find a good fit of the theory to the cash investment debacle in Orange County, California. Moreover, the authors provide an institutional framework for dealing with information asymmetry.

Principal-agent theory rests on transaction cost and questions of information asymmetry. The focus is to effectuate an efficient contract relationship between the principal and the agent as a way to avoid opportunistic behavior. Lawrence L. Marin applies this theoretical approach to service delivery contracting in general, and performance-based contracts in particular.

Instead of rational utility maximizing behavior, prospect theory offers a competing descriptive model of economic behavior under uncertainty and the attendant probability assessment. Kenneth A. Kriz defines prospect theory and applies the concepts to bond issuance and pricing. In doing so, he finds that loss aversion and status quo bias can help explain behavior that is contrary to rational economic behavior.

A second set of articles arises from an organizational perspective emphasizing process more than outcome. Individuals must make sense of their situation. In our context that means the process of making interpretations of an ambiguous financial context and putting these perspectives into practice. In the first article, Gerald J. Miller, Jonathan Justice, and Iryna Illiash outline this theory. Using examples from cash investment, debt issuance, and budget tradeoffs, they illustrate the interpretations that financial managers make.

Establishing governmental accounting standards may appear to be so technical that it could constitute one finance area uncluttered by theoretical offerings. However, William Earle Klay, Sam M. McCall and Curtis E. Baynes debunk this notion by examining the discourse among key participants in using accounting standards to focus on nonfinancial performance measurement reporting. Ambiguity permits competing groups to use powerful interpretive arguments.

Financial techniques and activities can be endowed with intrinsic values. William G. Albrecht and Thomas D. Lynch assert that a focus on the mix of such characteristics can separate perceptions from preferences in a "rational" manner. They develop these points using cash, debt, and capital budgeting techniques.

A third set of articles focuses on strategic financial behavior. Government financial management occurs within a framework of legal rules that guide behavior. It is easy to overlook the primacy of federalism in creating the opportunity for public financial management to flourish. Decentralization yields differences over capital market access, tax burdens, funding alternatives, and a myriad of other finance choices. By comparing several notions on fiscal decentralization, James Edwin Kee illustrates that hierarchy, not just markets, can influence financial choices.

Budget balance is the starting point of public financial strategy. Structural budget imbalances emerge when recurring revenues do not match recurring expenditures. Merl Hackbart and Jim Ramsey assert that policy choices create these imbalances, and that resolving the imbalances requires more than incremental decisions.

Faced with alternative ways of financing infrastructure, finance managers can learn from others. This form of best practices strategy is illustrated in Craig L. Johnson's chapter on financing information technology investments.

In the last chapter, L. R. Jones and Jerry L. McCaffery examine financial policy implementation. Specifically, they examine the status of reforms in the U.S. government that would create agency-level chief financial officers and efforts advancing performance measurement. Their analysis reveals a mix of success despite continuing barriers to reform in these critical areas of financial management.

Acknowledgments

This book is the result of collaborative efforts of many individuals, in particular the contributing authors, who not only took the time to write specifically for the book but also to serve as reviewers for many of the chapters that appear here. To each one of them, we extend our sincere appreciation. We also want to acknowledge the names of several individuals who read and commented on various chapters, in particular Professors Bradley T. Ewing, Robert J. Freeman, Brian Gerber, and Scott E. Hein, Texas Tech University; Professor Charles Coe, North Carolina State University; Professor Fred Thompson, Willamette University; Professor Robert P. Smith, Clemson State University; and Dr. John P. Forrester, the General Accounting Office. We extend our heartfelt thanks to them all.

CHAPTER 1

Managing Financial Transactions Efficiently
A Transaction Cost Model of Public Financial Management

John R. Bartle and Jun Ma

> Striving for efficient resource allocation is often thought of primarily as an investment problem–a matter of choosing the economic activities that yield the greatest net social benefits. Yet the more one focuses on how to make the choices and appreciates the difficulties involved, the more one is drawn to expand the view of the problem to include organizational as well as investment terms. (Friedman, 2002, p. 641)

As an area of study, public financial management (PFM) is in need of a theoretical orientation that would move it beyond the dominant normative "best practice" framework, which focuses on the rules of accounting, managerial control, and legal compliance. Typically this orientation outlines how financial management should be done in public agencies to achieve the goals of compliance with legal requirements, accounting standards, financial control, and, to some degree, resource optimization. These are important normative values, but are certainly not the only ones that are compelling. Further, positive theory–explanation and prediction of varying patterns of behavior–is not well advanced in PFM. In this chapter, we develop a transaction cost model of PFM that provides the basis for both a positive and normative theory. We ground the theory in financial transactions, which are the building blocks of public institutions. However, we also recognize the centrality of organizational capacity in the crafting of institutions, and like Friedman see the need to extend transaction cost models to take account for organizational learning.

First, we review literature that has applied transaction cost economics to PFM. Although several theorists have recognized the potential of transaction cost economics, such potential remains unrealized. Next we specify the promise of applying transaction cost economics to PFM. We then illustrate the types of transaction costs that are common in hierarchical and contractual governance structures. The ubiquitous management functions of coordination, motivation, and control imply costs for any governance structure, and a good institutional structure will minimize these costs. We then argue that traditional transaction cost economics has little to say about how effective governance structures develop, and argue for reinterpreting Coase's (1937) classic article on the nature of the firm and incorporating the recent rebirth of organizational capacity theory. We argue that governance structure is primary, but that management does matter. Good management will reduce the transaction costs of organizing and managing financial transactions, which have not been completely eliminated by effective governance structures. Therefore, what we propose is an enhanced transaction cost model. We then illustrate the application of this model to PFM using a historical study of tax collection. Finally, we discuss a research agenda applying this model to PFM.

Literature Review

Since the 1980s and especially the 1990s, transaction cost economics has been applied to explore many important issues in private financial management, including procurement (Bajari and Tadelis, 2001), management control (Spekle, 2001), capital structure (Williamson, 1988; Kochhar, 1996; Goswami, 2000), and capital budgeting (Arya et al., 2000). Several theorists have recognized the potential of transaction cost theory by implicitly or explicitly applying it to specific areas of PFM. Premchand (1993) has applied it to expenditure management, Reed and Swain (1997) to cash management, and Schwartz (1996) to inventory and cash management. This literature recognizes that several pecuniary and nonpecuniary costs are relevant in managing government finance, such as ordering, holding and outage costs in inventory management, and trade-offs among the costs associated with liquidity, security, and return in cash management. Recently, Bartle and Ma (2001) argued that transaction cost theory can be applied to many fields of PFM, such as managing cash, debt, investments, pensions, risk, and purchasing, because in these fields "it is not much of a leap of faith to assert that governments attempt to achieve their objectives in the most efficient way (including transaction costs), and not too bold to assert that they should" (p. 176). But none has made efforts beyond suggesting the potentials of transaction cost theory.

In PFM, there are two fields where formal transaction cost models are most developed: procurement and management control. A central theme in government procurement is the choice of procurement contracts. McAfee and McMillan (1988) develop a model of optimal contract, which takes into account four effects: the bidding competition effect, the risk-sharing effect, the moral hazard effect, and the cost-padding effect (pp. 23–45). Another issue is the role of post-contractual price adjustment in public procurement. The dominant view is that post-contractual price adjustment is one kind of inefficiency in government procurement, which is sometimes notoriously observed in large procurement projects. These post-contractual price adjustments are viewed as a result of commitment failure. But in their two-period model of procurement focusing on the hold-up problem, Bos and Lulfesmann (1996) challenge this view from the perspective of transaction cost economics, and argue that there is a rationale in the upward renegotiation of contractual prices in public procurement.

In the field of management control, Thompson and Jones (1986), and Thompson (1993) have applied the concepts of transaction cost theory to budget execution. They examine two variables: the cost structure of production and the heterogeneity of the outputs. This creates four typologies, which then helps determine whether responsibility should be placed with either individuals or organizations, and whether control should be *ex ante* or *ex post.* They argue that managers should then use these typologies in deciding what controls are feasible and desirable. They go on to suggest that substantial cost savings are possible by matching the proper control techniques to each public service. Thompson and Jones apply this conceptual framework to the relationship between the budget controller and the agency in the design, execution, and monitoring of budgetary contracts.

However, despite these early efforts, the theoretical potential of transaction cost theory is underdeveloped. Many issues of PFM have not been analyzed from this perspective. Even where it has been applied, transaction cost models have been developed by economists who have less interest in management issues. The control model developed by Thompson and Jones holds an ambiguous attitude about transaction cost theory because it seems that they, especially Thompson (1993), focus on control cost more than the impact of transaction costs.

PFM as Contracting

Transaction cost theory is a promising perspective for PFM for two main reasons: the ubiquity of transactions, and the widely accepted value of efficiency in this area. As Williamson (1993) argues, "any issue that can be posed directly or indirectly as a contracting issue can be addressed to advantage in 'transaction management' terms."

Many issues of revenue collection are essentially contracting issues. In principle, revenues could be collected with three different types of contracts between the revenue collecting authority and revenue collector: wage, share and fixed-rent contracts. Wage contracts mean that the government hires revenue collection agents on fixed wages, and the revenue collection agents agree to turn over to the government all the revenues they collect. Share contract occurs when *in lieu* of a wage payment, the revenue collection agent holds onto a prespecified share of the revenues collected. Fixed-rent contracts occur when the revenue collectors agree to pay a prespecified fixed sum to the government in return for the right to the entire revenue proceeds (Azabou and Nugent, 1988, p. 684). Before the 19th century, the fixed-rent contract was the dominant form of revenue collection. The wage contract is the dominant form of revenue collection in modernized systems, so much so that other methods of collecting revenues are seen as anomalous.

Many issues in expenditure management also are contracting issues. Expenditure management is a three stage administrative process: (1) determination of the policies, objectives, and resources needed; (2) allocation of resources needed for those objects; and (3) assurance that specific tasks are carried out economically, efficiently, and effectively (Premchand, 1993, p. 22). Transaction costs (bargaining and decision costs) are involved in determining expenditure policy because such policy is essentially an expenditure contract between elected officials (with the assistance of the central budgeting bureau, or CBB) and spending agencies. Therefore, what occurs in creating an expenditure contract is a "political transaction cost" (North, 1990).

After a budget is approved, an expenditure contract exists between the CBB (on behalf of elected officials) and spending agencies in which the CBB controls the policy making promises to supply funds under specific conditions, and the spending agency agrees to spend the money in ways that have been agreed upon. Both elected officials and spending agencies may behave opportunistically. Contract enforcement in this financial transaction has not been overlooked by academic scholarship; researchers from political science and public choice have produced a huge body of literature on this issue. However, almost all of this literature focuses on the opportunism of spending agencies, that is, "bureaucratic opportunism" (Niskanen, 1971 and 1975; McCubbins, Noll, and Weingast, 1987 and 1989), overlooking the potential that elected officials may behave opportunistically by not keeping their budgetary commitments to supply funds. Nearly 30 years ago, Caiden and Wildavsky (1974) vividly described a picture of noncredible budgeting commitment by politicians. In their study of budgeting in developing countries, they found that budgets were disappearing and instead that repetitive budgeting, under which budgets are made and remade throughout the year, was dominant because the financial environment was characterized by poverty and uncertainty (pp. 66–78). In such an environment, appropriations for an agency will not necessarily be available from the ministry of finance; as a result, expenditure contracts are not enforceable, and budgeting commitment is not credible. Government agencies living under repetitive budgeting will develop certain strategies to hedge themselves against risks arising from budgetary uncertainty and opportunism, such as creating autonomous funds under their own control.

In financial transactions occurring between the government and the private sector, such as procurement and debt issuance, contracting behaviors exist as well. In public procurement, financial transactions can be arranged by three kinds of contracts: the fixed-price contract, cost-plus contract, and incentive contract. Transaction costs exist in creating and enforcing these contacts, and will be an important determinant of contractual choices. In public debt management, there are contracts between the debt issuer (the government) and debt buyers, and a variety of institutional factors that reflect the uncertainties in these contracts, such as debt insurance and loan guarantees.

In sum, many if not all issues of PFM can be viewed as contracting issues. Financial transactions between the government and private firms are market transactions, whereas financial transactions between elected officials and spending agencies and between the central treasury and revenue collection agencies are hierarchical transactions. But they all involve contracting behaviors. Therefore, PFM can productively be approached from the perspective of transaction cost theory.

Transaction Costs in PFM

PFM involves effectively organizing, directing, and managing financial transactions in the public sector. However, it is carried out in a world where transaction costs are positive and where effective management and institutional design are relevant. Organizing and managing these transactions involve transaction costs. Financial transactions differ depending on both the nature of the transaction and the way they are organized and managed. A transaction cost model of PFM evaluates institutional and contractual arrangements and management innovation on the basis of how well they solve various transaction cost problems by the criteria of institutional, contractual, and management efficiency. As Milgrom and Roberts (1992) argue, "[U]sing efficiency as a positive principle requires taking care about whose interests are being served and what kinds of arrangements are feasible" (p. 49).

Following transaction cost economics, it is assumed that (1) actors in PFM exhibit bounded rationality; (2) actors may behave opportunistically in some circumstances; and (3) the risk preference of managers is a variable and not a constant (Bartle and Ma, 2001). The basic unit of analysis in PFM is the financial transaction, that is, the transfer of funds from one organization to another. Financial management can be viewed as a process of organizing and managing financial transactions. The variety of ways of doing so reflects the fact that financial transactions differ in some basic attributes. Financial transactions vary in dimensions such as frequency, uncertainty and complexity; the ability to measure output and performance; connectedness of transactions within an agency and to related organizations; asset specificity (which can include human or political assets as well as physical assets); and information distribution (Williamson, 1975, 1985; Milgrom and Roberts, 1992; Spekle, 2001; Bartle and Ma, 2001). These different dimensions are the building blocks of a transaction cost analysis of management, and a test of this theory would look to explain variation in the success of organizational structure using these variables.

In applying transaction cost theory to management, Milgrom and Roberts (1992) identify two basic management functions: coordination and motivation. Different organizational forms and institutional and contractual arrangements give rise to transaction costs in coordinating and motivation (p. 29). In PFM we add a third basic management function, control. These three costs are outlined in the following sections.

Coordinating Costs

The efficient management of financial resources requires specialization and an appropriate division of labor in executing financial transactions, giving rise to the need for coordination among various agencies. In revenue management, coordination between the central treasury and various revenue collection agencies is necessary. In managing expenditures, coordination is required between the CBB and various spending agencies, between high-level officials and administrative branches within an agency, and in some cases between government agencies and private firms.

But coordination is not cost free; transaction costs will occur. Coordination can be achieved through two basic mechanisms: market and hierarchy. A market mechanism is used when the government agency transacts with private firms. In this case, "transaction costs associated with coordination problems arise from the need to determine prices and other details of the transaction, to make the existence and location of potential buyers and sellers known to each other, and to bring the buyers and sellers together to transact" (Milgrom and Roberts, 1992, p. 29). Hierarchy is common in PFM of course, but this arrangement gives rise to transaction costs as well. As Milgrom and Roberts (1992) state,

> The transaction costs of coordination through hierarchies–whether private or governmental–are primarily the costs of transmitting up through the hierarchy the initially dispersed information that is needed to determine an efficient plan, using the information to determine the plan to be implemented, and then communicating the plan to those responsible for implementing it. These costs include not only the direct costs of compiling and transmitting information, but also the time costs of delay while the communication is taking place and while the center is determining the plan (p. 29).

Any serious student of bureaucracy understands the pervasive challenge of coordinating through hierarchy.

In expenditure management, the expenditure process reflects the conflicting desires and risk preferences of the CBB, spending agencies, outside principals, and outside contractors. The CBB and outside principals (like the public and the legislature) typically hope to control spending whereas spending agencies hope to spend. Within the spending agency, higher-level officials are more oriented toward controlling spending whereas lower-level officials are often more oriented toward spending (Reed and Swain, 1997, p. 169). In other words, they have different interests and risk preferences. In the expenditure process, policymakers first decide on general and specific spending plans, and the CBB and line officials will communicate expenditure authority from policymakers to spending agencies, who in turn communicate the expenditure plan to the subordinate branches. Information costs and decision-making costs are important in this process of expenditure coordination. Similarly, transaction costs of coordination through hierarchy will occur in revenue management, especially between the central treasury and revenue collection agencies. The central agency must first interpret legislation and write rules to operationalize legislation, and communicate such policies to revenue collection agencies, their agents, and taxpayers. Sometimes, the central agency needs to coordinate collections among the different agencies that collect revenue, such as motor vehicle departments or alcohol control commissions.

Transaction cost theory contends that transaction costs are determined by the attributes of contractors and of financial transactions. Coordination costs will be higher in situations where opportunism is prevalent, risk preferences of contractors differ, asset specificity exists, financial transactions are complex and uncertain, financial transactions are connected, and when information distribution is asymmetric. Nevertheless, sometimes coordination costs are institutionally determined. For example, in a system of multiple principals where checks and balances and separation of powers exist, financial management may be in the hands of many independent fiscal officials (McKinney, 1995, p. 9). This will increase transaction costs of coordination. As Milgrom and Roberts (1992) argue, there are also transaction costs of maladaptation when communication is beset with information impactedness, and the decision- makers have insufficient or inaccurate information (p. 29). This also exists in PFM. For example, in expenditure management, when policymakers have made an expenditure plan with insufficient or inaccurate financial information, transaction costs of maladaptation will occur when there is a need for transfers and reprogramming of expenditure authorities.

Motivation Costs: *Ex Ante* Incentive Alignment

In PFM, the existence of opportunism and the need for coordination suggests that motivation is vital. First, contractors need to be motivated to behave honestly. The inclination of contractors to behave opportunistically will be strong when financial transactions involve information asymmetry, infrequency, difficulty of measuring output and performance, and asset specificity. In these cases, motivation will affect performance. Second, as a result of specialization, different sectors of PFM have different interests; therefore, various parts of the administration must be motivated to coordinate.

One of the strengths of the market system is that it causes self-interested behavior to be channeled into a socially desired direction. But, there is no similar coordinating mechanism in the public sector. In this case, as Milgrom and Roberts argue,"[O]rganizations either must rely on individuals to ignore their own self-interests . . . or else they must devote ingenuity and resources to bring coherence between individual self-interest and the social or organizational objectives" (1992, p. 28). The former cannot be depended on. The latter, according to Huang (2002), is a kind of "implicit control mechanism," that attempts to cause the preferences of principals and agents to converge. A variety of devices used in the private sector to make preferences converge are generally not available in the public sector, such as stock options, incentive wages, bonuses, and promotion incentives. Because of these characteristics of the institutional environment of PFM, the transaction costs of designing and implementing preference-converging measures are high. Also, as has been discussed, in certain financial transactions, the transaction costs of motivating contractors to act honestly will be very high.

In summary, motivation involves several transaction costs of designing and running a motivation system: the costs of measuring effort and performance of financial managers, information costs of designing an effective incentive contract, information costs of linking managerial efforts with financial outcomes, and costs of enforcing agreements to ensure that financial managers and contractors will honor commitments. Transaction cost economics fully recognizes how high these transaction costs are and that it is impossible to address and resolve all of the relevant contracting issues in advance. It emphasizes that optimal incentive contracts are costly to design and implement, and *ex post* governance structures are necessary, whereas agency theory stresses designing optimal incentive contracts in advance and *ex ante* incentive alignment (Williamson, 1990, p. 111). We adopt the former perspective because we believe it is more realistic.

Control Costs: *Ex Post* Safeguard

The need for control is widely accepted in PFM, although there is no agreement on the degree of control. The need for control arises for two reasons. First, financial managers are not residual claimants, thus they may behave opportunistically. Second, effective motivation systems may be difficult to design and implement. Therefore, it is not difficult to understand that traditionally PFM, especially expenditure management, has focused on the importance of control. For a government agency, controlling expenditures includes external and internal control. External controls are exercised by outside agencies like the legislature, the CBB, the executive office, the central bank, or others. Ideally, internal controls are the operational controls that supplement the goals of the central financial agency. Once the expenditure plan is approved, the government agency will turn to management and operational control processes (Premchand, 1993, pp. 31–33). Both external and internal controls are needed because agency problems exist in the expenditure process. Spending agencies may not spend money economically, or not spend for the purposes agreed upon, or corruption may occur in this process. In revenue administration, taxpayers may seek to avoid paying taxes or bribe revenue collectors, whereas the latter may have interests in colluding with taxpayers to cheat the revenue authority. Therefore, effective control systems are necessary in revenue administration as well.

Control is not cost free. To effectively control opportunism in PFM, information about spending and revenue collection agencies' behaviors is required. Moreover, a system of control over the CBB and the central treasury is also needed because financial managers at this level may also be inclined to behave opportunistically by shirking and colluding with subordinates. In sum, transaction costs occurring in control are mainly information costs and monitoring costs. In certain situations, transaction costs of controlling opportunistic behaviors will be very high. Where opportunism is prevalent, transactions are specific, information distribution is asymmetric, transactions are complex and uncertain, and output or performance is difficult to measure.

Discussion

In PFM, because the central agencies tend to depend on the information provided by the administrative agencies, coordination is very important. The CBB or treasury agency cannot completely rely on information provided by spending agencies or revenue collection agencies because they may distort information provided. To alleviate the problem of information asymmetry, the central agencies may develop their own information collection methods to carry out various control mechanisms. But, the dilemma in PFM is that spending agencies or revenue collection agencies must be given sufficient incentives and autonomy to behave efficiently and effectively, because too many rules and controls may harm the performance of revenue and expenditure managers. Indeed, public managers–unlike their counterparts in private management–are often so tightly constrained that they are unable to use many incentive plans to motivate employees. As Premchand (1993) points out, compliance in public expenditure management depends upon not only control from the CBB but also on motivation and autonomy. Overly tight control can create disincentives for effective financial management in spending agencies. Moreover, to further effect internal control, the central agency must design a control system that "integrates incentives in such a way that participants find it easy and compelling to comply in enforcing their internal control duties" (McKinney, 1995, p. 93). This means that a motivation system is also necessary for the purpose of control. The challenge then is to design a governance structure and management tools to simultaneously solve coordination, motivation, and control problems.

Another question is relative magnitude of motivation and control. Huang (2002) argues that because explicit control mechanisms are usually compounded by difficulties of monitoring subordinates' efforts and outputs, new institutional economics tends to focus on implicit control mechanisms aiming to converge preferences between principal and agents. But this is not our focus. As Williamson (1990) points out, although agency theory stresses designing optimal incentive contracts to motivate agents, transaction cost economics contends that such a contract is costly to design and implement, and *ex post* control mechanisms are necessary (p. 111). Following Williamson, we argue that in PFM there are high transaction costs of designing and implementing contracts, therefore *ex post* control mechanisms are necessary.

Governance Structure, Organizational Competency, and Management in PFM

Governance Structure

Williamson (1990) argues that the underlying hypothesis of transaction cost economics is to "align transactions (which differ in their attributes) with governance structures (which differ in their costs and competencies) in a transaction cost economizing way" (p. 110). We now turn to a discussion of governance structures in PFM.

According to transaction cost theory, certain mechanisms are efficient instruments for achieving mutual cooperation: centralized coordination (Milgrom and Roberts, 1992, p. 32) and credible commitment (Williamson, 1983). First, centralized coordination means that it is necessary to develop a strong and effective central treasury and CBB to coordinate various revenue collection and expenditure activities. This is even true when revenue collection and expenditures activities are fragmented and dispersed as in the French *ancien regime* (Caiden, 1978; Bosher, 1970), in U.S local governments before the Progressive Era (Rubin, 1998), and when various government agencies established their own autonomous funds (Caiden and Wildvasky, 1974). We have taken the existence of the central treasury for granted; however, historically there was no central treasury in many countries. Different revenues were collected by different collection agencies, and from these collection agencies revenues went directly to various expenditures according to plans. Therefore, less money collected would go to the central agency, and the state never had a clear sense of how much revenue it had and how much it spent (Bosher, 1970). In this situation, coordination is very costly. Furthermore, as Caiden and Wildavsky (1974) indicate, even if the central treasury exists, it may be ineffective in coordinating revenue collection and expenditure activities when various spending agencies collect and spend their own autonomous funds at their own discretion.

Second, credible commitment is vital for effective coordination because when each actor honors his contract, coordination is easy to attain. Unfortunately, in PFM, many financial commitments are not credible. For instance, in expenditure management, "[O]nce the budgetary allotments are made, the administrative agencies view them as property rights or entitlements—unalterable and available for them to spend for a specified period" (Premchand, 1993, p. 83). In this case, if the CBB is unable to keep its budgetary commitment, spending agencies affected will have less incentive to coordinate.

As for motivation, it is difficult to design and implement optimal incentive contracts in government. This may be one reason for the control and rule orientation of PFM. For example, some have suggested that to motivate spending agencies to use their funds economically, spending agencies should be allowed to transfer unspent funds from one period to the next. However, it is very difficult to carry out such an incentive contract, especially when the agency managers and the CBB do not already have a trusting relationship because, as Weimer and Vining (1996) write, "[T]he manager must anticipate the possibility that the budget office will expropriate the savings by reducing the base budget in the next period" (p. 105). In this case, rules may be required to make credible a commitment not to expropriate the savings.

Finally, we address control-oriented governance structures. Ouchi (1980) identifies three basic mechanisms of control: markets, bureaucracies, and clans. Market control relies on prices and competition, bureaucratic control relies on rules, and clan control relies on an informal network and "a relatively complete socialization process that effectively eliminates goal incongruence between individuals." Riahi-Belkaoui (2002) also applies these three types of management controls in management accounting. All three mechanisms are at work in PFM. Market control works in the cases procurement and debt management, whereas clan control may operate through informal organization within government agencies. But, most often controls in PFM rely on rules. To implement rule-based control systems will result in information costs in designing rules, transaction costs of informational impactedness and asymmetry in implementing rules, and information and measurement costs to detect financial mismanagement and corruption in enforcing rules. Moreover, although rules in PFM contribute to reducing transaction costs when they help to protect the public funds from opportunism, at a certain point additional rules will increase transaction costs of organizing and managing financial transactions.

Organizational Capacity

Although transaction cost economics emphasizes *ex post* governance structure, it has little to say about the development or maintenance of governance structure. To understand the cost and competency variation of governance structures, it is necessary to draw on the recent rebirth of organizational capacity theory. This rebirth is partly built upon the reinterpretation of Coase's (1937) classic article on the nature of the firm.

Langlois and Foss (1999) argue that Coase explained the emergence of the firm by two dimensions of costs: transaction costs (i.e., "costs of using the price mechanism") and qualitative coordination costs. The latter has been a central topic of organization capacity theory. This theory states that production knowledge has two dimensions: (1) organization capabilities, that is, the knowledge about how to produce; and (2) qualitative coordination, that is, the knowledge about how to link together the productive knowledge of people and organizations. Although Coase "may have put aside the issue of capabilities, he did not neglect the issue of coordination" (Langlois and Foss, 1999, p. 203). However, transaction cost theory has overlooked the production side of the firm, "thus capturing only part of what Coase called 'the nature of the firm'" (Langlois and Foss, 1999 p. 202). Although transaction cost is an important dimension to explain the existence of firm, as Hodgson (1998, p. 181) states, transaction cost minimization is "the thin glue" holding the firm together, and it is not appropriate to place the entire or major burden of explanation on the concept of transaction cost.

This has important implications for applying transaction cost theory to PFM. It means that in identifying and designing efficient governance structures in response to transaction cost problems, we must go beyond transaction cost economics and apply the knowledge of organizational competency (Chandler, 1992). This will help us understand how government agencies develop competencies through individual and organizational learning. Transaction cost theory has ignored some fundamental features of organizations, and one such salient feature is "the distinctive kind and rate of group and individual learning that takes place within organizations" (Hodgson, 1998, p. 196). The emphasis on learning in organizational capacity theory supplements transaction cost theory. It attributes the existence of the firm to "the transmission of information and the generation of appropriate practical knowledge" (Hodgson, 1998, p. 192). The capacity of the firm to "safeguard and enhance group and individual competence" explains its existence (Hodgson, 1998, pp.192–193). Moreover, it argues that individual and group learning are undertaken within specific organizational frameworks, and thus are shaped by organization culture, organization structure, and prior existing knowledge, creating a path dependence. Therefore organization culture, organization structure, and path dependency determine the cost and competency of a governance structure. This enhancement helps us understand the evolution of effective routines in PFM. With an improved understanding of governance structures, it is possible to match governance structures to financial transactions with different attributes.

Management Matters

To Williamson (1999), the firm-as-governance structure argument, "certainly makes significant provision for management" (p. 1101). In an earlier article, Williamson (1998) argues for application of transaction cost theory to strategic planning and management. According to him, if transaction cost theory is to be more relevant to strategic management, it needs to push beyond the generic level at which it now operates and to consider particulars. Rather than asking what is the best generic mode (market, hybrid, firm, or bureau) for organizing a certain transaction, the question to be put instead is how the organization with pre-existing strengths and weaknesses should organize a certain transaction to achieve and sustain competitive advantages (Williamson, 1998, p. 48).

This line of inquiry holds great implications for PFM because, as Bozeman and Straussman (1990) argue, public managers must look beyond the budget and manage financial resources strategically. To do so means that a spending agency should organize and manage its financial transactions in ways that will create more political support, and therefore lower coordination costs in organizing and managing financial transactions.

The balance between governance and management becomes important. From the perspective of transaction cost theory, the governance choice is primary whereas management strategy is secondary. Williamson (1998) writes, "Transaction cost economics views strategic ploys and positioning as of second order of importance. Clever gambits will rarely save a firm in which serious governance misalignments are observed" (p. 47). However, this does not deny the importance of management. Design and implementation of effective governance structure is an important task for top-level public financial managers. In PFM, effective management will further minimize transaction costs of organizing and managing financial transactions that have not been completely minimized by effective governance structures.

Tax Collection: An Illustration

Transaction cost theory will not explain every issue of PFM—no such theory may exist. However, transaction cost theory should help us improve our understanding of many issues of PFM. It offers the opportunity to do so by providing a general framework within which the attributes of actors and transactions can be modeled. Its focus is on the organizational architecture and the incentives it creates, and how the building blocks of transactions affect the development of organizations and subsequent service delivery. Our model incorporates organizational capacity and learning in a way consistent with the basic principles of transaction cost theory. This section illustrates the potential for the application of transaction cost theory to PFM using historical research on a specific sub-field of PFM, tax collection.

Tax collection presents a choice among three types of contracts. The choice between the wage contract and either the share or fixed-rent contract is essentially a choice between a hierarchical form of governance structure and a market form (Ma, 2002). In the early modern historical period, governments often employed a market form of governance for tax collection ("tax farming"). Why? The transaction cost model of PFM would predict that it was because the costs, including transaction costs, of using wage contracts were higher than the costs of using fixed-rent or share contracts. The transaction costs of wage contracts are realized when the government decides to collect taxes itself; these costs include the costs of realizing compliance among taxpayers and tax officials. The transaction costs of using fixed-rent or share contracts occur when the government decides to privatize tax collection to the private sector. The costs of both options constrain and shape the government's contractual choices in tax collection (Ma, 2002).

If the government decides to collect taxes itself, it should minimize its internal transaction costs. In the early modern period when tax farming was dominant, most governments were unable to achieve this, and thus had to employ a market-type governance structure to collect taxes. Motivation and control costs of creating taxpayer compliance were very high largely due to the nondemocratic nature of the early modern regimes and the lack of loyalty to the evolving nation-states. These governments usually failed to motivate taxpayer compliance. Consequently, their taxpayers had strong incentives to avoid taxes by concealing assets, underreporting payments, and even revolting against taxation. In such circumstances, the governments would have to establish monitoring and enforcement institutions to induce compliance. Information and measurement costs are two major transaction costs of tax collection. As North (1981) observed, although the state increased its power to extract revenues from its constituents with a reduction in the power of external and internal rivals, it "was constrained by the costs of measuring wealth and income which were predominantly derived from local and regional production and trade" (p. 150).

Motivation and control costs of creating compliance among tax officials were also very high. Governments had to rely on tax officials to monitor taxpayers' behavior and enforce tax policies. However, tax officials can pursue their own interests through shirking and corruption at the expense of the state's revenues. In a zero transaction cost world, these agency problems will disappear. However, agency problems existed and affected the state's choices of tax collection mechanisms. In the early modern period, motivation costs of creating compliance among tax officials were prohibitive because of the dominance of patrimonial administration. Recruitment and promotion were not based on individual capacity but on favoritism and wealth, and in some places official positions had been institutionalized as private property. In these circumstances, the state would have had to establish costly control mechanisms to reduce agency costs. The information and measurement costs in monitoring tax officials' behavior was very high in this period because of underdeveloped transportation and communication systems, the lack of effective accounting and auditing systems, and the lack of standardized measurement systems (Ma, 2002).

Early modern governments also faced high coordination costs in tax collection if they decided to collect taxes themselves, that is, information and decisions costs of coordinating between the central treasury and other revenue collection agencies. Several structural elements contributed to this high coordination cost, including the underdevelopment of banking system and transportation and communication systems. It was largely due to these high coordination costs that many early modern governments had not established real and effective central treasuries (Ma, 2002).

The early modern administrative system was also unable to foster the development of organizational capacity. The lack of emphasis on merit selection in patrimonial administration systems had negative effects on individual and group learning, and in turn this inhibited organizational capacity to accumulate production knowledge. As a result, tax officials had little interest in learning and accumulating production knowledge (Ma, 2002).

Meanwhile, at the beginning of the early modern period, governments were able to keep the transaction costs of using fixed-rent contracts low. These costs were determined by the relative bargaining powers of tax farmers and the state. Many early modern states selected tax farmers from minority groups with relatively low bargaining powers, such as the Chinese business elite in Southeast Asia (from the 17th to the early 20th centuries), the Jewish businessmen in Egypt (Roman Empire), and French professionals in Prussia of Frederick the Great. Meanwhile, in some countries, such as *ancien regime* France before the late 16th century, the states forbid elite groups from participation in tax farming. This supports Levi's (1988) hypothesis that in revenue production, the rulers tended to increase their own bargaining powers. Furthermore, almost all countries using tax farming used competitive auction as the main method to grant fixed-rent contracts. Many early modern states also favored short-term leases and frequent public auctions in the hope of forcing the lease prices upward. To some extent, this helped reduce transaction costs of using fixed-rent contracts, raising the rent the state extracted from tax farmers (Ma, 2002).

In sum, in the early modern period, the transaction costs of using wage contracts were higher than the transaction costs of using fixed-rent contracts. Meanwhile, early modern administrative regimes impeded the development of organization capacity. Therefore, a wage contract governance structure was not as efficient as a fixed-rent contract, and tax farming was the common form of tax collection. Of course, transaction costs did not disappear with the use of tax farming. In the early modern period, although tax farming had made it unnecessary for the state to directly monitor tax collection, the state still had to develop an effective management system by designing proper contracts, auctioning out contracts, and enforcing tax contracts.

Therefore, this model does seem to explain the institutional structure of tax collection in this period. Although there were deviations from the efficient governance structure, over the long run of this period, governments made the cost-minimizing institutional choice. This is an example of the potential of this transaction cost model as a positive model to explain patterns and developments in governance structure. Later, when institutional incentives changed, the mode of tax collection changed in the modern state.

Other Applications of the Model

In this section, we discuss six other sub-fields within PFM to further illustrate the potential of this theory. One field where the enhanced transaction cost model readily applies is government procurement. The transaction cost model should provide a better explanation of contract choices (cost plus fixed-fee, fixed-price, and incentive contract) in public procurement. For instance, it should help to explain why some governments prefer fixed-price contract (a positive question), and also to assess whether this is the best contractual choice (a normative question). As Adler et al. (1998) argue, transaction cost dimensions should be able to differentiate governance structures along the contacting continuum. For example, it should be able to make positive predictions and normative judgments about the degree of participation of different U.S. states in cooperative purchasing on a wide continuum ranging from constitutional prohibitions against cooperative purchasing on the one end to multi-state purchasing pools at the other end (Bartle, 2002). It will also help to identify major transaction cost problems existing in public procurement, such as the adverse selection problems (finding good contractors) and moral hazard problems (*ex post* opportunism), and help to develop and enforce governance structures designed to reduce corruption, such as vendor-induced preferences and constrained competition (Bartle, 2002).

Debt transactions involve market-type financial transactions, in which competition and price serve to coordinate, motivate and control financial transactions related to debt financing. However, effective financial management is important for minimizing transaction costs. From the perspective of transaction cost theory, a historical problem of government debt is the potential opportunism of the government. As North and Weingast (1989) point out, in fiscal history, many governments behaved opportunistically when the sovereign would not credibly commit to repayment of debts. The financial market whenever it worked well would punish the government with higher interest rates. However, the market and reputation were not successful in constraining opportunism of the state, especially when it discounted the future heavily. In early modern history, it was the establishment of a new governance structure (limited monarchy) that allowed the state to credibly commit to its debt payment. This point is very useful for us to understand the institutional environment of debt management for modern governments. The various rules and procedures that are created to insure the government will commit to its debt contracts, such as requirements for credit quality, bond ratings, and other measurements to protect debt buyers, suggest that these institutions developed to reduce the transaction costs in this market. Moreover, the transaction cost model will help to understand the choices of bond types (general obligation and revenue bonds, which can be viewed as two basic types of debt contracts), debt maturity structure (different maturity structure may result from different transaction cost problems in different financial transactions), underwriting, and innovative financing where other entities are involved in a government's debt issuance.

In the mid-1980s, the major trend in risk management was the move from the traditional insurance market to self-insurance and intergovernmental insurance pools. From the perspective of transaction cost theory, the high transaction costs of using insurance may have induced the government to use self-insurance. Transaction costs exist in other fields of risk management as well, because effective risk management requires identifying, measuring, and controlling risks. To do so, it is important for the central office and spending agencies to coordinate with each other; as a result coordination costs occur. When an intergovernmental insurance pool is used, the coordination costs will be even higher. Moreover, various agencies must be motivated to coordinate with the central agency's need for information and protective efforts to remove and reduce risks. When motivation fails, the central agency has to carry out direct control and monitoring, in which information costs and monitoring costs are very high. Indeed, effective risk management depends on how successfully the government reduces transaction costs involved.

As works of Reed and Swain (1997) and Schwartz (1996) suggest, transaction cost theory can be applied to inventory and cash management. Schwartz (1996) incorporates the concept of transaction cost in his analysis of inventory management. He identifies three types of costs—ordering cost, holding cost, and outage cost—which are essentially transaction costs. In their chapter on cash management, Reed and Swain identify transaction costs in handling funds, such as depositing money, investing it, or making payments. Pooling can involve transaction costs as well. Similarly, Schwartz writes, "having sufficient cash on hand enables the local government to reduce transaction costs and to avoid the penalty costs that arise from being short of immediately available funds" (p. 395). He points out that the optimal cash balance is determined by transaction costs, along with the risks and costs of cash shortages and the net difference between interest rates on transaction balances and those available in the short-term securities market. Despite these efforts, there is a need to formalize transaction cost theory in this area. For example, transaction cost theory will help to assess whether consolidated or dispersed cash management is more efficient in any given situation, or if administrative agencies can commit to coordination when the CBB depends on the agencies to forecast collections and disbursements.

Transaction costs are relevant to capital budgeting as well. In the process of planning and allocating resources among competing capital investment projects, spending priorities create coordination costs. A full understanding of those coordination costs will help us to understand capital budgeting. Furthermore, as addressed before, capital budgeting is a field where asset specificity often happens, which will then bring about additional transaction costs.

Transaction cost theory is useful for improving our understanding of financial control. It may be desirable to design and implement different control mechanisms for financial transactions with different attributes. Here, as in other situations, trust is an important variable. There is a trade-off between trust and information. When PFM involves very complex financial information, managers or supervisors need to decide whom they can trust. The enhanced transaction cost model provides insights into such complex relations in PFM.

Conclusion

Fundamentally, many of the values of the normative best practices framework of PFM referred to earlier are manifestations of transaction cost theory. For example, accounting standards such as Generally Accepted Accounting Practices (GAAP) convey information to actors that reduce information asymmetry and uncertainty, allowing for lower transaction costs and more efficient contracting. In this case, the institutional structure improves efficiency in a static sense, but also makes easier impersonal contracts, creating a dynamic that enhances long-term economic growth. The apparent normative goal of compliance with GAAP is a manifestation of the deeper value of creating strong institutions that give appropriate incentives for social and economic development. But conflicts between best practices and the transaction cost model suggest that the latter model is more applicable. For example, while legal or accounting best practices might be appropriate for some governments, in many other cases best practice is unattainable and impractical because the transaction costs of compliance far outweigh the other benefits. The modifications that are required in applying best practices suggests that this norm is limited, and instead that the underlying value reflected by this enhanced transaction cost model is more applicable. That value is institutional efficiency in the broad sense that minimizes production, transaction, and external costs. The development of contracts that achieve institutional efficiency is a normative value that should be central to PFM. Transaction cost theory also allows the development of positive models that can better explain why practices evolve over time and vary across societies, as we have seen in some of the illustrations presented here. It can also better explain the presence of corruption and its persistence in some governments. Thus, this approach can allow public financial management to develop a more coherent normative justification while also allowing for development of a positive theory of the field.

References

Adler, Terry B., Robert Scherer, Sidney Barton, and Ralph Katerberg. 1998. "An Empirical Test of Transaction Cost Theory: Validating Contract Typology." *Journal of Applied Management Studies,* 7: 185–200.

Arnold, David. 1996. "Purchasing and Risk Management." In *Management Polices in Local Government Finance,* eds. Richard Aronson and Eli Schwartz. Washington, DC: The International City/County Management Association.

Arya, Anil, John Fellingham, Jonathan Glover, and K. Sivaramakrishnan. 2000. "Capital Budgeting, the Hold-up Problem, and Information System Design." *Management Science,* 46 (February): 205–216.

Azabou, M., and J. Nugent. 1988. "Contractual Choice in Tax Collection Activities: Some Implications of the Experience with Tax Farming." *Journal of Institutional and Theoretical Economics,* 144 : 684–705.

Bajari, Patrick, and Steven Tadelis. 2001. "Incentives Versus Transaction Costs: A Theory of Procurement Contracts." *Rand Journal of Economics,* 32: 387–407.

Bartle, John R. 2002. "A Transaction Cost Model of State Government Procurement." Presented at the Association for Budgeting and Financial Management annual conference, January 19.

Bartle, John R., and Jun Ma. 2001. "Applying Transaction Cost Theory to Public Budgeting and Finance." In *Evolving Theories of Public Budgeting*, ed. John R. Bartle. New York: JAI Press.

Bos, Dieter, and Christoph Lulfesmann. 1996. "The Hold-up Problem in Government Contracting." *Scan. Journal of Economics*, 98 : 53–74.

Bosher, J. F. 1970. *French Finances 1770–1795: From Business to Bureaucracy.* Cambridge: Cambridge University Press.

Bozeman, Barry, and Jeffrey Straussman. 1990. *Public Management Strategies.* San Francisco: Jossey-Bass Publishers.

Brehm, John, and Scott Gates. 1997. *Working, Shirking and Sabotage.* Ann Arbor, Michigan: University of Michigan Press.

Caiden, Naomi. 1978. *Patterns of Budgeting: The Experience of France 987–1830.* Unpublished dissertation. University of Southern California.

Caiden, Naomi, and Aaron Wildavsky. 1974. *Planning and Budgeting in Poor Countries.* New York: John Wiley & Sons.

Chandler, Alfred. 1992. "Organizational Capacities and the Theory of the Firm." *Journal of Economic Perspectives*, 6: 79–100.

Chiles, T. H., and J. F. McMackin. 1996. "Integrating Variable Risk Preferences, Trust, and Transaction Cost Economics." *Academy of Management Review*, 21: 73–99.

Coase, R. 1937. The Nature of the Firm." *Economica*, 4: 386–405.

Dunleavy, Patrick. 1991. *Democracy, Bureaucracy and Public Choice.* New York: Prentice Hall.

Friedman, Lee S. 2002. *The Microeconomics of Public Policy Analysis.* Princeton, NJ: Princeton University Press.

Goswami, Gautam. 2000. "Asset Maturity, Debt Covenants, and Debt Maturity Choice." *Financial Review*, 35: 51–68.

Hodgson, G. M. 1998. "Competence and Contract in the Theory of the Firm." *Journal of Economic Behavior and Organization*, 35: 179–201.

Huang, Yasheng. 2002. "Managing Chinese Bureaucrats: An Institutional Economics Perspective." *Political Studies*, 50: 61–79.

Kiser, Edgar. 1994. "Markets and Hierarchy in Early Modern Tax Systems: A Principal-Agent Analysis." *Politics and Society*, 22: 284–315.

Kiser, Edgar. 1999. "Comparing Varieties of Agency Theory in Economics, Political Science, and Sociology: An Illustration from State Policy Implementation." *Sociological Theory*, 17: 146–170.

Kochhar, Rahul. 1996. "Explaining Firm Capital Structure: The Role of Agency Theory vs. Transaction Cost Economics." *Strategic Management Journal*, 17: 713–728.

Langlois, R. N., and N. J. Foss. 1999. "Capacities and Governance: The Rebirth of Production in the Theory of Economic Organization." *KYKLOS*, 52: 201–218.

Levi, M. 1988. *Of Rule and Revenue.* Berkeley: University of California Press.

Ma, Jun. 2002. *Revenue Production and Transaction Costs: Contractual Choices of Tax Collection.* Unpublished doctoral dissertation. University of Nebraska.

McAfee, R. Preston, and John McMillan. 1988. *Incentives in Government Contracting.* Toronto: University of Toronto Press.

McCubbins, Mathew D., R. G. Noll, and Barry Weingast. 1987. "Administrative Procedures as Instruments of Political Control." *Journal of Law, Economics and Organization,* 3: 243–277.

McCubbins, Mathew D., R. G. Noll, and Barry Weingast. 1989. "Structure and Process, Politics and Policy: Arrangements and the Political Control of Agencies." *Virginia Law Review,* 75: 431–82.

McKinney, Jerome B. 1995. *Effective Financial Management in Public and Nonprofit Agencies.* Westport, CT: Quorum Book.

Milgrom, Paul, and John Roberts. 1992. *Economics, Organization, and Management.* Upper Saddle River, NJ: Prentice Hall.

Moschandreas, Maria. 1997. "The Role of Opportunism in Transaction Cost Economics." *Journal of Economic Issues,* XXXI: 39–57.

Niskanen, W. 1971. *Bureaucracy and Representative Government.* Chicago: Aldine Inc.

Niskanen, W. 1975. "Bureaucrats and Politicians." *Journal of Law and Economics,* 18: 617–643.

Noorderhaven, Niels G. 1996. "Opportunism and Trust in Transaction Cost Economics." In *Transaction Cost Economics and Beyond,* ed. John Groenweegen. Boston: Kluwer Academic Publishers.

North, Douglass C. 1981. *Structure and Change in Economic History.* New York: Norton.

North, Douglass C. 1990. "A Transaction Cost Theory of Politics." *Journal of Theoretical Politics,* 2: 355–367.

North, Douglass C. and Barry Weingast. 1989. "Constitutions and Commitment: The Evolution of Institutions Governing Public Choice in Seventeenth-Century England." *Journal of Economic History,* 49 (December).

Ouchi, William. 1980. "Markets, Bureaucracies, and Clans." *Administrative Science Quarterly,* 25: 129–141.

Premchand, A. 1993. *Public Expenditure Management.* Washington, DC: IFM.

Reed, B. J., and J. W. Swain. 1997. *Public Finance Administration.* 2nd edition. Thousand Oaks, CA: Sage Publications.

Riahi-Belkaoui, A. 2002. *Behavioral Management Accounting.* Westport, CT: Quorum Books.

Rubin, Irene. 1998. *Class, Tax and Power: Municipal Budgeting in the United States.* Chatham, NJ: Chatham House Publishers.

Rubin, Paul. 1990. *Managing Business Transactions: Controlling the Cost of Coordinating, Communicating, and Decision Making.* New York: Free Press.

Schick, Allen. 1996. "The Road to PPB: The Stages of Budgetary Reform." *Public Administration Review,* 26: 243–258.

Schwartz, Eli. 1996. "Inventory and Cash Management." In *Management Polices in Local Government Finance,* eds. Richard Aronson and Eli Schwartz. Washington DC: The International City/County Management Association.

Spekle, Roland. 2001. "Explaining Management Control Structure Variety: A Transaction Cost Economics Perspective." *Accounting, Organizations and Society,* 26: 419–441.

Thompson, Fred. 1993. "Matching Responsibilities with Tactics: Administrative Controls and Modern Government." *Public Administration Review,* 53: 303–318.

Thompson, Fred, and L. R. Jones. 1986. "Controllership in the Public Sector." *Journal of Policy Analysis and Management,* 5: 547–571.

Waterman, Richard W., and Kenneth J. Meier. 1998. "Principal-Agent Models: An Expansion?" *Journal of Public Administration Research and Theory,* 8: 173–202.

Weber, Marx. 1922/1968. *Economy and Society.* New York: Bedminster Press.

Weimer, David L., and Aidan R. Vining. 1996. "Economics." In *The State of Public Management,* eds. Donald F. Kettl and H. Brinton Milward. Baltimore: The Johns Hopkins University Press.

Williamson, Oliver E. 1975. *Markets and Hierarchies: Analysis and Antitrust Implications.* New York: Free Press.

Williamson, Oliver E. 1983. "Credible Commitment: Using Hostages to Support Exchange." *American Economic Review,* 73 (September): 519–40.

Williamson, Oliver E. 1985. *The Economic Institutions of Capitalism.* New York: Free Press.

Williamson, Oliver E. 1988. "Corporate Finance and Corporate Governance." *Journal of Finance,* 43: 567–591.

Williamson, Oliver E. 1990. "A Comparison of Alternative Approaches to Economic Organization." *Journal of Institutional and Theoretical Economics,* 146: 61–71.

Williamson, Oliver E. 1993. Foreword to *Managing Business Transactions: Controlling the Cost of Coordinating, Communicating, and Decision Making,* by Paul Rubin. New York: Free Press.

Williamson, Oliver E. 1998. "Transaction Cost Economics: How It Works; Where It Is Ahead." *De Economists,* 146 (April): 23–58.

Williamson, Oliver E. 1999. "Strategy Research: Governance and Competence Perspectives." *Strategic Management Journal,* 20: 1087–1108.

Wilson, James Q. 1989. *Bureaucracy.* New York: Basic Books.

CHAPTER 2

Information Asymmetry in Public Investment Management

Brian K. Collins and Aman Khan

Public organizations can invest idle funds to increase revenue flows in either the short or long term. Short-term investment opportunities arise when positive cash flows result from the timing of tax revenue collections relative to expenditures, or positive revenue flows from the receipt of bond proceeds before their expenditures. Because these positive cash flows are generally short-term, public investments begin and are concluded within a year. Long-term investments generally involve an allocation of funds to public agencies with the express purpose of generating investment income for current and future use. The most common example is government-managed pension funds. Other examples include endowment funds for university foundations, risk pool funds for self-insurance, or sinking funds for bond repayments (Reed and Swain, 1997).

For either short- or long-term investments, public managers must balance the objective of maximizing returns with protecting principal when realizing the time value of money. This balancing act requires public investment officials to manage investment risks, maintain sufficient liquidity, and maximize rates of return in a complex financial marketplace. Moreover, public managers must operate under legal restrictions and political pressures that add to the complexity. For example, public money managers are often bound by statutory or constitutional constraints limiting investments to low-risk instruments or geographic areas (Heller, Walton, and Will-moth, 2002).

In most cases, public investment managers are able to reap benefits from the time value of money within the constraints of the law and good investment practices. But the failure to do so can have catastrophic results, as the case of Orange County, California, illustrates (Jorion, 1995; Baldassare, 1998). As the elected county treasurer of Orange County, California, Robert "Bob" Citron managed the Orange County Investment Pool (OCIP), which drew deposits from the county coffers as well as 186 other public agencies, such as municipalities and school districts, who flocked to the investment pool in hopes of exceptionally high returns. In fact, during Citron's first 22 years as county treasurer, OCIP had an average return of 9.4 percent, a full percentage point higher than the state investment pool, which translated into about $755 million in revenues above that generated by the state investment pool (Jorion, 1995).[1]

Unfortunately for Orange County, past performance was no guarantee of future performance. By 1994, Citron managed about $7 billion in deposits that he had leveraged into a $20.5 billion portfolio. The logic of his investment activity centered on using reverse repurchase agreements in which he would sell securities in the pool as collateral for borrowed funds. He would then reinvest those funds in a variety of relatively low-risk notes of moderate to long-term duration, and thus exploit the difference between short and longer-term yields. At one point, Citron had borrowed and then invested twice as much as the equity in the investment pool (Jorion, 1995). Citron's strategy was successful as long as interest rates remained stable or declined, because he could profit from repurchasing the collateralized securities with returns from securities with higher yields and longer maturities. Once interest rates began to increase steadily, however, the high interest rate risk, low liquidity strategy failed, and OCIP lost $1.69 billion dollars. Orange County filed for Chapter 9 bankruptcy, and became the largest municipal bankruptcy in U.S. history.

As a result of Citron's management, the county was forced to sell physical assets, county payrolls were slashed, and schools lost millions in their operational budgets. Bob Citron and key staff resigned under pressure, and Citron eventually plead guilty to several felony counts regarding the operation of the investment pool, but he did not make any illegal investments. Ultimately the state legislature took action to prevent similar problems, because other local governments were vulnerable to the same set of public-finance managerial dilemmas that ended in bankruptcy for Orange County.

Such losses as the Orange County bankruptcy are rare examples of disastrous public investment failure, but the complexity of decision making in public finance suggests that the possibility of significant managerial failure is present when information asymmetries exist. Public investment management is a good example of this. Financial markets and instruments involve highly complex, fast-moving, and high-stakes decision making. Yet market theory is based on the assumption that there is full or complete information among buyers and sellers about the goods and services being exchanged, but this is not an accurate description of the realistic operation of financial markets. Buyers and sellers, or borrowers and lenders, generally do not have full or complete information about transactions, and thus market failures are likely to result from information asymmetries.

Information asymmetries can also affect the administration of public finance. Given the agency relationship between public managers, politicians, and the public, information asymmetries can create incentives for public managers to be opportunistic in the development of investment policies. Such opportunism can take the form of illegal actions, corrupt practices, or even investment that place public funds at unduly high risks.

The objective of this chapter is to elucidate the theoretical impact of asymmetric information on public finance management by examining the case of public investment. Because public finance management is integrally associated with dealing with information asymmetries in several arenas of choice (such as financial markets, the department managing investments, a local government investment pool, or even the state legislature), we will first use the IAD framework of analysis to define three arenas of choice in which asymmetric information will have a substantial impact on public finance. Then we offer a theoretical explanation of how information asymmetries affect public investment management in each arena. We illustrate the explanatory power of these theories with a discussion of the Orange County case. Finally, we show why it is important to understand the linkages between each arena of choice to reduce the pathologies associated with asymmetric information without unduly limiting the managerial discretion necessary for effective public finance.

Asymmetric Information in Public Investment Management

Understanding the impact of asymmetric information in a complex decision making environment such as public investment provides an analytic foundation for understanding both particular investment decisions in financial markets and associated managerial dilemmas for government investors. The assumption that information is important in complex decision making is axiomatic in rational-choice frameworks of analysis, even though individuals undoubtedly have limited information-processing capacity. We agree that humans possess bounded rationality; therefore, the information structure is a critical factor in any decision-making situation.[2] The following discussion provides an informal definition of one important information structure: asymmetric information.

What Is Asymmetric Information?

Information asymmetries arise when one actor in a decision-making situation has more, or better, information than another actor in that same situation. For example, one decision-making situation is a market where a seller has more or better information about the characteristics of a good than the seller, or a borrower who knows more about the likelihood of default than the lender. Another situation is the workplace where an employee may have more or better information about her job effort than her employer does. In short, asymmetric information arises when relevant information is known to some people (private or hidden information) in the decision-making situation, but not to everyone (public information).

Embedded within this relatively simple definition of asymmetric information is an enormous literature in economics and game theory that has produced numerous theories and complex mathematical models to explain a wide variety of phenomena.[3] In the quotation below, Milgrom and Roberts (1987, p. 184) begin to unpack the theoretical significance of asymmetric information with a discussion of three simple games to illustrate how incomplete information and the distribution of information between actors (i.e., asymmetry) create different decision-making situations.

> To get an idea of the role of information asymmetries in strategic behavior, consider three simple card games. In the first, each player is dealt five cards face up, the players make any bets they want, and then the best hand wins. In the second, each player receives five cards, some of which are dealt face up, and the rest face down. Without looking at their hole cards, the players make their bets, then the cards are turned face up and the best hand wins. Finally, the third game is like the second, except that players can look at their hold cards. Again there is betting, the hidden cards are revealed, and the best hand wins.

As Milgrom and Roberts explain, these games represent three configurations of incomplete information and the distribution of information between players. The first game represents decision making under complete and symmetric information. In short, there is no uncertainty (complete information), and all actors have all relevant information to the betting decision. In this particular game, the information structure of the game is such that both players can easily determine the outcome, and hence there is no incentive to bet at all. Thus the decision of how much to bet is transformed into a decision of whether to play the game at all.[4]

The second game represents decision making under incomplete information that is distributed symmetrically. In other words, both players have public information of the cards face up, but both face uncertainty about the cards face down. Uncertainty in this context arises from random nature of dealing cards, not the behavior of the other player. The information from the face cards enables players to assign probabilities to their unseen cards and thus calculate expected values. Hence, the game proceeds much along the lines of classic decision theory, with each actor able to make probabilistic assignments to potential outcomes (risk) and betting according to expected values and levels of risk assessment or risk aversion. Such an information structure is often used to model insurance and investment risk, according to Milgrom and Roberts (1987).

The third game represents decision making under incomplete information that is distributed asymmetrically, and is thus the point of our departure. In this game, both players have access to public information (visible cards), and each player has private information about each of their hole cards. Thus, each player has complete information about their own cards, but incomplete information about the other's cards.[5] In other words, information about each hand of cards is distributed asymmetrically. As Milgrom and Roberts (1987) suggest, it is the existence of this private information that leads to strategic behaviors such as bluffing, signaling, or reputation building.

In short, asymmetric information is an information structure that assumes some form of interaction among actors in a decision making context that is characterized by strategic uncertainty. If these actors are assumed to have at least partially conflicting goals or objectives, then there is an incentive not to reveal all relevant information to all the actors in the situation. In other words, asymmetric information generates strategic uncertainty.

In public investment, such strategic uncertainty may have an adverse impact on investment actions and outcomes. Public managers may not take full advantage of opportunities in financial markets, or they may make unduly risky investments like Bob Citron in Orange County. In either case, asymmetric information is a key component of decision making that makes poker a fun and interesting game to play and public investment management a challenging and potentially controversial game to play.

To facilitate the explication of how asymmetric information affects public investment, it is useful to specify decision-making arenas in the management of public investment. The operational and collective choice arenas, as identified in the IAD framework of analysis (Kiser and Ostrom, 1982) are useful conceptions for defining the different kinds of actions that public investment managers take under asymmetric information.[6] Each arena will be defined, and a theory will be offered to explain how the strategic uncertainty of information asymmetries affects the efficiency and effectiveness of public investment management. Examples from the Orange County case are used to illustrate the impact of information asymmetries.

Adverse Selection at the Operational Arena of Choice

The operational arena of choice describes the situation in which an action in the physical world flows directly from individual decision making (Kiser and Ostrom, 1982; Ostrom, Gardner, and Walker, 1994). For public investment, the operational arena of choice is a financial market in which managers decide whether to participate in buying, selling, borrowing, and lending, and if so, how. In general, public managers must decide whether to invest short-term positive cash flows at a particular point in time or not. If investment is chosen, they must select between financial instruments such as equities or bonds, and then decide for what duration those instruments will be held. Thus all financial market transactions are key actions in the operational arena of choice that create an outcome such as a change in cash flows, cash revenues, returns on investment, or portfolio holdings.

If asymmetric information is present in financial markets, then it can affect spot transactions or potentially cause complete market failure. Asymmetric information exists in any market when at least one actor in a potential transaction holds private information about the attributes of good or service before a transaction is completed. For example, partial or total market failure can result when sellers hold information about the quality of goods that a potential buyer does not hold. The classic example is the "lemon problem" in the used-car market, which is also known as *adverse selection* (Akerlof, 1970). Adverse selection occurs if the products most likely to produce an adverse outcome for the buyer are those most likely to be bought. For example, if the owners of used cars hold private information about the true quality of the used car and buyers do not, then there is asymmetric information in the used-car market. The problem is that all the cars would be sold if there were symmetric information, because the market would adjust prices to reflect the quality of the used cars. Under asymmetric information, however, buyers are so worried about the quality of the used cars that they reduce what they are willing to pay for any used car. As price offers decline, sellers have less incentive to make the transaction if they hold a high-quality car. Hence, the only cars likely to be offered are the lemons. The lemons push the high-quality used cars out of the market, which could ultimately lead to a total collapse of the used-car market if buyers are unwilling to purchase lemons, even at a low price.

Like other market actors, public investment managers must overcome information asymmetries to derive the benefits of mutually beneficial exchange in financial markets (Hillier, 1997; Forsythe, Lundholm, and Reitz, 1999). For example, borrowers often hold information about the risk of default that lenders do not and perhaps cannot know. Since lenders want to avoid a transaction that is detrimental to their interest, such as a high-default-risk borrower, they have a disincentive to participate in the market because of an adverse selection problem identical to the lemon problem, in that potential borrowers most likely to produce adverse outcomes to the investor are those most likely to seek financing and be selected by investors.

The problem of adverse selection in bond markets was at the core of the investment transactions that precipitated the Orange County bankruptcy. In this situation, the county treasurer, Bob Citron, acted as a borrower, selling various notes in the bond market. Citron held information about the risk of default that lenders did not possess, namely the extent to which reverse repurchasing agreements had increased the duration of his investments, thus making the OCIP investment pool subject to significant interest rate risk. Jorion (2001) estimates that there was a 5 percent chance of losing more than $1.1 billion over a year, but even Moody's and S&P rated Orange County bonds at AA and A1, respectively.

Under these conditions of asymmetric information, creditors were willing to lend money to Orange County as Citron attempted to leverage their way out of an over-leveraged position. As the OCIP fund became less solvent, Citron became more likely to borrow in the bond market. For example, as liquidity became an increasing problem in the summer of 1994, Citron, with the approval of the Board of Supervisors, issued a $600 million note to provide additional liquidity to the over-leveraged fund (Jorion, 1995). This attempt to raise capital was too little, too late, however. Interest rates continued to decline, and by October 1994, OCIP could not meet agreements to repurchase instruments and could not repay bond debt. By November 1994, the OCIP had defaulted on $100 million of bond payments. In an effort to avoid a potential $1 billion default on short-term debt, the Board of Supervisors authorized the filing for Chapter 9 bankruptcy protection in 1994.

In addition to the losses suffered by creditors, the impact of adverse selection in the Orange County case reverberated throughout financial markets as investors began to question whether other municipalities were issuing debt with hidden risks (Jorion, 1995). For example, the Texas state investment pool suffered a significant run when reports surfaced about their use of reverse repurchasing agreements, even though the Texas pool was not nearly as heavily leveraged as the OCIP pool. Municipal bond prices on average decreased 1 percent, and California-based bonds decreased between 3 and 4 percent. In short, like the lemon problem suggests, adverse selection can disrupt entire markets, and the Orange County bankruptcy had that impact in the short- to intermediate-term municipal bond market.

In summary, absent information asymmetries, public investment managers could produce, on average, higher rates of return, but the adverse selection is a powerful incentive to adopt investment strategies that may be too passive, and hence they forego the opportunity to increase rates of return, even at acceptable risk levels (Forsythe, Lundholm, and Reitz, 1999). However, in the real operation of financial markets, public managers must avoid selecting or offering investments with hidden risks that may be inappropriate for portfolios that value protecting principal.

One way to avoid these problems is either to avoid public investment altogether, or make investments in only the most safe and low-risk securities. Both of these approaches, however, come at the cost of lost revenues to a government and a deadweight loss to society in the form of underutilized financial capital. Citron's mistake was not the use of complex investment instruments, but leveraging those instruments created a liquidity problem. Nevertheless, recent surveys find support for the expectation that public managers are reticent to participate aggressively in financial markets. For example, 84 percent of public investors use a passive investment strategy, such as buying securities and holding them until maturity or investing in products designed to yield the market rate of return (Flahaven, 2002). These passive strategies are certainly appropriate since they are designed to protect principal, but the dominance of the passive approach is also consistent with the theoretical expectation that public investors will consciously forego more active participation in financial markets because of the adverse selection problem. McCue (2000) presents experimental evidence that local government investment managers, as individuals, act consistently with prospect theory by being risk seeking when facing losses; however, as organizational managers they violate the principles of prospect theory because they are not risk seeking when facing losses. McCue actually uses Citron as an example of what happens when individual preferences override the organizational behaviors associated with public organizations.

To avoid the inefficiencies associated with asymmetric information in financial markets, governments, intermediaries, and financial market participants themselves develop institutions to reduce information asymmetries. Governmental responses include regulatory actions that compel those offering investment instruments in financial markets to reveal information to potential buyers through financial statements using common accounting standards; however, note the financial subterfuge of Enron and other companies who, at best, skirted the rules of accounting and financial reporting. Violation of these rules and standards have cost investors billions of dollars, weakened confidence in financial institutions, and ultimately proved detrimental to the performance of the stock market at large. However, the Securities and Exchange Commission has authority to monitor and to enforce such regulations as a means of reducing asymmetric information (Forsythe, Lundholm, and Reitz, 1999).

Even individual market actors will take efforts to build a reputation as a credible investor or borrower through instruments such as bond insurance or public audits. Financial intermediaries such as Moody's, Standard and Poor's, or Fitch conduct extensive research and analysis that is summarized in bond ratings that reduce information asymmetries in the bond market; but, as the Orange County case demonstrates, these responses to information asymmetries are far from perfect.

In summary, public managers face adverse selection problems because of asymmetric information in financial markets. Although many institutional arrangements exist to reduce information asymmetries, public managers must still screen out those investments with unduly high levels of risk without foregoing active market participation to maximize rates of return. Yet, as the example above indicates, public managers can and do select investments with substantially negative effects on the government and citizens. Turning to the collective choice arena provides additional explanation of how information asymmetries can create incentives for opportunistic public investment management.

Moral Hazard in the Collective Choice Arena

In the collective choice arena, the actors are in the position to make authoritative decisions in three areas: (1) who is eligible to make the policy-rules that govern the operational decision making; (2) the process by which those policy-rules are made; and (3) the substantive policy-rules themselves. A legislative body with elected officials representing districts is perhaps the most common conception of a collective choice arena. Other examples include appointed judges who adjudicate disputes and offer legal opinions or police chiefs who determine that racial profiling will not be practiced in the department. In each example, the important actions taken in the collective choice arena are some form of rulemaking, which is usually thought of as policy-making, adjudication, or management that governs operational-level decision making (Ostrom, 1990).[7]

Therefore, in the collective choice arena, public investment management is about the development and implementation of public investment policies. These policies ultimately affect investment outcomes at the operational level of analysis because they are the rules that specify what actions public managers are required, permitted, or prohibited from taking. Sample investment policies offered by the Government Finance Officers Association and the Municipal Treasurers Association provide generic rules about investment objectives, delegation of authority, ethics, internal controls, reporting, instruments, collateralization, selection of brokers/dealers, allowable maturities, diversification, risk tolerance, and auditing (Heller, Walton, and Willmoth, 2002).

In this arena of public investment, information about hidden actions creates asymmetric information between a principal and agent, which creates the problem of moral hazard. Generally speaking, a principal contracts with an agent to provide a good or service in exchange for compensation. If the interests and objectives of the principal and the agent are not perfectly aligned, then the agent may take hidden or unobserved actions that are detrimental to the interest of the principal. Hence there is strategic uncertainty between a principal and agent. For example, a real estate agent may not put forth the bargaining effort to increase the sales price of a house because she has other clients with more lucrative property; a stock broker may suggest unnecessary investment transactions to increase her commission; or a clerk does not provide quality customer service because the effort is too costly and the boss will not discover the poor service. In each of these cases, the principal cannot perfectly observe an agent's quality of work, effort, or other parameters that are important for realizing the principal's objective. Consequently, the agent has an incentive to exploit that information asymmetry by shirking or being opportunistic (providing low quality or effort), but still receiving full compensation, which is also known as a *moral hazard problem*.

The moral hazard problem generates inefficiencies and other forms of agency losses. First, since the agent obtains the benefits of shirking behavior, the principal does not obtain the benefits derived from full effort or quality of work. Moreover, from a social welfare perspective, moral hazard entails a loss for society in the form of foregone production associated with agency shirking and the costs of monitoring agency behavior. For example, knowing that agents may have strong incentives to shirk, principals can allocate resources to monitor agent performance, but the cost of monitoring performance means that other productive activities are sacrificed. Taken to its logical extent, principals may forego agency relationships altogether because they may find that the potential benefits from delegating authority to agents is less than the costs of monitoring their actions.

Moral hazard is prevalent in the development and implementation of public investment policies because there are multiple, nested principal-agent relationships with significant information asymmetries. Below are three examples where moral hazard is likely to have a negative impact on investment policy-rules and investment outcomes at the operational level.

First, consider the case in which a public manager is the principal who uses agents such as brokers or other financial analysts to implement a common policy-rule requiring investments first to protect the safety of the principal (deposits), second to maintain adequate liquidity, and third to achieve a return on funds invested. In other words, a return on funds invested should be pursued only if objectives one and two can be met as well.[8] Public investment managers are often public finance generalists, and thus they may need the expertise of brokers or dealers in the private sector to assist in implementing a investment plan based on the previously stated objectives. In essence, the public manager authorizes private brokers or dealers to make investments in accordance with the policy above in exchange for commissions or other forms of monetary benefit. For example, in a recent survey of public investors, 80 percent of respondents claim to consult at least two broker/dealers regarding purchasing securities, and about two-thirds use three broker/dealers as purchasing consultants (Flahaven, 2002).[9] Moreover, it is increasingly common for local governments with a small finance staff and relatively little expertise to privatize all of their portfolio management services (Greifer, 2001).

In any situation with private brokers as agents, there is a high probability of asymmetric information and the potential for moral hazard, because gaining additional expertise is the justification for using brokerage services. In a recent survey of public investors, for example, more than 70 percent of the respondents admitted that they did not verify broker/dealer prices with real-time market data when pricing individual securities. Because most brokerage agents work on some form of commission basis, they have strong incentives to encourage many large transactions in the financial markets. Such transactions can easily conflict with a policy valuing the safety of principal or liquidity over returns.

For instance, Bob Citron, the Orange County treasurer, relied heavily upon two Merrill Lynch financial analysts for advice. As you recall, Citron's investment strategy was based upon the expectation that interest rates would remain low and stable or decline in the long term. According to Jorion (1995), Citron relied heavily upon the interest rate forecasts of Charles Cough, Jr., chief investment strategist for Merrill Lynch. With favorable interest rate forecasts, Citron continued to receive advice on borrowing and purchasing securities from Michael Stamenson, a broker for Merrill Lynch who benefited financially from dealing with Citron and OCIP. His advice, and the continued sale of securities that many deemed inappropriate for public investment, can be considered agent shirking. This interpretation is consistent with the Orange County legal action against several investment firms, including Merrill Lynch, for fraud. The suit against Merrill Lynch was eventually settled out of court for about $470 million. Although Merrill Lynch did not admit wrongdoing, Stamenson is no longer with the company, and the relationship between the Merrill Lynch and the county was statutorily terminated for nine years (Bloomberg, 2003).[10]

A second case of moral hazard arises when the public is the principal who delegates investment authority through an election, such as a state or local government treasurer. There is a severe information asymmetry in this context because the public has very little incentive to gather information about the activities of the public manager. The public manager can make policies and take actions that reflect a responsible, competent approach to public investment, but she can also make opportunistic policies that are hidden from the public observation.[11] For example, elected officials can exploit information asymmetries to create a portfolio with high levels of risk that can bring substantially higher returns than a lower risk portfolio does. If the investments are profitable, the elected public manager can use the results as a basis for re-election, even though the high-risk portfolio did not conform to the stated investment policies written to reflect the objectives of the principal, that is, the public. The public will not discover opportunistic behavior until there is a significant public failure, which is also the story of Orange County.

In Orange County, Citron was the agent of the public, and in some ways he was more accountable to the public than to other elected officials. The political structure of Orange County, California, during the period under question, placed the authority for the management of public investments in the elected office of a county treasurer with a term of four years. The public also elected a five-member Board of Supervisors, who represented districts in the county. The board retained the services of a CAO, but neither held any controlling authority over the county treasurer. The role of the board and CAO was one of oversight, not policymaking. In short, the office of county treasurer was functionally autonomous from the board and the CAO.

Public confidence in Citron's management of the county investment pool was strong and stable, as demonstrated by six consecutive terms as the county treasurer (Baldassare, 1998). The source of this long-term support was not his educational or work experience, because Citron had not completed any degrees related to public or private finance, and had only served as a loan officer in a failed investment company before joining the staff of the county treasurer's office. However, upon attaining the office of county treasurer, his record of high returns fueled strong and stable support. In the campaigns previous to 1994, Citron had run virtually unopposed, primarily because of his management of OCIP. Citron consistently received commendations from the Board of Supervisors, local newspapers, and other local governments because of the extraordinary returns of the investment pools, which obviated the need for tax revenue increases.

Baldassare (1998) suggests that the 1994 election was a referendum on the investment policies that Bob Citron had followed for nearly two decades. Those policies had been extraordinarily successful for two decades, but at an inordinate risk to the public fisc. In the 1994 election, John Moorlach mounted a fierce campaign that specifically highlighted the impending losses of OCIP and risk exposure of Citron's management. Moorlach's claims did not resonate with the public or press because they were attributed to partisan sniping, but some Wall Street firms stopped lending to Citron, and some cities began to withdraw their deposits.[12]

Some local governments even complained that the election rhetoric hurt their credit ratings, which showed the credibility of Moorlach's claims. Just before the election, Moorlach even wrote to the Board of Supervisors about Citron's policies, but the board dismissed the letter as a publicity stunt in a losing election effort. Citron won the election with 61 percent of the vote, but OCIP would collapse soon after the election ended. The reality was that Moorlach was correct in his assessments, and he was eventually appointed county treasurer after Citron resigned.

In short, the public's agent had adopted opportunistic investment policies for nearly two decades. During that time, there were no observable agency losses because investment bets paid off.[13] Ultimately however, Citron's shirking the obligation to protect deposits resulted in the largest bankruptcy in municipal history, reduced county services, the selling of county assets, and years of fiscal instability.

A third, and particularly problematic case of moral hazard, arises when public investment managers are the "common agent" for multiple principals (Dixit, 1996). For example, consider the situation in which the public investment manager is a civil servant appointed by a legislative body such as a city council, whose members are elected by

the public. In this case, the elected officials directly delegate the investment policy-making authority to an agent, but the public indirectly delegates that authority through their election of the city council. Hence,
the public manager is the agent of both the council and the public at
large. Even if the public manager develops and perfectly implements a
policy that reflects the goals and objectives of one principal, that policy
may not reflect the goals and interests of the other principal. For example, a model policy that values protection of financial principal and
liquidity over returns is generally considered to be in the public's interest, but may not be in the interest of other elected officials, because a
city council under fiscal stress may pressure for greater returns.[14] The
public manager must determine which policy to implement, and in
choosing one, will be shirking in relation to the other principal. Note
that both policies can legitimately be said to serve the public interests,
but they do so in contradictory manners, thus by definition shirking
must occur. The Orange County case illustrates two "common agency"
situations.

   In the first situation, the county treasurer can be considered the
common agent of both the Board of Supervisors and the general public. As previously discussed, Citron was clearly an elected agent of the
public. In general, the public's objectives in investment management
are to first protect principal; second, maintain liquidity; and third,
obtain a return on investments. This classic description of public objectives, however, was in conflict with the objectives of the Board of
Supervisors, who had been increasingly reliant on the Citron's investment returns as a significant and stable flow of revenue for county
operations (Baldassare, 1998).

   In reality, the board's objective was to obtain returns on investments
first. It is true that the Board of Supervisors had no direct control over
investment operations in Orange County, but the five elected members
of the board clearly had oversight authority and the ability to influence
investment operations. For example, the county government had to
authorize the borrowing of funds to be used by Citron for investment
purposes. During a post-bankruptcy hearing, the California state senate
grilled two board members about their oversight of county treasurer.
During the testimony, the two board members could not recall a $600
million taxable note issued in July 1994, that had been passed on the
consent calendar (Jorion, 1995). This activity by the board represents
the tacit agreement between the board as principal and the county
treasurer as agent to use investment policies for the goal of providing
substantial and stable revenue flows for the county government.
However, this objective is in conflict with what is typically prescribed
to be in the public's interest. Citron can be said to have disregarded

the typically defined public good, but he was in alignment with the Board of Supervisors.

The second example of common agency problem is seen in the structure of the OCIP. An investment pool is a financial institution designed to reduce the transaction costs of participating in financial markets and increase investment returns (Pasqual, Collins, and Reid, 1989). By pooling investment funds and exploiting group purchasing power, smaller public agencies act collectively to obtain more expertise, greater access to high-yield investments, and a greater level of portfolio diversification. Administrative costs are reduced by spreading the costs among many participants, and investment transaction costs are reduced because larger pools of capital will generate more competition among financial institutions seeking investment capital. In short, local governments can obtain investment economies of scale if they deposit funds in an investment pool that is under some centralized management. In the OCIP case, for example, 187 public agencies made deposits in the pool that Citron managed as the Orange County treasurer. These agencies included among others, 37 municipalities, 60 school districts, and 11 water districts that made deposits, and thus made Citron their investment agent (Jorion, 1995).

Despite the steady growth in the number of local governments joining the OCIP during Citron's tenure, the very structure of the investment pool demonstrates a pernicious common agency problem. When making a deposit in the investment pool, a local government essentially selected Citron as their agent for public investment. However, those local governments had different objectives for public investment. For example, school districts and other special districts were required by law to invest idle funds or have them held in trust, so these governments had virtually no choice but to make deposits in OCIP. It is fair to say that their objective was principal preservation. Other local governments, such as Santa Barbara and Claremont, however, openly stated that their primary reason for participating in the pool was to generate revenue flows to supplement tax revenues (Jorion, 1995).

Hence, the institutions that encouraged a mix of mandated and voluntary participation in OCIP generated a severe common agency problem that was left for Citron to resolve. His investment policies were consistent with the objectives of the voluntary participants and even benefited the mandatory participants, but formally he was not pursuing the objectives of mandatory participants. When the pool became insolvent, all of the principals paid actual and opportunity costs.

In summary, there are many principal-agent situations in public investment management that have a strong negative influence on investment outcomes. There are generally two strategies for ameliorating these problems: reduce information asymmetries and align the incentives of the agent with the objectives of the principal. In public finance, reducing information asymmetries is the most common strategy for overcoming moral hazard.

From a theoretical standpoint, the reduction of information asymmetries between a principal and agent will reduce the likelihood and severity of moral hazard. In practice, this means that principals must monitor the behavior of agents to ensure compliance. For example, public managers are often required to submit reports and undergo audits. These monitoring techniques are effective means of reducing information asymmetries if they are grounded in accounting rules that provide standard definitions of common terms like revenue, expenses, assets, and liabilities so that audits can conducted by third parties. Even this system, however, raises a second-order moral hazard problem, in that information asymmetries regarding accounting and financial statements create incentives for both public managers and auditors to make inaccurate reports, just as the Enron and other financial scandals in 2001–2002 demonstrate. Nonetheless, financial reports, audits, and accounting standards are fundamental to sound public investment management.

As the Orange County case illustrates, however, monitoring is not a panacea. First, the county treasurer did make reports to the Board of Supervisors, but those reports were generally only annual, verbal, and often incomprehensible (Jorion, 1995). Eventually, the Board of Supervisors asked for written reports and received reports which included comments that made little sense such as:

> We do not have the large inflationary wage increases, runaway building, both in homes, commercial, and those tall glass office buildings. . . . Few, if any, tall office buildings are being built. (Jorion, 1995, p.14)

In addition to the county treasurer reports, however, there were outside audits of the investment pool that failed to inform the board, the public, or participants in OCIP of the fundamental problems in the investment pool (Jorion 1995). In 1994 alone, there were four independent audits of OCIP. The SEC, financial intermediaries including S & P and Moody's, the auditor hired by the Board of Supervisors (KPMG's Pete Marwick), and the elected county auditor, Steve Lewis, all conducted audits without findings to suggest a fundamentally flawed investment operation.[15] Some auditors, such as Marwick, claimed that they were not hired to second guess the investment policy, just audit the internal controls or detect illegal activities (Jorion, 1995).

Even though monitoring public investment managers has the potential to reduce information asymmetries, and thus opportunistic actions, additional responses to moral hazard generally focus on financial incentives that are designed to align the incentives of the agent with the objectives of the principal. In market situations, financial incentives often include some form of profit-sharing among the principal and agent that are formalized in a contract. Alternatively, contracts may require an agent to be bonded as collateral against shirking. In either case, the logic is that agents will reduce opportunistic behavior if their behavior can be directly tied to the principal's preferred outcome, which is often modeled as profit. Even if there are contractual incentives, monitoring must occur to ensure compliance with the contract so the contract does not obviate the need for monitoring.

There are many other limitations to a contractual approach in general, and even more limitations for public investment management.[16] Consider first the notion of contracting between the principal and agent in public investment management. In many situations there is no formal contracting between the principal and agent, because the agent is an official who may be electorally bound to pursue the public good, but the terms of the "electoral contract" are vague at best. Moreover, there is no mechanism to offer or to enforce financial incentives for more effective public investment because elected officials serve under constitutionally or statutorily defined compensation.[17] Even in the case of managers in civil service positions, there is very little contractual space in which to provide financial incentives because civil service, by definition, standardizes contracts for government employees and limits variation in their compensation packages. Privatization of public investment management is the situation most likely to utilize financial incentives to align principal and agent interests, because such financial incentives could be written into the RFP as the compensation for investment services.

In summary, information asymmetries in the collective choice arena create severe political and managerial dilemmas for public investment managers. Although monitoring can reduce information asymmetries, and contracting has some potential to reduce the temptation for public managers to act opportunistically, both approaches have significant limitations. Consequently, more blunt policy instruments are often brought to bear. The next section examines how constitutional rules attempt to restrict managerial discretion in an effort to prevent some of the pathologies associated with asymmetric information in public finance management.

Responses to Moral Hazard in the Constitutional Arena of Choice

In the constitutional arena of choice, actors take actions that determine the constitutional rules that govern the collective choice arena

(Kiser and Ostrom, 1982). Constitutional-level rules define who is eligible to participate in collective choice arenas and what rules will govern the collective choice process. In addition, constitutions also specify substantive rules that can constrain policy-making or managerial discretion by prohibiting certain classes of actions or policies.

Constitutional rules are important for public investment managers because incentives and monitoring do not completely resolve moral hazard in the collective choice arena. For example, the California state government made multiple constitutional level responses to the Orange County bankruptcy. Because Orange County was a "general law" county, the California state statues are the body of constitutional rules governing public investment at the local level. In direct response to the bankruptcy, the state government passed two major pieces of legislation to address the moral hazard problems.[18]

The first set of reforms sought to enhance monitoring of public investment managers in an attempt to reduce the information asymmetries giving rise to moral hazard. Each county's board of supervisors was required to appoint an investment oversight committee to include the county treasurer, a county financial officer, representative from the board of supervisors, representatives from other local governments participating in investment pools, and members of the public. Moreover, the new provisions required county treasurers to present a written, annual investment policy statement to the oversight committee and board of supervisors. What had merely been good practice before the bankruptcy was codified as a constitutional requirement for general law counties.

A second set of reforms created an informal contract between elected county treasurers and the public with incentives to mitigate against moral hazard. First, there was legislation that constitutionally defined the goals and objectives of local public investment managers as safeguarding principal first, maintaining liquidity second, and obtaining returns on funds third. Legislation also endowed public investment managers with a legal trustee/fiduciary status. Thus, any violation of the constitutional investment objectives for general law counties would henceforth have legal ramifications and penalties. These potential individual sanctions are functionally equivalent to bonding an agent. In other words, public managers who violate their fiduciary status would suffer significant loss, whether in financial penalties or loss of freedom.

A final set of constitutional reforms sought to significantly diminish managerial discretion by removing policy and operational choices from an investment manager's domain of options. The logic is that information asymmetries are likely to be exploited in a systematic fashion. If those opportunistic actions can be identified, then some forms of shirking can be constitutionally prohibited. Thus, the California state government prohibited local public investment mangers from purchasing inverse floaters, one of the most damaging investments for OCIP. Prohibitions against using short-term debt to purchase long-term maturities were also instituted. Managers could use reverse repurchase agreements, but such securities were limited to 20 percent of the total portfolio value. Moreover, there were many new rules governing the process of depositing and withdrawing funds from an investment pool, including lengthier periods for providing notice of withdrawals. In short, the state attempted to constitutionally prohibit other counties from adopting Citron's investment policies.

This last set of constitutional reforms pose a dilemma for public finance. On one hand, it is important to prevent the type of investment failures that occurred in Orange County, and limiting managerial discretion is one solution. In contrast, public managers need discretion to perform their duties. For example, during periods of very low interest rates, limiting managerial discretion may effectively eliminate policies and operational decisions that are effective in that financial environment. Moreover, rules may inadvertently restrict public managers from using innovative financial strategies that were unforeseen when the rules were developed. Hence, there remains a conundrum of how to balance the benefits of constitutional constraints on public managers with the costs of restricting managerial discretion.

Therefore, constitutional constraints are, in many cases, a response to moral hazard problems arising from information asymmetries that occur in the collective choice arena. Yet, even if constitutional constraints, monitoring, and incentive contracts resolve moral hazard problems in the collective choice arena, information asymmetries can entail adverse selection problems in the operational arena of choice. However, adverse selection can be mitigated with a variety of responses if independent intermediaries or policy-making bodies take appropriate actions. The important implication of these analyses in each arena of choice is that a full understanding of public finance management requires a perspective that is broader than market operations only, public administration only, or politics only. The next section explores how these arenas are linked in to structure the complex decision making of public finance under asymmetric information.

An Institutional Analysis of Public Finance under Asymmetric Information

The IAD framework of analysis has been instructive about how asymmetric information creates strategic uncertainty in three arenas of choice.

Yet these arenas are only separable units for analytic purposes because public finance is practiced in an environment of nested institutions that structures decision making under asymmetric information. In particular, we can define the key elements of an arena of choice and show how those elements link arenas of public finance and how information asymmetries operate within and across these arenas of public finance.

Figure 2.1 provides a conceptual map to illustrate how arenas of public finance are linked, and Table 2.1 presents examples of the framework from the Orange County case.[19] There are four elements in the diagram below: action situations, outcomes, rules-in-use, and monitoring and sanctioning. First, the *action situation* is the social context in which individuals make decisions or take actions. The decisions or actions taken are contingent upon the arena of choice. Describing an action situation requires knowledge of the participants who are in positions to make decisions about potential actions they can take *given the information they possess* about how those potential actions are linked to potential outcomes, and the costs and benefits of those actions and outcomes to the participants.[20] This is the context in which *information asymmetries* affect decisions and actions in public finance.

Thus, *outcomes*, the second component of the framework, are the results of decisions or actions taken in the action situation. These outcomes are often evaluated according to criteria such as efficiency, equity, effectiveness, fiscal equivalency, or accountability. Outcomes in the operational arena serve as the primary feedback mechanism for decisions and actions in all arenas of choice. In other words, performance affects decisions and actions in constitutional, collective choice and operational arenas of choice.

The final two elements are rules-in-use and mechanisms of monitoring and sanctioning. In the constitutional arena and collective choice arena, the key outcomes are rules that are used to govern decisions and actions in lower arenas of choice. For example, constitutional rules govern policy-making in the collective choice arena, and those policies govern operational decisions and actions. Since rules are not "self-formulating, self-determining, or self-enforcing" (V. Ostrom, 1980, p. 312), however, the mechanisms of *monitoring and sanctioning* determine the *rules-in-use*, which are how rules are actually applied in governing the action situations in which decisions and actions are taken in any arena of choice. In summary, actors are making decisions and taking actions in response to a specific set of governing institutional arrangements (i.e., rules-in use, monitoring, sanctioning mechanisms), and action situations, which are often characterized by information asymmetries.

Thus, this framework of analysis demonstrates how nested rules can structure the impact of information asymmetries in public financial man-

Figure 2.1
An IAD Conceptual Map for Public Finance Decision Making
Adapted from Rules, Games and Common-Pool Resources *by Ostrom, Gardner, and Walker (Ann Arbor: The University of Michigan Press, 1994).*

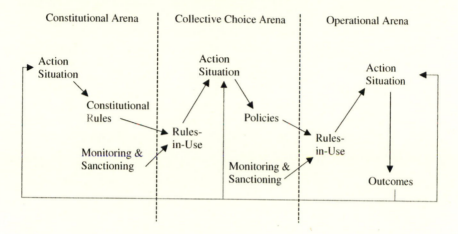

agement. Table 2.1 provides a short summary of the Orange County case to illustrate how the framework can be applied to demonstrate how public managers and political officials respond to information asymmetries that permeate public financial management. For example, the summary story of Orange County is one of an elected county treasurer with an investment policy (collective choice arena) that requires borrowing funds to make high-risk, low-liquidity investments in the financial markets (operational arena). There was virtually no monitoring or sanctioning of his behavior by the public, Board of Supervisors, or auditors (collective choice arena), and thus Citron continued the investment strategy until investors started a run on OCIP in fear that the fund was not solvent (operational arena). In light of mounting losses (outcome in operational arena), the board declared bankruptcy (outcome feeds into collective choice arena) and the California state government restructured rules governing public investment in general law counties (outcome feeds into constitutional arena).

In summary, an institutional analysis structured through an IAD framework provides a deep contextual understanding of both discrete decisions and the interactions of financial markets, public bureaucracies, and politics, which lend both theoretical and practical insights into public finance management. First, the framework of analysis presented here provides a means of organizing theoretical inquiry into public finance management. Whereas Table 2.1 illustrates its application to an interesting case study, Table 2.2 demonstrates how the framework organizes major concepts in public investment management. A similar exercise can be applied to public finance in general.

Table 2.1
An Institutional Analysis of the Orange County Bankruptcy

	Operational Level	Collective Choice Level	Constitutional Level
Key Decisions or Actions in Arena	• Citron issues $600 million in debt in summer of 1994 to cover liquidity problems • Citron extends the duration of some investments from 5 years to 10 years in mid-1994 in an effort to make up for earlier losses and liquidity problems	• Public votes on county treasurer and Board of Supervisors • Board of Supervisors determines county budget and revenue sources • County treasurer uses autonomy to make investment policy • Other local governments determine investment policies	• State legislature determines whether general law governments have too much discretion in public investment. • State legislature determines whether changes should be made to qualifications for county treasurers.
Key Outcomes of Decision Making and Actions	• OCIP defaults on bond payments • Board of Supervisors file for Chapter 9 bankruptcy as run on OCIP is beginning	• Citron elected county treasurer • Citron adopts high-risk, low-liquidity investment policy designed to provide substantial, stable revenue flows to OCIP participants • Local governments join OCIP • Board of supervisors do not raise taxes to ease reliance on investment revenues	• Two pieces of legislation redefined the "general law" provisions for county governments, i.e., changed the constitution for general law governments

Table 2.1 (Continued)
An Institutional Analysis of the Orange County Bankruptcy

Rules in Use	• Citron's high-risk, low-liquidity policy of leveraging reverse repossession agreements to exploit the difference between short and longer term interest rates	• General law status of Orange County • Charters of municipalities participating in OCIP • State statutes requiring school district to invest idle funds • Proposition 13, which limited county taxing authority	• Rules and procedures governing the California state assembly
Monitoring and Sanctioning	• Failure of Citron to report properly • Failure of Board of Supervisors • Failure of ratings agencies • Failure of the public via elections	• Independent judiciaries after the bankruptcy • Board of Supervisors after bankruptcy • Oversight committee after bankruptcy • Voters after bankruptcy	• Public • Powerful groups • Other elites • Independent judiciaries

The practical import of this framework of analysis for public managers is the recognition that distinct arenas of choice will impact their administration of public finance in three ways. First, public managers must recognize that constitutions often limit managerial discretion. Although there are strong justifications for limiting discretion in when asymmetric information is present, constitutional constraints are still blunt instruments that easily stifle innovation and tie the hands of public investment mangers during periods of low interest rates. Consequently, managers should play an active role in the creation or re-creation of constitutional constraints, or else risk the loss of important investment tools and techniques.

Second, both political officials and public managers must recognize the critical importance and limitations of monitoring and sanctioning. Monitoring public financial management is the primary means by which information asymmetries are reduced in the operational and collective choice

Table 2.2
A Conceptual Overview of an Institutional Analysis of Public Finance

	Operational Level	Collective Choice Level	Constitutional Level
Key Decisions or Actions in Arena	• Investing at particular time • Issuing debt at particular time • Participation in an investment pool • Selection of instruments • Selection of maturities	• Investment objectives: safety, liquidity, returns • Selection of public investment managers or those who will appoint managers • Definitions of classes of acceptable financial instruments and maturities	• Investment objectives: safety, liquidity, returns • Eligibility requirements for public managers and those who select public managers • Definitions of classes of acceptable financial instruments and maturities
Key Outcomes of Decision Making and Actions	• Return on investments • Capital raised • Debt burden • Exposure to risk	• Investment policies (Heller et al., 2002) • Laws, statutes or ordinances	• Constitutional rules
Rules in Use	• Investment policies, laws, statutes, or ordinances as implemented in the collective choice arena	• Constitutional rules as enforced through monitoring and sanctioning	• Wide variety of rules that are contingent upon form of constitutional decision making.[21]
Monitoring and Sanctioning	• Decisions and action lead directly to outcomes.	• Independent judiciaries • Constitutionally appointed agents • Voters	• Public • Powerful groups • Other elites

arenas of public finance. However, the mechanisms for monitoring and sanctioning are not perfect. Accounting standards can be ignored or misunderstood. Ratings agencies may not be vigilant in their analyses. Auditors can be sloppy or unethical. Politicians may pressure managers for greater returns when that is an inappropriate policy, and the public may not know or fully understand the implications of such actions.

Therefore, public managers are best served by multiple and even redundant mechanisms for monitoring public investment management. Multiple mechanisms reduce the possibility of collusion between public managers and their monitors. Redundant mechanisms provide a quality control for monitoring mechanisms. Even though there is no perfect way to reduce information asymmetries, multiple redundant mechanisms are an appropriate, but expensive, goal.

Finally, public managers and political officials should not consider the challenges of asymmetric information insurmountable. Implicit in the framework of analysis presented above is the premise that people can create institutions to resolve problems and improve the decision-making situation. In other words, public finance and public investment are not static. Financial markets are fast-paced, dynamic institutions that are constantly innovating. Public managers and political officials must be willing to do the same if the benefits of public investment are to be realized. This means that managers and political officials in all arenas of choice must seek to develop innovative institutional arrangements that encourage active participation in financial markets that is both responsible and responsive to the public.

Conclusion

In conclusion, it is important to recognize that information asymmetries impact public finance in different ways, which can be conceptualized according to arenas of choice. At the operational level, asymmetric information can result in adverse selection that affects the outcomes of financial transactions in various markets. In the collective choice arena, asymmetric information can create moral hazard among principals who contract with agents to conduct public finance. This situation is exacerbated by the nested principal-agent relationships among the public, elected officials, and professional managers in both the public and private sectors. The strong incentive for agent shirking and resultant losses has led to constitutional provisions that limit the discretion of public managers.

The Orange County case is perhaps the worst-case scenario of what happens when information asymmetries are not effectively addressed. Although the county has recovered very quickly from its bankruptcy, the case is still instructive today because many other public managers face information asymmetries in a similar institutional context that does not provide an effective response to the problems associated with information asymmetries. Like the Orange County case, these problems may not become apparent until there is a financial disaster. Hence, it is incumbent upon public managers, political officials, and the public to recognize the danger signs associated with information asymmetries and respond appropriately with actions in every arena of choice: operational, collective choice, or constitutional.

Notes

1. There have been many accounts of the Orange County bankruptcy. This chapter relies heavily upon the Jorion (1995) and Baldassare (1998) accounts.

2. There are certainly other factors that affect decision making, actions, and outcomes in public finance. The IAD framework also suggests that attributes of the physical world and community will also impact decision making in the arena of choice (Kiser and Ostrom, 1982; Ostrom, Gardner, and Walker, 1994). The attributes of the physical world include the physical limitations of transforming actions into outcomes or the nature of goods and services, such as whether a good is subtractive in nature (private, common pool resources) or not (public toll goods). For example, basketball is a game of strategic interaction in which players must make decisions about their actions, such as whether to pull up for a short jump shot or dunk the basketball. The action arena will definitely influence the decision to shoot or to dunk, but the physical attributes of height and gravity may foreclose the possibility of some of some actions, such as dunking a basketball. Attributes of the community can best be summarized as the prevailing culture and shared history, if any, of the participants. To simplify the presentation above, we have excluded the impact of these important factors.

3. See Phlips (1988) and Hillier (1997) for a good overview of the economics of asymmetric information in a market context. Bebczuk (2003) provides a detailed application of asymmetric information to financial markets. Rasmusen (2001) provides a game-theoretic foundation for understanding the implications of information asymmetries in a variety of contexts.

4. Chess has the same information structure as the first game mentioned in Milgrom and Roberts (1987), but the complexity of calculations makes the game very challenging to play and perhaps more amenable to wagering.

5. In this game, uncertainty arises from the incomplete information about the cards held in the opponent's hand. Information asymmetries can also arise from the uncertainty associated with games in which one player does not know the behavior (moves or choices) of other players. In general, game theory distinguishes this type of uncertainty as a product of imperfect information, which focuses upon player behavior. Incomplete information arises

from a player's understanding of elements of the game, such as number of players, payoffs, or available strategies (Phlips 1988).

6. The IAD framework has a long and deep intellectual history associated with rational choice institutional analysis and the Workshop in Political Theory and Policy Analysis (Kiser and Ostrom, 1982; Ostrom, Gardner, and Walker,, 1994; McGinnis, 2000). As a framework of analysis, the IAD helps to organize inquiry by positing broad relationships that are used to address many questions. Many different theories can be developed from a single framework of analysis, just as many different formal models can be derived from a single theory.

7. For the purpose of this analysis, the following broad definition of rules applies: "Rules, as we use the term, are prescriptions that define what action (or outcomes) are required, prohibited, or permitted, and the sanctions authorized if the rules are not followed. All rules are the result of implicit or explicit efforts to achieve order and predictability among humans by creating classes of persons (positions) who are then required, permitted, or forbidden to take classes of actions in relation to required, permitted, or forbidden states of the world" (Ostrom, Gardener, and Walker, 1994, p. 38).

8. There are obviously other very important public investment objectives that value returns much more highly. Public pensions are one important example. Because Orange County is the example in this chapter, we focus on a set of investment objectives that would be appropriate for this case.

9. Such principal-agent arrangements may be formal or informal. Privatization generally requires a formal contract and RFP process, but there are many informal "contracts" between public managers and their investment consultants. The form of the contract is straightforward: in exchange for advice from the consultant, the public manager will use the broker to make market transactions. Thus, the moral hazard problem: more transactions benefit the broker, but may not be consistent with the public manager's policy, but the manager probably is not fully capable of determining whether the advice is consistent with the policy, else she would not be seeking advice.

10. In June 2003, Orange County resumed a working relationship with Merrill Lynch. County Treasurer John Moorlach stated that "There's no use in fighting an old war . . ." especially since Lynch has "the largest inventory of any broker-dealer (Bloomberg, 2003, p. C5)."

11. This does not indicate a cover-up or a failure to disclose information per se. Information about governmental activities and policies is a public good, nonrivalrous and not packageable. Hence, there is a collective action problem and public information is rarely produced without vigilant press corps or interest groups.

12. Although county elections were nonpartisan, it was well known that Citron was a Democrat, and the only elected Democrat at the county level. Moorlach was backed by Republicans.

13. Other agency losses became apparent during the legal investigation that resulted in a plea agreement requiring Citron to plead guilty to several felony counts of fraudulent activities surrounding the distribution of investment returns to various accounts. Citron did not violate any laws regarding public investments (Baldassare, 1998).

14. Of course, one resolution is to presume that elected officials perfectly represent the public, so that what elected officials prefer is, by definition, what the public prefers. This is problematic on several levels, including Arrow's impossibility theorem and the information asymmetries that create a moral hazard problem between the public and their representative agents.

15. County auditor Lewis did highlight unusual and risky investments in a 1991 audit that detected investments in below investment-grade securities, which was contrary to state statutes. Citron removed those securities from the portfolio.

16. See Williamson (1985) for a classic analysis of the problems of incomplete contracting and principal-agent problems and institutional responses to them. Dixit (1996) also provides a model of how ineffective these approaches are in a common agency situation.

17. Heller, Walton, and Willmoth (2002, p. 20) call for governments to indemnify "investment officers from personal liability so long as they adhere to the tenets of their respective policies." This is contrary to the logic of having an agent be bonded to induce incentive alignment with the principal, especially if the agent has significant discretion in setting the investment policy. It also assumes that a well-defined investment policy is in place or outside the discretion of the public investment manager.

18. The two pieces of legislation were SB 866 and SB 564. See Baldassare (1998) for a detailed summary for both state and local level reforms, including a movement to become a charter government, which would enable the citizens to make the county treasurer an appointed position under a county executive. The charter proposal failed in a referendum with 61% of the voters against a charter government.

19. This figure is adapted from Ostrom, Gardner, and Walker's (1994) description of the IAD framework of analysis. This chapter makes an application of the IAD framework to public finance in general and public investment in particular.

20. A full description of the action situation also includes a description of the actors (Ostrom, Gardner, and Walker, 1994). The actors are the participants who have preferences, information processing capabilities, selection criteria, and resources. The actors and the action situation create patterns of strategic interaction that directly affect outcomes in the real world.

21. For example, there are constitutional conventions, referenda, initiatives, and other forms of amending a previously existing constitution. Creating a constitution *sui generis* also involves rules, but they are rarely formal and often embedded in the norms of a community's elites.

References

Akerlof, G. A. 1970. "The Market for 'Lemons': Quality Uncertainty and the Market Mechanism." *Quarterly Journal of Economics*, 84, no. 3: 488–500.

Baldassare, M. 1998. *When Government Fails: The Orange County Bankruptcy.* Berkeley: University of California Press.

Bebczuk, R. 2003. *Asymmetric Information in Financial Markets: Introduction and Applications.* Cambridge: Cambridge University Press.

Dixit, A. K. 1996. *The Making of Economic Policy: A Transaction Cost Politics Perspective.* Cambridge: MIT Press.

Flahaven, B. 2002. "Survey Reveals Preference for Passive Investing." *Government Finance Review*, 18, no. 5: 39–40.

Forsythe, R., R. Lundholm, and T. Rietz. 1999. "Cheap Talk, Fraud, and Adverse Selection in Financial Markets: Some Experimental Evidence." *Review of Financial Studies*, 12, no. 3: 481–518.

Greifer, N. 2001. "Revising Treasury Management Strategies." *American City and County*, 116, no. 11: 12.

Heller, F., S. Walton, and J. Willmoth. 2002. "Back to Basics: Making the Case for Investment Policies." *Government Finance Review*, 18, no. 4: 20–23.

Hillier, B. 1997. *Economics of Asymmetric Information.* New York: Palgrave Macmillan.

Jorion, P. 1995. *Big Bets Gone Bad: Derivatives and Bankruptcy in Orange County.* San Diego: Academic Press.

Jorion, P. 2001. "Orange County Case: Using Value at Risk to Control Financial Risk." Case study, http://www.gsm.uci.edu/~jorion/oc/case.html (accessed June 6, 2003).

Kiser, L., and E. Ostrom. 1982. "The Three Worlds of Action: A Meta-theoretical Synthesis of Institutional Approaches." In *Strategies of Political Inquiry*, ed. E. Ostrom, 179–222. Thousand Oaks, CA: Sage Publications.

Lerner, J. 2002. "When Bureaucrats Meet Entrepreneurs: The Design of Effective 'Public Venture Capital' Programmes." *Economic Journal*, 122, no. 477: 73–84.

McCue, C. P. 2000. "The Risk-Return Paradox in Local Government Investing." *Public Budgeting and Finance*, 20, no. 3: 80–101.

McGinnis, M. D., ed. 2000. *Polycentric Games and Institutions: Readings from the Workshop in Political Theory and Policy Analysis.* Ann Arbor, MI: University of Michigan Press.

"Merrill Lynch Gets Back into Orange County's Good Graces." 2003. *Seattle Times*, 4 June, C5.

Milgrom, P., and J. Roberts. 1987. "Information Asymmetries, Strategic Behavior, and Industrial Organization." *American Economic Review*, 77, no. 2: 184–193.

Ostrom, E. 1990. *Governing the Commons: The Evolution of Institutions for Collective Action.* Cambridge: Cambridge University Press.

Ostrom, E., R. Gardner, and J. Walker. 1994. *Rules, Games, and Common Pool Resources.* Ann Arbor, MI: University of Michigan Press.

Ostrom, E. 1996. "An Agenda for the Study of Institutions." *Public Choice,* 48, no. 1: 3–25.

Ostrom, V. 1980. "Artisanship and Artifact." *Public Administration Review,* 40, no. 4: 309–317.

Pasqual, S., B. K. Collins, and M. Reid. 1989. *Local Government Investment Pools.* Lexington, KY: National Association of State Treasurers.

Phlips, L. 1988. *The Economics of Imperfect Information.* Cambridge: Cambridge University Press.

Rasmusen, E. 2001. *Games and Information: An Introduction to Game Theory.* London: Blackwell Publishers.

Reed, B., and J. W. Swain. 1997. *Public Finance Administration.* Thousand Oaks, CA: Sage Publications.

Weimer, D. L., and A. R. Vining. 1999. *Policy Analysis: Concepts and Practice,* 3rd ed. Upper Saddle River, NJ: Prentice Hall.

Williamson, O. E. 1985. *The Economic Institutions of Capitalism.* New York: Free Press.

CHAPTER 3

Bridging the Gap Between Contract Service Delivery and Public Financial Management
Applying Theory to Practice

Lawrence L. Martin

Governments at all levels today (federal, state, and local) operate in a privatized environment. A substantial proportion of public services are now delivered through contractual arrangements with for-profit businesses and non-profit organizations. For example, the Commercial Activities Panel of the U.S. General Accounting Office (GAO, 2001) reports that total federal contracting reached $216 billion in fiscal year 2001, divided as follows: services (43 percent), supplies and equipment (37 percent), research and development (12 percent) and construction (8 percent) (GAO, 2002). The federal government is one of the world's largest purchasers of services.

Specific data on service contracting for state and local governments are not readily available. However, contracting for both goods and services is estimated at $275 billion annually (Cooper, 2003, p. 11). Studies of state and local government contracting suggest that a substantial proportion of this $275 billion figure involves services (Martin, 1999a; Chi and Jasper, 1998). It is not too strong a statement to say that without its cadre of contractors, governments today could not discharge their basic service responsibilities.

The trend in the use of contracting to provide public services shows no sign of decreasing. At the federal level, President Bush's management agenda calls for subjecting some 850,000 positions identified as commercial in nature to competition and potential contracting. The Office of Management and Budget (OMB) has established a goal of having all federal department and agencies compete at least 10 percent of these positions during fiscal year 2003 (OMB, 2002, p. 18). At the state and local government levels, studies suggest that service contracting will continue to trend upward. Some 56 percent of state agencies and 66 percent of local governments (municipalities and counties) indicate that they intend to increase their use of service contracting (Martin, 1999a, p. 12; Chi and Jasper, 1998, p. 4).

Service Contracting as Public Financial Management

Service contracting has become a "core competency" of governments (McCue and Gianakis, 2001; Kelman, 2001). Consequently, it is difficult to understand why service contracting continues to receive so little attention in the public financial management literature (Martin and Miller, 2005; Kelman, 2002; MacManus, 1991; MacManus and Watson, 1990). At its most fundamental level, public financial management is concerned with the basic pursuit of the so-called three Es: economy, efficiency, and effectiveness (Premchand, 1993, p. 292). How can public financial managers purport to pursue government economy, efficiency, and effectiveness in today's privatized environment without including service contracting?

The argument can be made that the lack of attention paid to service contracting in the public financial management literature is at least partially the result of a lack of theory. As Cooper (2003) notes, most of the literature addressing service contracting falls into one of two categories: (1) *policy* debates, much of which are polemical in nature, on the relative merits of service contracting vis-à-vis direct government delivery (e.g. Sclar, 2001; Moe, 1987); or (2) *administrative* debates over how to conduct valid cost comparisons between government and contract service delivery (traditionally referred to as "make-or-buy" decisions) (e.g., Martin and Miller, 2005; Anthony and Young, 2003; Martin, 1999c; Kelly, 1984).

Only make-or-buy decisions can be said to truly address a public financial management issue. The larger, and equally important, area of service contract administration has been largely ignored in the public financial management literature. Without at least some theoretical basis to serve as a bridge between service contracting and public financial management, governments would appear to be relegated to an endless series of trial and error experiments with little hope of gaining insight into, and developing an understanding of, the economy, efficiency, and effectiveness of this mode of alternative service delivery. As Brown and Potoski (2003, p. 153) suggest, "The success or failure of any alternative service delivery arrangement likely depends on how well governments can manage the entire contracting process." The General Accounting Office (GAO) has framed the issue more succinctly, "Put simply, the poor management of service contracts undermines the government's ability to obtain good value for the money spent" (Cooper, 2003, p. 105).

This chapter looks at the application of two theoretical frameworks that hold promise for improving our understanding of the public financial management aspects of service contracting, with particular emphasis on contract administration. The first framework, "principal/agent" theory, comes from the realm of economics. The second, the "expanded systems framework," is derived from the traditional engineering concept of efficiency (the ratio of outputs to inputs) as extended by the government performance accountability literature and movement. Principal/agent theory provides normative guidance as to how service contracting relationships should be structured and contract administration activities carried out. The expanded systems framework provides normative guidance on how the concept of performance should be conceptualized and operationalized in service contracting.

Principal/Agent Theory

Principal/agent theory is derived from the field of economics (e.g., Spence and Zeckhauser, 1971; Ross, 1973). The basic problem addressed by the theory is how to best structure principal/agent relationships so that the latter will act in the best interests of the former. Among its many public sector applications, principal/agent theory has been used to study the relationships between: elected officials and public managers (Feldman and Khademian, 2002); city councils and city managers (Selden, Brewer, and Brudney, 1999); auditors and clients (McCall, 2002); actors in the budgetary process (Forrester, 2002); and health care reform (Sekwat, 2000). Principal/agent theory has also been used to study contracting. However, much of this work has appeared in nonpublic financial-management–oriented publications or addressed defense contracting (Bajari and Tadelis, 2001). As a result, this literature appears to have largely escaped the attention of many public financial managers.

In applying principal/agent theory to service contracting, governments (principals) delegate functions or activities (service delivery) to contractors (agents). Principal/agent theory has generated a number of important insights that have implications for service contracting, including: transaction cost analysis; the problems of information asymmetry, incomplete contracts, and agent opportunism; the use of *ex ante* incentives and penalties; and approaches to *ex post* monitoring. These concepts in turn provide normative guidance relative to the structure and administration of service contracts.

Transaction Cost Analysis

Transaction costs are said to be inherent in any principal/agent relationship (Brown and Potoski, 2001; Sclar, 2001; Kettl, 1993). They can be defined as the costs principals incur to insure that agents act in their best interests. Transaction costs can be internal to an organization (employer/employee relationships) or external (government/contractor relationships).

The foundation work on transaction cost analysis is generally credited to Williamson (e.g., 1985, 1975). According to Williamson, the costs of producing any good or service is a combination of both production costs and transaction costs. Applied to service contracting, *production costs* are those costs governments incur in paying or reimbursing contractors to deliver services. *Transaction costs* are those costs governments incur in the administration and monitoring of service contractors and contract service delivery. The concept of transaction costs and their analysis may be the most important insight provided by principal/agent theory.

Governments are said to engage in service contracting for a variety of reasons, including promotion of competition, flexibility in service delivery, restricting the size of government, access to outside expertise, and others (e.g., Savas, 2000; Kettl, 1993). However, the reason most frequently cited by governments themselves for using service contracting is to reduce costs (Martin and Miller, 2005; McDavid, 2001; Martin, 1999a; Chi and Jasper, 1998; Stone, Bell, and Pool, 1997). Following Williamson's guidance, contract service delivery only makes economic sense when the combination of contractor production and transaction costs are less than the combination of in-house production and transaction costs. For this reason, the public financial management literature on make-or-buy decisions (e.g., Anthony and Young, 2003; Martin, 1999c, 1993) provides guidance relative to the inclusion and calculation of production costs and transaction costs for both in-house and contract service delivery.

What the public financial management literature does not do is provide guidance on the *management* of transaction costs. It is a necessary, but not sufficient, condition to simply identify and calculate transaction costs; they must be managed during contract administration. Otherwise, transaction costs can increase beyond original calculations and undermine the economics of service contracting. Fortunately, many of the insights provided by principal/agent theory provide normative guidance on the management of transaction costs.

The Problem of Information Asymmetry

Information asymmetry refers to the imbalance of information that always exists between principals and agents. Information asymmetry is related to Herbert Simon's (1997, 1976) notion of "bounded rationality." Governments (principals) seldom, if ever, possess all the information needed to make rational choices. In the case of service contracting, contractors (agents) always have more knowledge about their day-to-day service delivery operations than governments do. The ability of governments to acquire detailed day-to-day information about contract service delivery is largely a factor of what contractors are willing to divulge voluntarily and what governments are able to independently discover as a result of contract monitoring. Thus, contract monitoring is a major component of contract administration. Contract monitoring also has major implications for transaction costs and their management. The more difficult a service contact is to monitor, the greater the transaction costs incurred.

The problem of information asymmetry gives rise to two other problems in service contracting, the problem of incomplete contracts and the problem of agent opportunism.

The Problem of Incomplete Contracts

Because of information asymmetry, neither governments nor contractors can accurately foresee all the problems that may occur during contract service delivery (Kavanagh and Parker, 2000). Information asymmetry thus gives rise to what principal/agent theory refers to as "incomplete contracts."

Incomplete contracts lack sufficient precision (specificity) to cover all service delivery contingencies. Incomplete contracts must therefore be amended or changed to deal with unanticipated service delivery problems when and as they arise. According to information asymmetry, all service contracts are incomplete to some extent. However, principal/agent theory suggests that the greater the degree of completeness (the greater the degree of precision or specificity) that is achieved in service contracts, the lower the transaction costs.

Government service contracts are usually divided into two main types: cost reimbursement (CR) and fixed-price (FP). Under CR contracts, contractors are reimbursed for necessary, reasonable, and allocable costs incurred in the provision of services. Under FP contracts, contractors are paid a fixed (price, fee, or unit cost) for service provision (NIGP, 1996). Incomplete contracts are generally of the CR type, while complete contracts (if any service contract can ever be said to be truly complete) are generally of the FP type. Both CR and FP contracts present dilemmas for governments (Brown and Potoski, 2001):

- CR contracts tend to *increase* production costs, but *decease* transaction costs. CR-type contracts generally increase production costs because contractors have no incentive to control costs. Conversely, CR-type contracts generally reduce transaction costs because contractors have no need to renegotiate cost adjustments when contract amendments or changes are made.
- FP contracts tend to *reduce* production costs, but *increase* transaction costs. FP-type contracts generally decrease production costs because the compensation of contractors is fixed. Conversely, FP-type contracts generally increase transaction costs because contractors invariably attempt to renegotiate their compensation when contract amendments or changes are made.

A normative solution to the dilemmas of CR/FP type contracts is suggested by principal/agent theory. The solution is for governments to develop more precise service contracts through the use of performance specifications and performance-based contracting. Service contract requirements are usually divided into two types: *design* specifications and *performance* specifications. Design specifications tell contractors how to deliver services (e.g., considerations relative to staff, facilities, equipment, service delivery strategies, and so forth). Performance specifications spell out what is expected in terms of results, but leave the "how" up to the contractors. Denhardt (2003) describes this approach as the government deciding on the destination but leaving the road map up to the contractors. According to the National Institute of Governmental Purchasing (NIGP, 1996) and the National Association of State Purchasing Officials (NASPO, 1997), a *performance-based contract* is one that stresses the use of performance specifications over design specifications. Unfortunately, both NIGP and NASPO are hazy in terms of exactly what constitutes "performance."

As used in performance-based contracting, the shift from design to performance specifications means that governments stop trying to control the process of service delivery. A process-oriented approach to service contracting (characterized by a heavy reliance on design specifications) must necessarily always lead to incomplete contracts. Instead, in performance-based contracting governments focus on a small number of performance specifications that are as precise as possible. This approach actually lends itself well not only to general government services (e.g., solid waste collection, street cleaning, custodial, fleet maintenance), but also to more specialized types of services (e.g., research and development, the creation of new knowledge, and others). Theoretically, it should be easier to develop a small number of performance specifications focusing on results than to describe in detail (using design specifications) how research and development activities are carried out or new knowledge developed.

The Problem of Agent Opportunism

Information asymmetry can also give rise to agent opportunism. *Agent opportunism* refers to the phenomenon that contractors (agents) sometimes pursue their own interests rather than the interests of governments (principals). For example, one form of agent opportunism is for contractors to provide lower-quality services than are called for in their contracts, thereby increasing their profit margins (Kavanagh and Parker, 2000). Agent opportunism is also the primary reason that "cost plus a percentage of cost" contracts are no longer used by most governments; these types of contracts create perverse incentives, in that contractors increase their profits by increasing their costs.

Principal/agent theory suggests that the problem of agent opportunism in service contracts can be overcome by the use of *ex ante* (before the fact) incentives and penalties that are tied to *ex post* (after the fact) monitoring.

The Use of *Ex Ante* Incentives and Penalties

Ex ante contract incentives and penalties are those that are decided upon up front by governments and included in contract documents. Principal/agent theory suggests that *ex ante* incentives and penalties can be used to create an alignment of interests between governments and contractors. When interests are aligned, no advantages accrue to contractors for engaging in agent opportunism (Bajari and Tadelis, 2001). Aligning the interests of governments and contractors also helps to control transactions costs by reducing, *but not eliminating*, the need for contract monitoring.

Ex ante incentives are used to reward contractors for meeting the needs of governments relative to such service delivery considerations as quality, timeliness, efficiency, effectiveness, and so forth. *Ex ante* penalties are used to discipline contractors for failing to meet the needs of governments. *Ex ante* incentives and penalties most often take the form of additional compensation contractors can earn for superior performance or compensation denied contractors for sub-standard performance. However, *ex ante* incentives can take other forms, including (1) the granting of contract extensions and renewals, (2) the award of additional work without competition, and (3) exclusivity arrangements whereby contractors are awarded additional work of either a particular type or in a specific geographical area.

Ex Post Monitoring

The word *monitoring* comes from the Latin *monere,* which means "to warn" (Kettner and Martin, 1986). *Monitoring* is essentially an early-warning system designed to alert governments when contractors stray too far from the contract specifications and the best interests of governments. As far back as Williamson (1975), the difficulty principals have in monitoring the actions and behaviors of agents was identified as a major driver of transaction costs. It follows, then, that governments (principals) have little or no economic incentive to monitor their contractors (agents). Monitoring *increases* transaction costs, which in turn *increases* service contracting costs. The challenge is for governments to develop relatively inexpensive, yet valid, approaches to monitoring.

Yet another insight provided by principal/agent theory is that governments can better manage transactions costs by making *ex ante* incentives and penalties the focus of *ex post* monitoring. This prescriptive guidance is at odds with the traditional approaches to the monitoring of service contracts, which rely heavily on a combination of process monitoring and financial monitoring. Because design specifications focus on process, monitoring focuses on process. And because cost-reimbursement (CR)–type contracts focus on costs and their necessity, reasonableness, and allocability, monitoring also focuses on contractor finances. However, *if* governments use performance-based contracting to identify the most important aspects of contract service delivery, operationalize them through the use of performance specifications, and attach *ex ante* incentives and penalties, *then ex post* monitoring should be primarily concerned with determining and validating the extent to which the desired performance is achieved.

Principal/Agent Theory and Performance-Based Contracting

Based on principal/agent theory and its normative prescriptions, the Public Management Committee of the Organization for Economic Cooperation and Development (OECD) has developed a set of guidelines for structuring internal or external principal/agent relationships

(OECD, 1999). By refocusing and extending somewhat the work of the OECD, a set of guidelines (see Figure 3.1) can be formulated for structuring service contracting relationships, carrying out contract administration activities, and managing transaction costs.

As Figure 3.1 illustrates, the first guideline states that contractual relationships should be "performance-based." This is an implicit *a priori* assumption, as made explicit by the title of the OECD (1999) source document, "Performance Contracting . . ." This interpretation is further supported by the second guideline, which states that contractors should be given increased discretion over inputs while being held accountable for performance. The third guideline (contracts should use performance specifications instead of design specifications) logically follows from the first two.

With the idea of avoiding to the greatest extent possible the problems of incomplete contracts, the fourth guideline states that the duties and responsibilities of governments and contractors should be clearly delineated in contracts. The premise is that governments should make service contracts as complete as possible by focusing on a few precise performance specifications while minimizing the use of design specifications.

Figure 3.1
Guidelines for Structuring Principal/Agent Relations in Service Contracts

1. Contractual relationship should be performance-based.
2. Contractors should be given increased discretion over inputs while being held accountable for performance.
3. Contracts should use performance specifications instead of design specifications.
4. The duties and responsibilities of governments and contractors should be clearly delineated in contracts.
5. The preferred contract type is fully-specified fixed price (FP).
6. *Ex ante* incentives and penalties should be aligned with the needs of governments.
7. Contractors should understand fully the consequence of superior and inferior performance.
8. *Ex ante* incentives and penalties should provide the basis for *ex-post* monitoring.

Source: Adapted from OECD., *Performance Contracting–Lessons from Performance Contracting Case Studies: A Framework for Public Sector Performance Contracting.* Paris: OECD, 1999, 57-58.

The fifth guidelines states that the preferred contract type is fully specified fixed price (FP). The use of performance specifications and performance-based contracting enables governments to use fixed-price (FP)–type contracts, thus avoiding the dilemma of the higher production costs associated with CR-type contracts. Precisely defined performance specifications, used in conjunction with performance-based contracting, reduce contract administration and monitoring activities–thereby enabling governments to avoid the dilemma of the higher transaction costs generally associated with FP-type contracts. The relationship between performance specifications, performance-based contracting, and transaction costs is specifically addressed in the guidelines by the emphasis placed on the use of *ex ante* incentives and penalties which should be aligned with the needs of governments (sixth guideline); the stipulation that contractors should understand fully the consequences of superior and inferior performance (seventh guideline); and finally, that *ex ante* incentives and penalties should provide the basis for *ex post* monitoring (eighth guideline).

Although the guidelines in Figure 3.1 provide normative direction as to the structure and administration of service contracts, they do not provide direction as to how "performance" itself should be conceptualized and operationalized. For normative guidance in this area, it is necessary to turn to the expanded systems framework and the government performance accountability literature and movement.

The Expanded Systems Framework

The basic systems framework (inputs, service, outputs) has long been used in public administration and policy analysis (e.g., Easton, 1953), public budgeting and financial management (e.g., Lynch, 1979) and the evaluation of government programs and services (e.g., Swiss, 1991). In the basic systems framework, performance is a unidimensional concept focusing on outputs and efficiency (the ratio of outputs to inputs). The expanded systems framework (see Figure 3.2) extends and expands the basic systems framework by adding two additional elements: quality and outcomes. Thus, the expanded systems framework views performance as a multi-dimensional concept consisting of three dimensions: *outputs, quality,* and *outcomes.*

Figure 3.2
The Expanded Systems Model

INPUTS ⟶ │ SERVICE │ ⟶ OUTPUTS ⟶ QUALITY ⟶ OUTCOMES

The theoretical basis for the expanded systems framework and the multi-dimensional conceptualization of performance comes from the government performance accountability literature and movement (e.g., Osborne & Gaebler, 1992), the work of former Vice President Al Gore (1993) and the National Performance Review, and in particular from the *Government Performance and Results Act* at the federal level, and the service efforts and accomplishments (SEA) reporting initiative of the Governmental Accounting Standards Board (GASB) at the state and local levels (GASB, 1994).

The Government Performance and Results Act

The Government Performance and Results Act (GPRA) (Public Law 103-62) requires that all federal departments and agencies report annually to the U.S. Congress on the performance of their programs and major service activities. Section 1115 (4) of GPRA states that each federal department and agency shall "establish performance indicators to be used in measuring or assessing the relevant *outputs,* service levels and *outcomes* of each program activity." Outputs are defined as measures of "activity or effort." Applied to services and service contracting, an *output* can be conceptualized as a measure of how much service is provided, while *outcomes* are defined as the results of services compared to their intended purposes. As used in GPRA, the terms *output* and *outcome* are sufficiently broad so that they also encompass issues of *quality* (emphasis added).

Governmental Accounting Standards Board

The Governmental Accounting Standards Board (GASB) is the organization that establishes generally accepted accounting principles for state and local governments. In 1994, GASB released an exposure draft of its proposed rules governing "service efforts and accomplishment" (SEA) reporting (GASB, 1994) The purpose of SEA reporting is essentially the same as GPRA–the promotion of performance accountability in government. SEA reporting at the state and local government levels is the functional equivalent to GPRA at the federal level.

SEA reporting has still not been formally mandated by GASB, but state and local governments have been strongly encouraged to prepare for its inevitable implementation. SEA reporting identifies two major types of performance measures, *outputs* and *outcomes.* As defined, outputs include quality. SEA reporting defines *outputs* as measures of the "quantity of service provided" and *quality* as measures of the "quantity of a service that meets a *quality* requirement." *Outcomes* are defined as measures of "the results that occur (at least partially) because of services provided" (GASB, 1994, p. 22) (emphasis added).

GPRA and SEA Reporting and Service Contracting

SEA reporting and GPRA are highly complementary. Although they come at the issue from slightly different perspectives, they both view government performance accountability as a multi-dimensional concept consisting of the tripartite dimensions of outputs, quality and outcomes.

According to both GPRA and GASB SEA reporting, the provision, measurement, and assessment of feedback on outputs, quality, and outcomes represents the way government services should be evaluated (see Figure 3.3). The monitoring and assessment of outputs compared to the consumption of inputs provides a measure of the *efficiency* of government programs, services, and activities. The monitoring and assessment of quality in relationship to the consumption of inputs provides a measure of the *quality* of government programs, services, and activities. And the monitoring and assessment of outcomes compared to the consumption of inputs provides a measure of the *effectiveness* of government programs, services, and activities.

The expanded systems framework, and the government performance accountability literature and movement, thus provide normative guidance on how performance should be conceptualized and operationalized in performance-based contracts. Using this approach, a performance-based contract can be defined as one that *focuses on the outputs, quality, and outcomes of service provision and may tie a portion or all of contractor's payments, as well as contract extensions or renewals, to their achievement.* (Segal, Moore, and Summers, 2002; Martin, 2002; Liner,

Figure 3.3
The Expanded Systems Model and Service Contract Administration and Monitoring

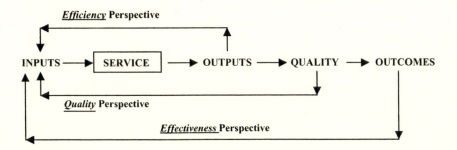

Figure 3.4
The Expanded Systems Model and Design and Performance Specifications

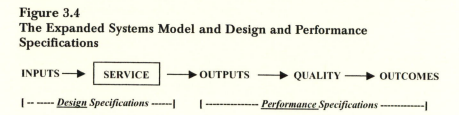

Dusenbury, and Vinson, 2000; Martin, 1999b). Guidance is also provided on service contract administration in general and *ex post* monitoring in particular; the focus should be on the extent to which contractors achieve the government's desired output, quality, and outcome performance. Thus, as Figure 3.4 illustrates, measures of output, quality, and outcome can—and should—become the manner in which performance specifications are conceptualized and operationalized in performance-based contracts.

Conclusion

This chapter has argued that a gap exists between service contracting and public financial management. The chapter further argued that the blame for this gap can be attributed, at least partially, to a lack of theory to guide the public financial management aspects of service contracting. To address this gap, two theoretical frameworks were presented and discussed: principal/agent theory and the expanded systems framework.

In the discussion of principal/agent theory, the concepts of transaction cost analysis, information asymmetry, incomplete contracts, agent opportunism, *ex ante* incentive and penalties, and *ex post* monitoring were discussed and their implications for service contracting examined. From this discussion, a set of guidelines was generated that provide normative guidance as to how service contracts should be structured and administered with an emphasis on the management of transaction costs.

In the discussion of the expanded systems framework, the concepts of outputs, quality, and outcomes were introduced and illustrated. Building upon the expanded systems framework and the concepts of outputs, quality, and outcomes, operational definitions of "performance" and "performance-based contracting" were proposed.

The result of both efforts is a set of prescriptive actions that should enable governments to better deal with the public financial management aspects of service contracting. By so doing, the hoped for goal is to increase the economy, efficiency and effectiveness of this mode of alternative service delivery.

References

Anthony, R., and D. Young. 2003. *Management Control in Nonprofit Organizations*. 7th ed. Boston: Irwin/McGraw-Hill.

Bajari, P., and S. Tadelis. 2001. "Incentives Versus Transaction Costs: A Theory of Procurement Contracts." *RAND Journal of Economics*, 32, no. 3: 386–407.

Brown, T., and M. Potoski. 2001. "Managing Contract Performance: A Transactions Cost Approach." Working paper. Available online at http://www.ppm.ohiostate.edu/brown/Jpammmm-12%5B1%D.htm (accessed September 19, 2002).

Brown, T., and M. Potoski. 2003. "Managing Contract Performance: A Transactions Cost Approach." *Journal of Policy Analysis and Management*, 22, no. 2: 275–297.

Chi, K., and C. Jasper. 1998. *Privatization Practices: A Review of Privatization in State Government*. Lexington, KY: Council of State Governments.

Cooper, J. 2003. *Governing by Contract: Challenges and Opportunities for Public Managers*. Washington, DC: CQ Press.

Denhardt, K. 2003. *The Procurement Partnership Model: Moving to a Team-Based Approach*. Arlington, VA: IBM Endowment for the Business of Government.

Easton, D. 1953. *The Political System*. New York: Knopf.

Feldman, M., and A. Khademian. 2002. "To Manage Is to Govern." *Public Administration Review*, 62, no. 5: 541–554.

Forrester, J. 2002. "The Principal-Agent Model and Budget Theory." In *Budget Theory in the Public Sector*, eds. A. Khan and W. B. Hildreth. Westport, CT: Quorum Books.

General Accounting Office (GAO). 2001. "Current Condition of Federal Contracting." PowerPoint presentation to members of the Commercial Activities Panel. Available online at http://www.gao.gov/a76panel/meeting.html (accessed July 14, 2002).

General Accounting Office (GAO). 2002. *Improving the Sourcing Decisions of the Government—Final Report of the Commercial Activities Panel*. Washington, DC: GAO.

Gore, A. 1993. *From Red Tape to Results, Creating a Government That Works Better and Costs Less: Report of the National Performance Review*. Washington, DC: U.S. Government Printing Office.

Governmental Accounting Standards Board (GASB). 1994. *Concepts Statement No. 2 of the Governmental Accounting Standards Board on Concepts Related to Service Efforts and Accomplishments Reporting*. Norwalk, CT: GASB.

Kavanagh, I., and D. Parker. 2000. *Contracting Out of Local Government Services in the UK: A Case Study of Transaction Costs*. Aston Business School Research Institute, Aston University, Birmingham, UK. Available online at http://www.research.abs.aston.ac.uk/working_papers/wpMENu4.html (accessed August 2, 2004).

Kelly, J. 1984. *Costing Government Services: A Guide for Decision Making.* Washington, DC: Government Finance Officers Association.

Kelman, S. 2001. "Remarking Public Procurement: Working Paper No. 3." John F. Kennedy School of Government, Harvard University, Cambridge, MA. Available online at http://www.ksg.harvard.edu/visions/publications/kelman.pdf (accessed July 1, 2002).

Kelman, S. 2002. "Contracting." In *The Tools of Government: A Guide to the New Governance,* ed. L. Salamon. New York: Oxford University Press: 282–318.

Kettl, D. 1993. *Sharing Power: Public Governance and Private Markets.* Washington, DC: Brookings Institution.

Kettner, P., and L. L. Martin. 1986. "Issues in the Developing of Monitoring Systems for Purchase of Service Contracting. *Administration in Social Work,* 9, no. 3: 69–82.

Liner, B, P. Dusenbury, and E. Vinson. 2000. *State Approaches to Governing-for-Results and Accountability.* Washington, DC: Urban Institute.

Lynch, T. 1995. *Public Budgeting in America.* Englewood Cliffs, NJ: Prentice-Hall.

MacManus, S. "Why Businesses Are Reluctant to Sell to Governments." *Public Administration Review,* 51, no. 4 (1991): 328–343.

MacManus, S. and S. Watson. 1990. "Procurement Policy: The Missing Link in Financial Management." *International Journal of Public Administration,* 13, no.1 and 2: 155–179.

Martin, L. L. 1993. *How to Compare Costs Between Government and Contract Service Delivery.* Los Angeles: Reason Foundation.

Martin, L. L. 1999a. *Contracting for Service Delivery: Local Government Choices.* Washington, DC: International City/County Management Association.

Martin, L. L. 1999b. "Performance Contracting: Extending Performance Measurement to Another Level." *PA Times,* 22, no. 1: 1, 8.

Martin, L. L. 1999c. *Determining a Level Playing Field for Public-Private Competition.* Arlington, VA: PricewaterhouseCoopers Endowment for the Business of Government.

Martin, L. L. 2002. *Making Performance-Based Contracting Perform: What the Federal Government Can Learn From State and Local Governments.* Washington, DC: PricewaterhouseCoopers Endowment for the Business of Government.

Martin, L. L, and Miller J. 2005. *Contracting for Public Sector Services.* Herndon, VA: National Institute of Governmental Purchasing.

McCall, S. 2002. "The Auditor as Consultant." *Internal Auditor,* 59, no. 6: 35–39.

McCue, C., and G. Gianakis. 2001. "Public Purchasing: Who's Minding the Store? *Journal of Public Procurement,* 1, no. 1: 71–95.

McDavid, J. 2001. "Solid-Waste Contracting-Out, Competition, and Bidding Practices Among Canadian Local Governments." *Canadian Public Administration,* 44, no. 1: 1–25.

Moe, R. 1987. "Exploring the Limits of Privatization." *Public Administration Review,* 47, no. 6: 453–460.

National Association of State Purchasing Officials (NASPO). 1997. *State and Local Government Purchasing: Principles and Practices.* Lexington, KY: NASPO.

National Institute of Governmental Purchasing. 1996. *Dictionary of Purchasing Terms.* Herndon, VA: National Institute of Governmental Purchasing.

Office of Economic Cooperation and Development (OECD). 1999. *Lessons from Performance Contracting Case Studies: A Framework for Public Sector Performance Contracting.* Paris: OECD.

Office of Management and Budget (OMB). 2002. *The President's Management Agenda.* Washington, DC: OMB.

Osborne, D., and T. Gaebler. 1992. *Reinventing Government.* Reading, MA: Addison-Wesley.

Premchand, A. 1993. "A Cross-National Analysis of Financial Management Practices." In *Handbook of Comparative Public Budgeting and Financial Management,* eds. T. Lynch and L. L. Martin. New York: Marcel-Dekker.

Ross, S. 1973. "The Economic Theory of Agency: The Principal's Problem." *American Economic Review,* 63, no. 2: 134–139.

Savas, E. S. 2000. *Privatization and Public Private Partnerships.* New York: Chatham House.

Sclar, E. 2001. *You Don't Always Get What You Pay For: The Economics of Privatization.* Ithaca, NY: Cornell University Press.

Segal, G., A. Moore, and A. Summers. 2002. *Can Massachusetts Still Afford the Pacheco Law?* Boston: Pioneer Institute.

Sekwat, A. 2000. "Principal-Agent Theory: A Framework for Improving Health Care Reform in Tennessee." *Journal of Health and Human Services Administration,* 22, no. 3: 277–291.

Selden, S., G. Brewer, and J. Brudney. 1999. "The Role of City Managers: Are They Principals, Agents, or Both? *American Review of Public Administration,* 29, 2: 124–148.

Simon, H. 1976. *A Study of Decision-Making Processes in Administrative Organizations.* 3rd ed. New York: Free Press.

Simon, H. 1997. *Models of Bounded Rationality.* Vol. 3. Cambridge, MA: MIT Press.

Spence, M., and R. Zeckhauser. 1971. "Insurance, Information and Individual Action." *American Economic Review,* 61, no. 2: 380–387.

Stone, M., A. Bell, and J. Pool. 1997. *Perspectives on Privatization by Municipal Governments.* Washington, DC: National League of Cities.

Swiss, J. 1991. *Public Management Systems: Monitoring and Managing Government Performance.* Englewood Cliffs, NJ: Prentice-Hall.

Williamson, O. 1975. *Markets and Hierarchies: Analysis and Antitrust Implications.* New York: Free Press.

Williamson, O. 1985. *The Economic Institutions of Capitalism.* New York: Free Press.

CHAPTER 4

Prospect Theory and the Municipal Bond Market

Kenneth A. Kriz

Research on municipal bonds largely centers on the behavior of partici-pants in the municipal bond market–from issuers and underwriters to various bond purchasers. Most previous municipal bond research has assumed that the participants follow classically defined rational eco-nomic behavior (specifically, the assumptions are made that individuals follow vonNeumann-Morgenstern utility functions, and that they assess changes in risk in a risk-neutral and consistent manner when assessing risky investments). When deviations from "normal" behavior are detected, they have been explained by appealing to some other set of motivations. To take one example, when the stated goals of bond issuers were found to deviate from what a classically rational issuer "should" have as their goals, principal-agent theory was invoked to explain the deviation (Simonsen and Hill, 1998). Principal-agent theory relies heavily on the assumption of rational economic agents and views any deviation in behavior from what an agent should do on behalf of the principal as *prima facie* evidence of opportunistic behavior.

However, it is known that classical definitions of rational behavior are not the only predictive models of human behavior, especially in situa-tions of uncertainty. One of the most frequently cited alternative schools of thought is known broadly as *prospect theory* (Kahneman and Tversky, 1979). Prospect theory seeks to explain the factors that lead to deviations from the predictions of classical models that incorporate subjective expected utility functions.

In this chapter, traditional models of municipal bond issuers and investors are first developed, along with the predictions that they make about the behavior of market participants. After reviewing prospect theory and developing the notion of the applicability of the model for predicting bond market behavior, the paper closes by discussing how prospect theory may be applied in the municipal bond market, focusing on deviations from traditional models. Some of these deviations include pricing anomalies and behavioral anomalies regarding decisions made during the course of issuing bonds. We will see that the traditional model of bond pricing tends to predict yield spreads between risk-free and risky bonds that are smaller than observed in the market, and that price changes respond to increased risk more strongly than to decreased risk. We will also see that some issuer behavior that cannot be explained by traditional models, such as the use of negotiated offerings, credit ratings, and bond insurance, can be explained using tenets of prospect theory.

Traditional Bond Pricing and Market Participant Behavior Models

Traditional models of bond pricing predict that investors will price risky bonds based on the expected cash flows received from the bond investment. Further, traditional models of bond issuance predict that issuers will seek to reduce the cost of raising funds to provide public goods. In this section, we review the traditional models of bond pricing and issuer behavior. Until the middle of this century, discussions about the pricing of bonds far outweighed the amount of research on the topic. Fisher first analyzed the incentives faced by bond buyers and some of the ways in which they evaluated alternative investments. His model can be represented as:

$$c_i^f = f(ir, \ d, \ -m) \tag{4.1}$$

where c^f is the cost of financing for issuer i, ir is the default free rate of interest, d are factors affecting the perceived default risk of the bond issue, and m are factors affecting the perceived marketability of the issue. Fisher measures the perceived default risk as a function of variables related to the variability of an entities debt service capability, its leverage (amount of debt outstanding), and its past reliability in meeting obligations. Fisher defines the risk of default as the probability that the entities funds available for debt service will not be sufficient to meet its debt service obligations. The variables noted above are those measurable variables that Fisher hypothesized entered into an investor's estimation of the default probability. However, he ignored the theoretical basis for how investors determine a proper price for bond issues. Still, Fisher's work provided an important early understanding of how market participants view the default risk of an issuer and how these participants' actions affect financing costs (Fisher, 1959). However, his model did not analyze the impact of the use of third parties to market or certify the credit quality of a bond issue. All of the information possessed by an investor in the Fisher model was generated exogenously or because of past issuer decisions.

Bierman and Hass (1975) were among the first to formalize the model of bond pricing based on investors' expectations of default risk. In their model, the expected present value of a bond (B) is a function of the interest payment to be received (I), the market rate of interest (i) used for discounting receipts of interest, the time until receipt of interest (t), and the probability that the bond will "survive" (not default) until the interest payment is received (p^t). For a bond with no maturity (a perpetuity), this can be represented as:

$$B = \sum_{t=1}^{\infty} \frac{Ip^t}{(1+i)^t} \tag{4.2}$$

This can be rewritten as the sum of an infinite series:

$$B = \frac{Ip}{1+i}\left[1 + \frac{p}{1+i} + \left(\frac{p}{1+i}\right)^2 + K\right] \tag{4.3}$$

Since p is less than one by definition, the value $\frac{p}{1+i}$ will also be less than one. Given this, the infinite series will converge and Equation 4.3 can be rewritten as:

$$B = \frac{IP}{1+i}\left(\frac{1}{1 - \frac{p}{1+i}}\right) \tag{4.4}$$

Collecting terms, we can rewrite Equation 4.4 as:

$$B = I\left(\frac{p}{1+i-p}\right) \tag{4.5}$$

If the bond is purchased at its par value, then the expected interest payment will be equal to the contractual rate of interest (r) times the value of the bond: $I = rB$. Inserting this into Equation 4.5, we obtain:

$$B = rB\left(\frac{p}{1 + i - p}\right)$$

(4.6)

Solving Equation 4.6 for r, we find that the contractual rate of interest will be set at as a function of the market rate of interest and the probability of survival:

$$r = \frac{1 + i - p}{p} = \frac{1 + i}{p} - 1$$

(4.7)

Bierman and Hass go beyond Equation 4.7 to analyze the setting of equilibrium contractual rates (Bierman and Hass, 1975). There are at least two significant conclusions that emerge out of this analysis. First, and quite obviously, the contractual rate is decreasing in the probability of survival:

$$\frac{\partial r}{\partial p} = -\frac{1 + i}{p^2}$$

(4.8)

Figure 4.1 shows how r changes in response to a change in p (assuming that $i = .05$). It offers some important insights into the theoretical relationship between default rates and bond prices. The slope of the leftmost part of the curve is the steepest, indicating a smaller responsiveness of contractual interest rates to changes in perceived default risk. For example, from the riskless baseline ($p = 1.00$) it would take a drop in perceived survival rates of nearly 15 percent (to $p = 0.858$) in order to create a 100 basis point change in the contractual interest rate. However, as perceived default risk increases (probability of survival decreases), interest rate increases are much more pronounced (formally, the second derivative of the contractual rate with respect to changes in perceived survival is positive). For example, a drop in perceived survival rates of 15 percent from an initial perceived survival rate of 60 percent ($p = 0.6$) would produce a 310 basis point increase in the contractual interest rate.

Taking Equation 4.8 and Figure 4.1 together with tenets of public economics, one gains insight into the theoretically optimal actions of bond issuers. The incentives of municipal bond issuers in the process of debt issuance can be illustrated by a simple economic model (Kriz, 2000c). We assume that municipal bond issuers attempt to maximize the social welfare function of the jurisdiction that they serve. The utility of the jurisdiction U is a known function of the amounts of public and private goods that are produced and their associated costs:

$$U = U(G_{Pr}, G_{Pu}, -c_{Pr}, -c_{Pu})$$

(4.9)

Figure 4.1
Relationship Between Probability of Survival (p) and Contractual Rate (r) in Bierman and Hass Model

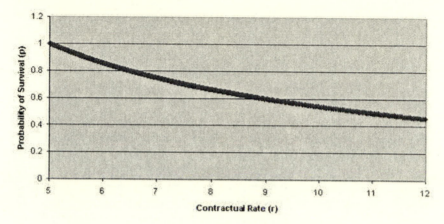

where G_{Pr} and G_{Pu} are the amounts of public and private goods produced with costs of c_{Pr} and c_{Pu} borne by the jurisdiction. We further assume that the costs of producing the goods can be split into two components–the "hard" costs of producing the goods c_i^h (such as construction of facilities, operations costs, and maintenance costs) and the costs of financing production c_i^f where i is either private or public production:

$$c_{Pr} = g((1 - \gamma_{pr})c_{Pr}^h, \; \gamma_{Pr}c_{Pr}^f)$$
$$c_{Pu} = g((1 - \gamma_{Pu})(c_{Pu}^h, \; \gamma_{Pu}c_{Pu}^f)) \tag{4.10}$$

In this equation and hereafter, γ_i is the percentage of total costs made up by financing costs. If we assume that these costs are additively separable, we can rewrite Equation 4.10 as:

$$c_{Pr} = (1 - \gamma_{Pr})c_{Pr}^h + \gamma_{Pr}c_{Pr}^f$$
$$c_{Pu} = (1 - \gamma_{Pu})c_{Pu}^h + \gamma_{Pu}c_{Pu}^f \tag{4.11}$$

Inserting Equation 4.11 into Equation 4.9, we can see that the utility of individuals in the jurisdiction is a decreasing function of both hard costs and financing costs:

$$U = (UG_{Pr}, \; G_{Pu}, \; -((1 - \gamma_{Pr})c_{Pr}^h + \gamma_{Pr}c_{Pr}^f)$$
$$-((1 - \gamma_{Pu})c_{Pu}^f + \gamma_{Pu}c_{Pu}^f)) \tag{4.12}$$

Assuming that the goal of municipal bond issuers is to maximize the utility of its residents, we can take first order conditions with respect to public financing costs:

$$\frac{\partial U}{\partial c_{Pu}^{f}} = -\gamma_{Pu}$$

(4.13)

Equation 4.13 shows that municipal bond issuers seeking to maximize the utility of their jurisdiction will seek to reduce financing costs for its public goods. Figure 4.1 suggests that the way to reduce financing costs is to act to reduce investors' perceptions of default risk. Therefore, one should see issuers taking actions to reduce perceived default risk in order to maximize taxpayer utility. If reducing perceived default risk is costly, then issuers should balance the cost of perceived risk reduction with the benefit of increased taxpayer utility caused by reduction in interest cost. Traditional theories therefore predict that issuers will act to reduce perceived default risk in order to reduce borrowing costs, to the point where further reductions in perceived risk are not cost-effective.

Prospect Theory

The economic models developed above belong to a class of models known as *expected utility models*. Specifically, when agents are faced with a decision involving risk in expected utility models, they maximize their expected utility by weighting the utility of various outcomes by the perceived probability that the outcome will occur. For example, if a risk-neutral agent is faced with the following decision between two alternatives:

Alternative 1:   A gain of \$11 with a probability of 0.5 and a loss of \$10 with a probability of 0.5; or

Alternative 2:   \$0 with certainty (probability of 1)

The agent would choose Alternative 1 because the expected utility of the alternative is positive:

$$E(U_{Alternative\ 1}) = 0.5(11) + (0.5)(-10) = \$0.50$$

(4.14)

Prospect theory is one alternative to expected utility theories. This theory (really a group of theories) developed from traditions of psychology in which experiments were conducted to try to identify behaviors consistent with the rational behaviors predicted by expected utility theory. When anomalous behaviors were detected, new theories of behavior with respect to uncertain prospects were developed (Kahneman and Tversky, 1979). Therefore, prospect theory developed not from a synthetic model of human rationality, but from an observed model of human behavior. In this way, one can describe the differences in the "ideal type" of economic agent in the two types of theory. In expected utility theory, economic agents are perfectly rational and exceedingly clever. They can immediately analyze a risky prospect and not only come to the correct conclusion about the probability distribution of outcomes, but they also "properly" value each outcome according to its economic merits. In prospect theory, as we shall see, agents are bounded by the limits of their abilities. They often resort to heuristics in order to determine the appropriate course of action. And as it turns out, their behavior is often at odds with the predictions of strictly rational models (Thaler, 1994).

There are many aspects of prospect theory; in this chapter we will discuss only those that seem most applicable to the municipal bond market. Readers interested in studying the topic more thoroughly are encouraged to read introductory papers and books (see especially the papers by Kahneman and Tversky (1979) and Rabin (1998), and the book by Thaler (1994)). Two of the more important candidates for use by those studying the municipal bond market are loss aversion and status quo bias. We next consider each in turn.

Loss Aversion

One of the implications of the expected utility model is that economic agents are predicted to behave similarly regarding potential losses as they do regarding potential gains. One simply totes up the value of the outcomes weighted by their expected probability of occurrence. However, it has been shown that individuals tend to place higher weights on losses than they do on gains. Consider again the risky choice that started this section:

Alternative 1:   A gain of $11 with a probability of 0.5 and a loss of $10 with a probability of 0.5; or

Alternative 2: $0 with certainty (probability of 1)

Alternative 1 has an expected payoff of $0.50. Therefore, it should be chosen by most economic agents. However, experimental research has shown that most individuals would take Alternative 2 over Alternative 1. In fact, there is support for the notion that there would need to be at least a 2:1 ratio in gains to losses to entice even a bare majority to take the risky alternative. In other words, Alternative 1 would likely be rejected by a majority of economic agents unless the gain rose to $20 or the loss fell to $5.50. This phenomenon has been named loss aversion in the prospect theory literature (Tversky and Kahneman, 1991).

The fact that a monetary loss is felt more than a same-sized monetary gain can also be explained through rational models of individuals demonstrating risk aversion. Risk aversion says that individuals will prefer a certainty equivalent gain (an option with probability 1) to a risky option at all levels of wealth, but will prefer a risky option to a certainty equivalent with respect to losses. Risk aversion produces the familiar S-shaped curve shown in Figure 4.2. This figure shows how a hypothetical economic agent would respond to uncertain propositions by charting the relationship between the changes in utility that an agent gets from various changes in wealth (gains are to the right of the vertical axis and losses to the left). With respect to gains, the agent has higher utility from not taking a risk (a point on the curve) than from accepting a risky proposition (this would be a straight line connecting any two points on the curve, the strict mechanics indicate that because the curve is concave it is higher—indicating greater utility—than any point on a straight line connecting two of its points holding change of wealth constant). However, with respect to losses, the agent has higher utility from a risky gamble (any point on any straight line is greater than the point on the curve corresponding to the same change in wealth). This indicates that agents would prefer risky prospects involving gains to risky prospects involving losses of the same amount.

Figure 4.2
Value Function for a Risk-Averse Individual

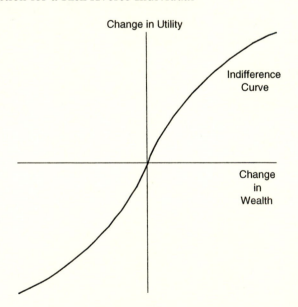

Where risk aversion fails to explain behavior is where the choice involves a combination of losses and gains, or when there are different sized gains and losses. Consider another risky choice:

Alternative 3:   A $2,000 gain with probability 0.5, $0 with probability 0.5; or

Alternative 4:   A $3,000 gain with probability 0.5, a $1,000 loss with probability 0.5; or

Alternative 5: $1,000 with certainty

Since each alternative has the same mathematical expectation ($1,000), risk-neutral or risk-averse agents should be indifferent between the choices. However, it has been shown that agents are much less likely to choose Alternative 4. This cannot be explained by expected utility models, even those that incorporate risk aversion. The only plausible explanation for the noted preference patterns is that agents have utility functions like that shown in Figure 4.3. This figure shows that while individuals may have standard concave utility functions in the range of gains, the function makes an abrupt shift of slope at the origin, indicating that potential losses are valued much greater than potential gains. In Figure 4.3, note the importance of the reference point. The perception of whether a gamble involves a potential loss and a gain or two gains (one of lesser magnitude) is a function of the individual weighing the decision. The analyst cannot derive from first principles what someone feels is their reference point. Still, in the case of municipal bonds, it is straightforward to assume that someone evaluating a potential for default will likely see the loss of principal and interest payments as a loss.

Status Quo Bias

Loss aversion has been noted in experimental settings (Kahneman, Knetsch, and Thaler, 1990; Tversky and Kahneman, 1991) as well as in empirical research (Shea, 1995). It is related to phenomena referred to in the literature as *endowment effects.* Endowment effects are where an individual's valuation of a good increases once they obtain it. In other words, owners of a good will often demand greater compensation to sell a good than potential buyers are willing to pay (Kahneman, Knetsch, and Thaler, 1990). Together, these phenomena may lead to status quo bias in decision-making. In decisions where multiple goods are involved, status quo bias implies that individuals will weight most heavily their current allocation of goods. In other words, individuals will prefer their current mix of goods to the loss of some goods, even when they are compensated by gains in other goods. Returning the choice between Alternatives 3, 4, and 5 above, if the problem was

Figure 4.3
Value Function for an Individual with Loss Aversion

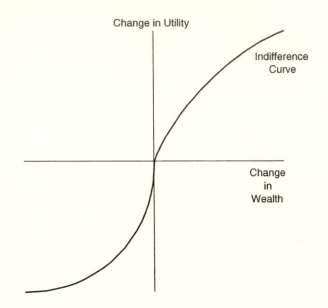

framed such that Alternative 5 was the basic alternative and Alternatives 3 and 4 were potential choices, status quo bias suggests that even an otherwise risk-neutral agent would have a greater probability of accepting Alternative 5 than we would expect from the certainty equivalent outcomes.

Status quo bias can be thought of as a deviation from "normal" preference relations as shown by "normally shaped" indifference curves. In Figure 4.4, the indifference curve I1 is "smooth" in the sense that small changes in the relative price of the two goods will produce a shift in planned consumption from the initial consumption point A. However, curve I2 is "kinked" at point A, implying that large changes in the relative price of goods are necessary to induce a shift in consumption patterns. This indicates status quo bias. In other words, an economic agent demonstrating status quo bias will have to be compensated greatly to shift consumption. Status quo bias has also been demonstrated both in experimental research (Samuelson and Zeckhauser, 1988; Knetsch, 1989) and in empirical research (Samuelson and Zeckhauser, 1988; Hartman, Doane, and Woo, 1991).

Applying Prospect Theory to the Municipal Bond Market

Traditional models of bond pricing and issuer behavior predict an orderly market, where bonds are valued by investors according to risk-

Figure 4.4
Normally Shaped Indifference Curve (I1) and Indifference Curve under Status Quo Bias (I2)
Based on Raymond S. Hartman, Michael J. Doane and Chi-Keung Woo, "Consumer Rationality and the Status Quo," The Quarterly Journal of Economics *106:1 (February, 1991), pp. 141–162. © 1991 by the President and Fellows of Harvard College and the Massachusetts Institute of Technology.*

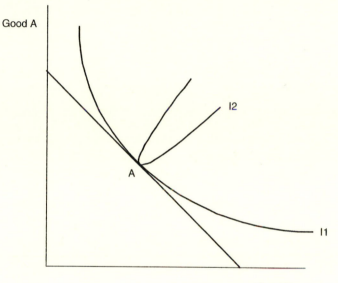

neutral models and issuers act in the best interest of taxpayers by minimizing interest costs on each issue. We next look at the empirical evidence that is emerging on bond pricing and issuer behavior and analyze consistency with the predictions of the traditional expected utility and the alternative prospect theory models.

In the area of bond pricing, Wu (1991) found that the spread between municipal bonds and Treasury securities of the same maturity indicated an implied default probability greater than that predicted using a risk-neutral model. He finds, however, that the deviations from the traditional model are small and not statistically significant. More recently, research by Kriz (2000b) has produced evidence of "mispricing" by bond purchasers, with risk premiums ranging from 29 to 94 basis points above those predicted by the risk-neutral pricing model. One further piece of evidence is offered by investor reaction to the Orange County bankruptcy. Denison (2000) analyzed whether bond fund investors anticipated the county's bankruptcy announcement. He found evidence of a large decrease in fund share price below that predicted by previous historical trends.

Though Denison's research looked at "excess" share prices as deviations from a market model (and is likely to be stronger empirically), some evidence can be offered simply by looking at returns of California municipal bond funds. Figure 4.5 below charts the daily returns calculated for the Lipper California Municipal Bond Fund Index for the 30-day period surrounding the county's bankruptcy announcement on December 7, 1994. The returns are calculated as the one-day percent change in the net asset value (NAV) of the Fund Index. Figure 4.5 shows that in the period just prior to the bankruptcy announcement, daily returns had been mostly positive. Then on December 7, the annual return drops by 157 basis points. Taken as a certainty equivalent measure, this means that investors would have had to have received 157 basis points in compensation for taking on the additional risk of holding funds in the Index. At this time, municipal bonds were trading at a national average of 128 basis points over a tax-free equivalent Treasury bond yield with the same average maturity. So an additional 157 basis points represents a large premium (using Figure 4.1, we can calculate that investors had to feel that default rates would more than double in order to justify the increase assuming that the initial perceived default probability was near its long-term average of 1 percent).

Figure 4.5
Daily Return on the Lipper California Municipal Bond Index, September 1–December 31, 1994 [FS](Author's calculations from data supplied by Lipper, A Reuters Company)

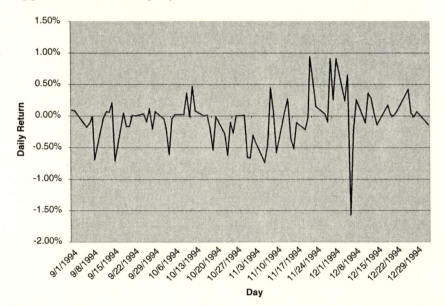

The results above indicate deviations from the results of the traditional risky bond-pricing model based on expected utility maximization. The results may indicate the presence of loss aversion among investors. Loss aversion would predict that investors would be extremely sensitive to the risk of losses. However, extreme risk aversion could also explain the reaction of markets to negative news. The key in understanding which theory best explains the behavior lies in the symmetry of pricing reactions. If the market responds in a dramatic fashion to negative news while not reacting as much in the face of positive news, this would lead us to favor a loss aversion explanation. If the reaction is more or less symmetric, in that the responses are of a similar magnitude, risk aversion may be a better model.

Figure 4.6 offers some insight into the symmetry issue. This figure charts the frequency of percent changes in the calculated default premium between October 1, 1993, and December 31, 1999 (Kriz, 2000b). The default premium was calculated by taking the spread between the Bond Buyer 20-Bond Index and the 20-Year Treasury Constant Maturity rate grossed up for tax effects. The Bond Buyer 20-Bond Index has an average maturity of 20 years, so over time maturity effects drop out.

Figure 4.6
Frequency Distribution of Daily Change in Implied Default Premium Between Bond Buyer 20-Bond Index and Treasury Constant Maturity Series, October 1, 1993–December 31, 1999

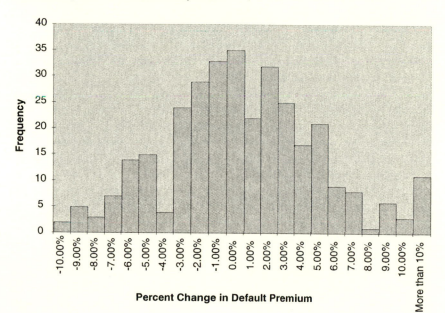

Percent Change in Default Premium

Figure 4.6 shows that there is a slight asymmetry in responses to perceived default risk. The distribution is skewed slightly positive (the calculated coefficient of skewness is 0.56). This indicates that there are more
strong market reactions in the direction of increasing yields due to the
perception of increased risk than there are strong reactions that reduce
yields due to the perception of decreased risk.

With regard to issuer behavior, deviations from predictions of the
expected utility model have also been noted. The first and most obvious
area is in the decision to use competitive bid or negotiated offer method
of sale along with the choice of an underwriter if the sale is negotiated.
There is some evidence that issuers may choose method of sale not only
to reduce interest costs of issuance, but also for other reasons. One piece
of evidence comes from Simonsen and Hill (1998), who surveyed bond
issuers in the state of Oregon. Even though issuers felt that minimizing
interest costs of issues was extremely important, they also cited past positive experience as an important determinant of method of sale (especially for those that used negotiated offerings). Also the most cited
reason by the issuers for using a specific underwriter was the previous
working relationship with the government. Elsewhere, Kriz (2000a) finds
that 22 out of 39 state bond issuers use one method of sale for 90 percent
or greater of their issuers over an eight-year sample period (some of this
is accounted for by the fact that some states are constrained by law to
issue only one way, but there is still a remarkable consistency in states
without such constraints).

This type of behavior is not predicted by expected utility theories and
traditional public economics. These models would predict that issuers
would weigh all of the costs and benefits of a proposed method of sale
and choose the method that would have the *ex ante* expectation of lowest
interest costs. Therefore, they should be some variability in the method
of sale. However, when viewed from a prospect theory perspective, it is
evident that there is a tremendous status quo bias in favor of using the
same method of sale, and perhaps the same underwriter, as the previous
issue. One key to why this might be the case is the perception by issuers
that they will not receive much in the way of interest cost savings from
shifting their method of sale. Several papers have questioned the size of
the savings realized by one method of sale over another, finding that differences in interest costs are small and not statistically significant (Peng
and Brucato, 2001; Leonard, 1996).

Another area where prospect theory may offer insights is the use of
credit ratings. Credit ratings represent a third party's certification of the
credit quality of a bond issue. The use of credit ratings should be related
to investors' need for information about an issuer. Therefore, it would
make sense that larger issuers who issue more often should need credit

ratings less than smaller issuers that issue often. In fact, the pattern supported by research is just the opposite. Johnson and Kriz (2002) document that most state bond issuers get at least two credit ratings on their general obligation issues, while Ziebell and Rivers (1992) show that the smallest city issuers are less likely to get ratings. This pattern is completely opposite from one that might be predicted from an expected utility model. However, if one allows that issuers may have a status quo bias toward getting credit ratings, the pattern becomes somewhat more explicable. Small issuers may not see a large enough benefit in getting ratings to counteract the inertia of not having obtained bond ratings in the past. Moreover, large issuers may become "locked in" to a pattern of getting multiple ratings.

A final area where prospect theory may manifest itself is the pricing of insured bonds. Despite the fact that insured bonds get a AAA rating from all rating agencies (all insurers are currently rated AAA), insurance does not lower interest costs to the level of a "natural" AAA rated bond. There is a small interest cost differential between insured bonds and moderate grade municipal issues (Moore, 2002). From an expected utility standpoint, this pricing differential does not make sense. With an insured bond, the default risk should be lowered to the same (if not lower) level as any other AAA bond. Loss aversion may offer a strong explanation for this phenomenon. With loss aversion, investors are hypersensitive to downside risk. So if investors perceive that there is any chance of a loss (either in dollar terms from not being paid, or in time having to wait for insurers to pay on the bond insurance policy), they will demand higher interest costs as compensation for taking on the risk. It appears that the market feels that there is still some residual risk left after insurance and bidding up the interest rate on the bonds.

In this chapter, we have introduced a new set of theories regarding how bond investors and bond issuers respond to risky prospects. We have seen how these theories can help explain some seemingly anomalous behavior in the municipal securities market. However, there is much more work to be done. Experimental and empirical research should be undertaken to try to evaluate whether loss aversion and status quo bias are present in the market and to try to measure the effect of their presence. Prospect theory has been applied in many different asset markets and in evaluating how economic actors make many types of decisions. This theory holds boundless opportunity for explaining behavior in the municipal securities market. Nevertheless, like any theory, it needs to be open to testing and evaluation. This is the best way to develop a set of theories that explains the world around us.

References

Bierman, Harold, and Jerome E. Hass. 1975. "An Analytic Model of Bond Risk Differentials." *Journal of Financial and Quantitative Analysis,* 10 (December): 757–773.

Denison, Dwight V. 2000. "Did Bond Fund Investors Anticipate the Financial Crisis of Orange County?" *Municipal Finance Journal,* 21 (fall): 24–39.

Fisher, Lawrence. 1959. "Determinants of Risk Premiums on Corporate Bonds." *Journal of Political Economy,* 67 (June): 217–237.

Hartman, Raymond S., Michael J. Doane, and Chi Keung Woo. 1991. "Consumer Rationality and the Status Quo." *Quarterly Journal of Economics,* 106 (February): 141–162.

Johnson, Craig L., and Kenneth A. Kriz. 2002. "Impact of Three Credit Ratings on Interest Cost of State GO Bonds." *Municipal Finance Journal,* 23 (spring): 1–16.

Kahneman, Daniel, Jack L. Knetsch, and Richard H. Thaler. 1990. "Experimental Tests of the Endowment Effect and the Coase Theorem." *Journal of Political Economy,* 98 (December): 1325–1348.

Kahneman, Daniel, and Amos Tversky. 1979. "Prospect Theory: An Analysis of Decision Under Risk." *Econometrica,* 47 (March): 263–292.

Knetsch, Jack L. 1989. "The Endowment Effect and Evidence of Nonreversible Indifference Curves." *American Economic Review,* 79 (December): 1277–1284.

Kriz, Kenneth A. 2000a. "Do Municipal Bond Underwriting Choices Have Implications for Other Financial Certification Decisions?" *Municipal Finance Journal,* 21 (fall): 1–23.

Kriz, Kenneth A. 2000b. "Risk Aversion and the Municipal Securities Market." Paper presented at the Association for Budgeting and Financial Management Conference. Washington, DC.

Kriz, Kenneth A. 2000c. "Financial Certification in the Municipal Securities Market." Dissertation, Indiana University, Bloomington.

Leonard, Paul A. 1996. "An Empirical Analysis of Competitive Bid and Negotiated Offerings of Municipal Bonds." *Municipal Finance Journal,* 17 (spring): 37–67.

Moore, Frank. 2002. "Does Bond Insurance Make Sense for You?" *Government Finance Review,* 18 (August): 16–19.

Peng, Jun, and Peter F. Brucato, Jr. 2001. "Do Competitive-Only Laws Have an Impact on the Borrowing Cost of Municipal Bonds?" *Municipal Finance Journal,* 22 (fall): 61–75.

Rabin, Matthew. 1998. "Psychology and Economics." *Journal of Economic Literature,* 36 (March): 11–46.

Samuelson, William, and Richard Zeckhauser. 1988. "Status Quo Bias in Decision Making." *Journal of Risk and Uncertainty,* 1 (March): 7–59.

Shea, John. 1995. "Union Contracts and the Life-Cycle/Permanent-Income Hypothesis." *American Economic Review,* 85 (March): 186–200.

Simonsen, William, and Larry Hill. 1998. "Municipal Bond Issuance: Is There Evidence of a Principal-Agent Problem?" *Public Budgeting and Finance,* 18 (winter): 71–100.

Thaler, Richard H. 1994. *The Winner's Curse: Paradoxes and Anomalies of Economic Life.* Princeton, NJ: Princeton University Press.

Tversky, Amos, and Daniel Kahneman. 1991. "Loss Aversion in Riskless Choice: A Reference-Dependent Model." *Quarterly Journal of Economics,* 106 (November): 1039–1061.

Wu, Chunchi. 1991. "A Certainty Equivalent Approach to Municipal Bond Default Risk Estimation." *The Journal of Financial Research,* 14 (fall): 241–247.

Ziebell, Mary T., and Mary Jean Rivers. 1992. "The Decision to Rate or Not to Rate: The Case of Municipal Bonds." *Journal of Economics and Business,* 44 (November): 301–316.

CHAPTER 5

Practice as Interpretation in Public Financial Management

Gerald J. Miller, Jonathan B. Justice, and Iryna Illiash

Connections between ends and means in public-policy–making can emerge from analysis, bargaining, learning, or interpretation. Finance is only one factor in making connections; however, every policy depends on money. Money is scarce. Necessity forces the question: Is the activity worth the money? Need establishes finance as the ultimate contingency and leads policy makers to depend on finance officials for expertise and practical advice.

Finance officials use a lens for seeing the issues, one that's highly developed and tempered through time. Norms direct the use of specialized knowledge and define financial management. This chapter explores the application of expertise, relying on finance officials to tell how they practice financial management, how they interpret ambiguous phenomena, and how they enact a world that their views of ends, means, and priorities dominate.

What Is Financial Management, According to Practice?

Two major authorities can help define financial management. One is composed of the texts provided for financial managers (Lehan, 1991). The other is the view financial managers take in focus groups and surveys

(Miller and Evers, 2002; Alexander, 1999; Miller, 1998). From these sources, we find three definitions of financial management.

Definition One

An optimizing logic appears as received wisdom in the training materials finance officers use. Lehan (1991, p. 35) offers three major issues in which financial managers optimize: the availability of money, the cost of money, and the productivity of money. Availability may be defined as liquidity. Maintaining liquidity "focus[es] on a jurisdiction's credit repute, reserves, tax strategies, billing cycles, payment procedures, past-due receivables, and the investment of loan proceeds and cash balances. Liquidity is the *sine qua non* of finance management" (p. 35). Cost of money implies reduction of costs and may involve reducing interest costs on borrowed funds as well as reducing the cost of government work. Increasing the productivity of money may apply generally in raising "the net benefit earned by the allocation of funds to the various purposes of . . . government" (p. 35).

The liquidity, cost, and investment goals often suggest behavior to maximize outcomes. These goals have strict efficiency tests, in other words. Efficiency can also carry a more relative test. Administrative efficiency traditionally hinges a given amount of performance on least cost or maximum performance on a given amount of resources (Thompson, 1967, p. 86).

In the relative sense, efficiency has become synonymous with a managerial emphasis rather than an economic one. As a way of defining the purpose of financial management, managerial ideas stress most heavily "the pursuit of maximum output with minimum inputs"; a "faith in the tools and techniques of management science and an ability to use them to resolve problems"; and faith in managers' skills and knowledge in acting as moral agents "to achieve the greatest good, not only for their organizations, but for society as a whole" (Edwards, 2001, p. 4).

The managerial position argues that a finance office operates as an institution with a right to operate in the public sphere independently. The primary institutional value is neutral competence, a concept combining managerialism with economizing values and certainly with the willingness and ability to generate policy alternatives for debate.

In focus group discussions, CFOs agreed that they must act instrumentally, most of the time, to achieve consensus priorities (Miller and Evers, 2002). The rest of the time, finance officers must act as stewards or fiduciaries for the public. One CFO said it best when he defined the purpose as "doing everything possible, with as little help from the taxpayer as necessary, to give citizens what they want." The CFO echoes a

Latin proverb on choices and reality: No gain is so certain as that from the economical use of what you already have.

Definition Two

Focus-group work led CFOs to suggest three purposes financial management could serve. The CFOs identified the three as loyalty to the elected elite, particularly mayors and chief executives; greater democracy and participation; and economic efficiency and financial control. The greatest amount of support grew for the loyalty purpose, that good finance officers should serve and support purposes established by mayors and chief executives.

The reason for this support is not hard to understand given these respondents. More than once, CFOs indicated that their job was to give advice, to produce options for elected officials–to "give them what they need to get what they want," one said. That person explained that a CFO cannot stand in the way of a politician bent on doing something; the best that can be done is to advise him on how to do it with the least financial damage. Ultimately, to have advice taken, to be viewed as a source of expertise and good judgment, the CFO must build confidence in this expertise among elected officials.

Supporting republican government follows a political logic. That logic hews closely to a modern-day "ubiquitous" budget strategy vividly described by Wildavsky (1964, pp. 74–84). Advocates everywhere try to build confidence among those examining their budget requests, he said. While it is a strategy related to the politics of budgeting, building confidence underscores the finance officer's role as an expert, conditioning political leaders to a reality that only the finance officer can divine. In building confidence, the normative basis moves beyond instrumentalism and neutral competence, the ordinary definition of expertise, to an interactive form of influence, with parts equally deferential, referential, and domineering.

Definition Three

CFOs did not reject citizen participation. Similar to and yet different than Alexander's (1999) respondents, these CFOs had significant doubts about some ways to bring it about. In fact, they defined successful participation far more broadly than the word *citizen* suggests: participation should involve the important stakeholders in the organization, whether the stakeholder is a taxpayer, an employee receiving a paycheck, the various parties in the debt market, or a vendor in the purchasing system. The CFOs also pointed out the necessary first step in participation–making financial information and processes clear and understandable to taxpayers, citizens, employees, elected officials, investors, and vendors.

In focus group discussions, however, CFOs argued that stakeholder participation often has roots in politics. They asked: Will demagogues take advantage of the tenuous control officials have over events to embarrass, or will political rivals take finance transactions out of context to defeat elected leaders? Not only are rivals a menace, taxpayers and bond market professionals have leverage over important issues also, and the three groups are sometimes at odds with each other.

The CFOs also explained that budgeting frequently operates as a closed system, excluding many groups. Budgeters can intentionally bury decision making from outsiders to ensure a simpler affirmation of community goals and a more resolute effort to accomplish them. Only in the cases of referenda on bond issues, on the issue of tax increases, and the disclosure of budget and financial reports required by various legal and financial authorities did CFOs concede to broadening public knowledge, with some participation, to solve problems.

What texts argue and what managers report are dependent on context. The context may include dimensions related to instrumental ideas—maintaining liquidity, reducing costs, and increasing productivity—that dominate a finance officer's thinking, making efficiency an absolute or relative measure of good choices. As a primary advisor and executor, CFOs encounter an agency dimension when they consider acting for local leaders or important stakeholders, such as taxpayers, vendors, and investors. The finance official often stresses precedent, consistency, and predictability in the advice he or she gives, and other times associates experience with issues and problems. As a necessity of law and a sense of fair play, the dimensions at other times may relate to balancing a variety of interests, due process, creative participation, and equity for those without voice.

Which Definition?

It is fair to ask which norm, which definition of public financial management, prevails? From what we understand, financial managers deal with decisions involving money, and through money they profoundly influence the work of government organizations. Analysis reveals that CFOs do not see the world in the same way.

Differences exist among CFOs because they have differing amounts of discretion when compared across state and local governments. Some CFOs have very basic, core-level responsibilities running routine operations. Others have a more policy-oriented role and may have become high-level advisors to chief executives. Still others may be elected executives themselves, particularly state treasurers. These differences became apparent in the budgeting office research of Thurmaier and Willoughby (2001) and Rubin (1998), in which large differences in the structures and expectations of budgeting officials emerged. Differences in place and time form a contingency theory of budgeting and, perhaps, financial management. Such differences may arise from legal structural sanction, political ideology, or the level of development of the profession locally, but the differences definitely exist.

Another strategic view argues that CFOs must capitalize legitimacy, functionalism, and independence. McCaffery and Jones (2001, pp. 62–65) argue that some budget officers and staff members are not useful enough and others are too useful. In not being useful enough, the budget office could exist as one part of an entire government regime dedicated to economizing. In such a situation, a budget office may not be useful in being just another voice for economy. In some circumstances, budget officers may not be believable enough, and in this way much less useful, in arguing impractical, inflexible managerial theories of organization or constitutional power in opposition to those who have managerial expertise at least equaling, if not surpassing, budget and finance officers, agency managers or outside consultants, all of whom have their own views of what will or will not work (p. 65). McCaffery and Jones spot instances where budget offices may be too useful, so good at what they do, that they tend "to get drawn into the role of general staff advisor, or even roles that would seem to be more political and belonging to . . . political staff," allowing fiscal values to be suppressed (p. 65). The inference? Budget officers must find a way to avoid being either useless or too useful to guard their legitimacy, functionalism and independence.

Success lies in a sense of aptness. Financial managers can interpret the need to act appropriately as economy, management control, policy and politics, or democracy imply. The interpretation emerges from the context in which issues have materialized. Contexts differ over time and reflect the financial manager's openness to politics and reference groups, as well as the risks associated with problems and solutions (Schneider and Ingram, 1997, pp. 36–38; Thompson, 1967, pp. 84–98).

Yet the basic motive behind structure and strategy remains: to preserve the institutional power of the finance office. The effort in building financial management theory bottoms on professionalization, institutionalization, and institutional survival premises, all of which are fundamental to understanding institutions universally (Scott, 2001; Merton, 1936, 1957; Selznick, 1957; Silverman, 1971; Zucker, 1991; Berger and Luckmann, 1966). How finance offices continue to be valuable–to avoid being useless or too useful–may seem to be irrelevant, since knowledgeable people can hardly conceive of a consequential government decision with no fiscal values at stake. If finance office influence is the issue, we can investigate whether influence serves fiscal values, managerialism, political masters, or democracy.

Theories about Financial Managers' Work

To investigate the meaningful content of public financial management, we use decisions as a unit of analysis, assuming that decision making can encompass most of what financial managers do. The decision-making view has a long tradition. In general, decision making "is the core of administration, [all administration] being dependent on, interwoven with and existent for the making of decisions" (McCamy, 1947, p. 41; Simon, 1947). Considerable effort has led to orthodox, prevailing, and alternative explanations of decision processes and outcomes (Miller, 1991; Wildavsky, 1964; Jones, Sulkin, and Larsen, 2003; Kant, 1992; Smith, 1991; Schneider and Ingram, 1997; Martinez-Vazques, 2001; Miller, Hildreth, and Rabin, 2001; Forrester and Adams, 1997; and Buchanan, 1977).

A theoretical view broad enough to build on existing theories must explore the connection between decisions and the social reality in which they take place. This approach involves interpretations. As Martin (2002, p. 261) points out, "Constructing a correct decision, a sound one, is always an interpretive project. Interpretation . . . must range over a great number of dimensions . . . and interpretive choices have to be made within each dimension." With the theoretical view taken in this chapter, we explore how financial managers make sense of reality in reaching decisions. We look at how managers recognize the possibility for making a decision, and the interpretive choices they make over numerous dimensions.

What Is an Interpretation?

A focus on interpretations comes from the body of research concerned with the construction of reality. That is, much of the world of financial managers exists because they want it to exist and because it customarily exists in the form in which they refer to it or grasp it. They—all financial managers in league with institutional leaders—could socially negotiate a change in many of the facts in their world if they wanted them changed.

Such a view comes from analytic philosophy. As Searle (1995, pp. 1–2) says "[T]here are portions of the real world, objective facts in the world, that are only facts by human agreement. In a sense there are things that exist only because we believe them to exist." Searle's examples are money, property, governments, and marriages. At first glance, these four concepts are very much objective in that they do exist for each of us. He explains that although all four "are 'objective' facts in the sense that they are not a matter of your or my preferences, evaluations, or moral attitudes," they could be changed by human action, specifically human action through institutions. Other media for exchange than money might be used if we prefer; a five-dollar bill may not exist for anyone other than those who prefer it. Property is defined by constitutions as existing for private persons or not; if it does not exist for private use, it no longer exists as property. Governments exist by the social contracts that emerge among individuals, and when the contract is written, it may be written with the specific authority of the governed to change it or do away with it. Marriages exist in many different forms, based on many different attitudes, as a civil action, a religious action, a human growth action in developing families, or simply an agreement to cohabit. Any of these forms may be changed by human action. Searle calls the facts that exist by human agreement "institutional facts."

He contrasts institutional facts with "brute facts." He illustrates brute facts as "Mount Everest has snow and ice near the summit" and "hydrogen atoms have one electron," both facts completely independent of human opinions. Institutional facts contrast with brute facts "because they require human institutions for their existence."

Searle recognizes that even brute facts depend upon human recognition and speech for part of their existence. Scientific research has to take place and the results reported, refereed, and accepted. A brute fact exists even though we may not know it fully or be able to say precisely what it is. He says, "Of course, in order to state a brute fact we require the institution of language, but the fact stated needs to be distinguished from the statement of it."

The more humans agree, the more institutional facts they accept, and, therefore, the more reality humans perceive. In areas where there seems to be full agreement among humans, we have "shared subjectivity" or a shared interpretation (Saaty, 1980, p. 15). Saaty argues (p. 15), "however we try to be objective in interpreting experience, our understanding is perceived and abstracted in a very subjective way. . . . Shared subjectivity in interpretation is actually what we mean by objectivity. Thus [the social constructions] we form are objective by our own definition because they relate to our collective experience." The world's finance officials know are constructed to benefit from their collective professional views, the opinions developed through social interaction in organizations, and the beneficial ideas they have accumulated through experience.

Golembiewski (1999, pp. 14–17) has straightforward arguments about interpretations and social constructions. He agrees with those theorists who "note that reality does not exist 'out there': it is enacted (or socially constructed) by each of us, and in some unspecified ways these individual enactments somehow come to constitute reality until they are somehow unenacted by enough of the appropriate people." He argues that, at least in some senses, social construction of reality applies since "much that constrains and motivates behavior exists by social consensus." He illustrates with Sherif's autokinetic experiment (Sherif, 1935) and recalls (p. 14):

> a point of light in a dark room seems to move; a consensus about distance moved often develops among groups observing that light; and that consensus persists when individuals are later brought back alone to observe the same light.

Although dramatic, the Sherif experiment is a narrow one, and Golembiewski points out that social construction of reality has "sharp limits." He notes (p. 14), "enact as you will, stepping out of a seventh floor window is unlikely to have sanguine effects." He argues further that even when subject to human action, social constructions may be extremely hard to change. He uses slavery as the ultimate example of hardened social constructions.

Golembiewski identifies the root of socially-constructed reality as power. He notes (p. 14) that "We are not . . . equal when it comes to enacting some . . . perhaps even the most important realities. Indeed, some power-wielders might be able to enact realities for many of us, most of the time."

His argument that power-wielders enact reality has a potential significance for financial managers. Following an economic or managerial logic, financial managers' analyses and recommendations to leaders have certain legitimacy within the limits of what economic theory holds. Following a political logic, financial managers' actions to build confidence among their superiors may often serve to speak the truth that financial managers believe, or interpret as truth, to powerful leaders.

The products of financial management—cash investments, debt structures, budgets, and all others—are socially-negotiated ones (Astley, 1985, p. 499). That is, there is no one best way, no objective truth on which to base management; there are very few "brute facts." This chapter argues that finance decision makers do much to create a reality for their organizations by strategically, symbolically, ritualistically, and rhetorically coping with the most critical problem facing them—resource constraints. Coping gives finance "rights" or legitimacy, the clout to be able to enforce the use of a special language and to force the justification of actions in unique ways. In that language, "financial management" becomes a general metaphor, one in which scarce means finance the highest and best ends chosen by the polity, through elected leaders who depend on reservoirs of expertise in bureaus, think tanks, consulting firms, and universities. Creating a reality in which resources are contingent and in which finance is the critical agency for commanding resources and wisely allocating them among uses, the financial manager provides many of the institutional facts in public organizations.

As for arguments that finance officials, or any other officials, are "rational actors," we have the counterargument by Olsen (2003, p. 2) that "theory may benefit from taking into account . . . a great diversity in human motivation and modes of action. Actors are driven by habit, emotion, coercion, interpretation of internalized rules and principles, as well as calculated expected utility and incentive structures. Human character is variable and changeable, not universal and constant." The working hypothesis of many researchers, as with Olsen, may be characterized here as "finance officials interpret." The financial official's world is one in which he or she has customary ways of seeing objects, people, and their interaction. Customs and even norms come from interpretations that have a more vivid sense of fact as consensus grows among those people the finance official influences and is influenced by.

For almost a half century, theorists have argued that managers play a major role in interpreting critical contingencies, in giving meaning or sense to phenomena they find, and in interpreting the phenomena they find when problems, solutions, and people meet in random ways. We argue here that finance officials' interpretations act to assign phenomena in ways in which the phenomena can be acted on, especially in controlling the critical financial contingencies the government organization faces. Finance officials can interpret phenomena to require computation, learning, bargaining, inspiration, or rationalization. What they choose depends on the amount of agreement about goals and about the technology most reasonably suited to achieve agreed upon goals (Miller, 1991, pp. 59–61; Burchell, Clubb, Hopwood, Hughes, and Nahapiet, 1980; Thompson and Tuden, 1959). By assigning the phenomena in a particular way, the finance officials dictate a way to deal with them. A simple interpretive system appears in Table 5.1.

The simple process outlined in Table 5.1 attributes credibility and legitimacy to the financial manager. The ambiguous events that occur lead to a cycle of interpretation or making sense for the organization. Brute facts and institutional facts help, but considerable ambiguity remains, enabling the financial manager to interpret through the views of his or her networks. The networks include those others with whom

Table 5.1
A Model of Interpretation by Financial Managers

Ambiguity prevails with few constraints.

Interpretations make sense of ambiguity.

The financial manager interprets ambiguity as the expert.

Financial managers construct interpretations from what they know and sense, pushing ambiguous phenomena into categories where they can be handled with computation, bargaining, or learning.

They communicate their interpretations through narratives, symbols, rituals, and myths.

They enforce their interpretations through the work others expect them to do—making decisions about taxing and spending—to rationalize interpretations, especially when they encounter punctuated equilibria.

---

the financial manager works closely, and the particular network chosen depends on the norm the financial manager senses as aptly fitting the ambiguous circumstances—economizing, building confidence among political leaders, or bringing the narrow or broad stakeholder public into the situation. The interpretations themselves depend on a variety of means through which the financial manager's frame of reference gives the interpretation intelligibility, projecting precedent, experience, general public feeling, political history, community climate and culture, and simple, compelling arguments. The financial manager can project the logic of appropriateness rooted in popular, political, and professional norms, trial and error, precedent, custom, habit, and the meaning of experience (March, 1994); general feelings such as tax revolts (Lowery and Sigelman, 1981), fiscal individualism or fiscal socialism (*Economist*, 2000); a dominating fiscal illusion (Downs, 1959–1960; Buchanan, 1977), or the premier conception of the community's social contract (Wildavsky, 2001); the particular point in the cycles of political history (Phillips, 1990); good policy arguments (Meyers, 1994, pp. 159–189); the extent of deference to expertise (Schneider and Ingram, 1997, pp. 158–159); and the sense of discretion one may have to take or oppose risky decisions (Miller, 1991, pp. 158–160; Thompson and Jones, 1986). Interpretations once chosen evolve into narratives or texts, rituals evoking and manipulating symbols, and ultimately myths (Miller, 1991; Czarniawska and Gagliardi, 2003; Roe, 1994). The financial manager has substantial authority to enforce interpretations in the work related to taxing and spending, often rationalizing interpretations or deftly handling punctuating events that alter stable interpretations and create new equilibria that give altered interpretations power in the future (Jones, Sulkin and Larsen, 2003, pp. 151–169; Jordan, 2003, pp. 345–346, pp. 358–360).

Case Studies

In the next sections, I survey supporting evidence for an interpretive theory. The three cases reflect the ways financial managers use the three definitions the chapter described initially. These three definitions reflect an efficiency logic, a political logic in which finance officials give political leaders "what they need to get what they want," and a variation of the democratic logic in which finance officials were "responsive to citizen demands" and anticipated citizen demands and acted in citizen interests.

In the first section, cash investment becomes an activity framed in such a way that the appearance of taking risks is greater than the risk itself. In the second section, debt management acts as a referential activity– a resort to members of a network for constructing interpretation–specifically in determining how much debt a government authority can afford and how that debt might be structured. In the final section, tax expenditure budgeting becomes a moral philosophy lesson in the superiority of incentives (in the form of tax expenditures) to gifts (the outright entitlement of individuals to a financial grant), all of which serve to reveal the relationship between finance officials and citizens.

Cash Investment

My research (Miller, 1991) investigated cash management practices, particularly those involving investment. My work investigated the acceptability of futures and options, early forms of derivatives, in cash investment practices of public managers. I found controversy over acceptance at two levels. At the ideological level, acceptance of financial innovations depends as much on the role and size of government in society as the inherent productivity potential of the techniques. A government that does little more than what is necessary may regard these innovations as irrelevant. A government that does everything may not need financial management, let alone financial innovations, since it faces no scarcity. In between, most financial managers find the language of risk and loss controlling their choices. At the instrumental level, in the public sector, risk is not opportunity which, when exploited, defines gain. Rather risk refers to the chance of mishap, the avoidance or prevention of which has a high priority. In fact, in public administration theory, risk may carry ethical connotations, one of the most traditional of which regards risk-taking as a violation of a fiduciary relationship to the polity.

In the research financial officials were asked their ranking of the goals of cash investment and then their use of derivatives. In the rankings (Miller, 1991, p. 165), officials considered as most important the preservation of capital. In a significant sense, the first goal became the frame for all other goals and for all investments and investment risks. As Tversky and Kahneman (2000) suggest, most individuals, and in this case, public cash investment managers, are loss averse. In an experiment with Ohio investment officers, McCue (2000) confirms these prospect theory predictions, as does Denison's survey (2002) and the comparative research by Mattson, Hackbart, and Ramsey (1990).

Debt Networks and Principal-Agent Relationships

Most orthodox theories portray principals as fully and completely knowledgeable about ends and means. Principals employ direct agents as instruments of implementation. In prevailing theories there are often information asymmetries between principals and agents, making the relationship a problem of bounded rationality, calculated risk taking, opportunism, and rent seeking. Financial accountability issues arise when the information asymmetries increase. When debt financing issues get attention, the observed behavior reveals less of a hierarchical relationship among parties than a deferential one among those we normally think of as principals and their various agents. The relationships involved in debt financing of public infrastructure projects may resemble a network more than principal-agent connections; approaching debt financing in this way forces several accountability issues to rise to prominence.

My colleague Jonathan Justice and I investigated a recent effort by the New York Metropolitan Transportation Authority to refinance its debt (Miller and Justice, 2002). The essence of the restructuring was the consolidation of previous debt issues under a simplified set of bond covenants, the lengthening of the debt repayment period, and the lowering of debt service. Stretching out the principal repayment for the MTA's existing debt appears to comply with conventions calling for the matching of asset useful life with the period of debt repayment, but not with injunctions to minimize total costs of debt service. This refinancing proposal carries a negative net present value, and so is not one that would be employed if cost minimization were the primary consideration. Beyond this technical consideration, the proposal has drawn attention for the role of the investment bank Bear Stearns in developing and promoting the refinancing plan. The fullest general interest newspaper account of the proposal describes it as "a striking example of the way in which Wall Street can shape public policy to its own benefit" (Pérez-Peña and Kennedy, 2000). At the same, there appears to be general agreement that absent a resumption by the State of New York in a major funding role in MTA capital budgeting, the agency has few other options for raising the funds called for by its capital spending plan.

Although there has not been a great deal of detailed information available, and MTA officials and their advisers have been cautious in their public remarks, there seems to be little doubt that the restructuring plan was conceived and detailed by Bear, Stearns. There is no doubt at all that on April 16, 2000, the proposed financing plan was presented to the CPRB and others in Albany on the MTA's behalf by Robert Foran of Bear Stearns, acting apparently in an informal advisory capacity, but evidently with a very large investment of time and effort. As an informal advisor, the firm would not be precluded from bidding on or negotiating for a large and profitable role in the underwriting of the proposed $12 billion of bond issuance, as it would have been if acting in a formal capacity as financial advisor to the MTA. At roughly 0.6 percent of issue amount, underwriting fees for the restructuring issue(s) are expected to total as much as $100 million if the deal is executed.

So who is the principal and who the agent? Are the bankers helping themselves or the MTA? Interpretations vary widely. " 'It makes me nervous that a private firm has structured a multibillion-dollar deal that will impact on the future of the transit system for three decades, that they thought it up, pitched it, did all this work to flesh it out, lobbied the State Legislature directly, and they're the ones who stand to make tens of millions of dollars off of it,' said Gene Russianoff, staff attorney at the Straphangers Campaign and an ardent critic of the plan. 'They have an inherent conflict of interest' " (Pérez-Peña and Kennedy, 2000, p. B6). Alternatively, other informed observers suggested, that this kind of informal advising is in fact a useful way for public agencies to get the benefit of free technical advice from financial experts who are otherwise very expensive.

Bear, Stearns has on at least a few past occasions been involved in advising and then doing business with bond issuing authorities in New York. In 1997, the firm resigned a formal financial advisory role in order to bid on the underwriting for the Long Island Power Authority's acquisition of Long Island Lighting Company (LILCO) assets. Bear, Stearns ended up as lead underwriter for that deal, which at $7 billion was the largest municipal issue up to that time (Pérez-Peña and Kennedy, 2000). In 1998, the firm advised the MTA on the creation of a "swaption" structure which enabled the MTA to take advantage of a low interest rate environment for outstanding debt which was not yet callable and had already been subject to the one advance refunding permitted by federal law. In return, Bear, Stearns was permitted to match the winning bidder and purchase half of the available options when it came in second in a competitive bid process (Kruger, 1998; Sherman, 1998).

Foran, in particular, had gained the trust of the MTA through a long-standing working relationship, according to at least one well-informed source. Our source argued, in keeping with the debt networks hypothesis, that long-term client-intermediary relationships and institutional knowledge are important in the small world of municipal finance. The MTA, like other issuers, continually gets advice from financial firms; the only unusual aspect of this particular proposal was the way in which the pitch was made, which may simply have reflected a desire to have the explanation of the plan given by the party with the most expertise and knowledge of the details of the proposal. As in any instance where relationships involve personal trust, reciprocity, and mutual expectations of goal fulfillment, this case may not lend itself to easy analysis within the framework of conventional principal-agent models of public finance.

The irony of this situation, of course is that the independent public authority device in general, and the financial maneuverings of the MTA in financing its capital program in particular, appear to primarily represent efforts to satisfy the demands of voters and ratepayers. Through the fare box and through their elected representatives (and the appointments made by those representatives), citizens have demanded that the MTA invest enough to remedy past underinvestment and forestall a future infrastructure crisis, but without obviously increasing its fares or demand for general tax revenues. In so doing, the demands may effectively have led the agency to become more accountable to the financial markets than to the constituencies more widely recognized as legitimately commanding the fealty of public organizations in a democracy. More recently, the fare increase took place anyway (Metropolitan Transportation Authority, 2003).

Orthodox observers suggested little controversy in what the leaders of the MTA did. It was said that a good idea is a good idea wherever it comes from, and that MTA's activities constituted "the best way to get free use of this very high-priced talent" (Pérez-Peña and Kennedy, 2000, p. B6). However, the reaction from the press and from mass transit user groups said that a good idea has to come without an obligation; with the obligation, the idea is suspect. Certainly, less orthodox observers say, suspicion would not grow to such a refinancing idea if it had come through open and fair competition among ideas to solve a problem.

Constructing the Basis for Budgeting Trade-Offs

Budgeting involves trade-offs between equity and efficiency. Budgeting also involves trade-offs between guns and butter. In modern times, budgeting has developed to involve trade-offs among the *means* of spending: directly by government agency, by grants to private and non-profit organizations, by loans or loan guarantees, or by tax incentives. How does a public finance official decide the means of spending? In a piece of research with my colleague Iryna Illiash, we found that the trade-off between conventional spending and tax expenditures often depends on the social construction of target groups.

From the War on Poverty in the 1960s to the late 1980s, the poor became less deserving than the run up to the War on Poverty had implied. From the period when such conservatives as Milton Friedman proposed a negative income tax, the sense that poor people had little or no responsibility for their plight lost credence in public opinion surveys (Miller and Illiash, 2001, p. 30) diminished. Budget constraints dictated that spending submit to statutory constraints and severe priority setting having high barriers to deservingness. Conservative opinion about welfare programs forced even neo-liberals such as President Bill Clinton to consider alternatives to federal spending for direct aid to the poor (Ventry, 2000). Facing demands to abolish welfare, the president could have considered an incremental change in which direct aid gave way to strong job creation incentives for organizations hiring former welfare recipients, as well as stronger job training programs.

Instead of incremental changes, the president worked a trade-off among the means of budgeting for the poor, abolishing direct welfare spending, and substituting stronger reimbursable tax credits, called earned income tax credits (EITC). The EITC had proved popular since its institution in 1975–1978, reducing budget spending in a superficial, but all too real statute-required scoring, sense. The credit had also proved popular because it went to those who worked rather than to those who did not, the latter those who leaders often portrayed as opportunists, unwilling to work and get off the dole.

By 1996, the EITC had proved sturdy enough to allow President Clinton to submit to the Republican Congressional majority-inspired Personal Work and Responsibility Act (PWORA) and its Temporary Aid for Needy Families (TANF) provisions with devolution to the states for welfare grants and with time limits on receipt of these grants. The PWORA, of course, came with numerous supports for the new TANF recipients as well as numerous provisions for the waiver of the limitation of direct benefits.

Fiscal and social welfare policy partisans could feel a sense of accomplishment. Those interested in deficit reduction could argue that spending fell with the end of the Aid to Families with Dependent Children and the income maintenance strategy. Some of those in favor of a safety net for the poor could argue the efficacy of incentives and the sturdy net that survived the fight over welfare.

The *New York Times* recently reflected on President Clinton's term of office and respectfully reported on his broad approach to welfare reform, and more broadly to the problems of poverty and race (DeParle and Holmes, 2000). The authors of the article observed (p. A1, A16) that President Clinton arguably created greater poverty with his reform, and perhaps for political reasons. Others denied expedience as a cause and argued instead the fortunate consequences reform might have for poor people. That is,

> The restrictions [time limits and work requirements imposed by reform] would help create a political climate more favorable to the needy. Once taxpayers started viewing the poor as workers, not welfare cheats, a more generous era would ensue. Harmful stereotypes would fade. New benefits would flow. Members of minorities, being disproportionately poor, would disproportionately benefit. . . . Mr. Clinton has presided over an unprecedented expansion of aid for poor families who do work. He won billions of dollars in wage supplements and smaller subsidies for everything from child care to children's health insurance, all framed as a moral obligation to "make work pay."

In reality, the poor became two groups. By 1996, the working poor were thought a deserving group, the nonworking poor, an undeserving group. The earned income tax credit served to reinforce the boundaries of the deserving group because the poor had to work to get the tax credit. The direct expenditure program became a state, not federal, responsibility–even though federal rules still existed to ensure that the "race to the bottom" among the states to shed welfare caseloads did not occur too quickly.

A trade-off occurred between direct expenditure and tax expenditure in the budget. Budget reduction advocates forced the idea of scarcity into the process. In the context of the presidential re-election race, the context emerged to get a problem "solved." In this context, the social constructions that had developed to that time led to the choice of the group on the back of whom one part of the budget would be balanced. The trade-off took place, and the criterion was deservingness.

Events crystallized social constructions. Government authorities perceived the need for budget deficit reduction and welfare reform at the same time, and they faced a presidential re-election campaign with an uncertain outcome. Opinion at the time–the social construction of target groups–led to close examination of the poor. The social constructions of the working poor were positive, and negative of the nonworking poor. The working poor gained a tax expenditure that also reinforced the definition of deservingness. The nonworking poor–the undeserving–became the casualties and were left to fend for themselves or adjust their behavior to become the working poor.

The attack on the earned income tax credit that followed welfare reform provided the rationalization for the trade-off. Faced with apparent fraud, the advocates of the working poor quickly found that increasing the number of audits would have an ameliorative effect. The audits would deliberately intimidate those of the poor who were seeking the tax credit but who were not working. However, the audits would and did turn up many more of the working poor who had failed to apply for their just share.

To summarize, the social construction of target populations as deserving or undeserving can dictate the fundamental criterion in any trade-off among budget tools. The greater the growth in spending, however translated through financial tools, the more one hears about government control of the governed. The opposite is really the case. The greater the effort to control conventional and nonconventional spending, the more leaders depend on social constructions of target populations to control government, and in the welfare reform case, to control utilitarian constructions.

Accounting for the Findings

Far from a dominant view of the world based on rational choice, financial managers–broadly defined–have some interpretations that lead them to maximize wealth and some that maximize the continuation of consensus gained in the past. However, context is just as important to remember. On a given day, interpretations can range widely, leading to a unique combination of observations from the three case studies. First, cash investment managers value the avoidance of losses more than the maximization of gains under conditions of risk. Second, debt restructuring can follow a rational strategy, even when achieving a less than optimal net present value. Third, tax expenditures can reduce budget deficits while rewarding those targeted groups socially constructed to be worthy or deserving.

The three cases join other research. For example, revenue forecasters attempt to create a self-fulfilling prophecy through an agenda set to estimate revenue in a "dynamic" way to account for the behavior the revenue estimates comprehend and follow from higher spending or greater tax rate reductions (Miller, 1991, pp. 207–228). Spending in the conventional sense mirrors the priorities of a strong executive and a budgeting process that pursues ritual in the interest of preserving a strong executive's power (Miller, 1991, pp 105–113). Information systems have little self-correcting ability in the command and control system sense and produce far more randomness of people, problems, and solutions (Miller, 1991, pp. 175–193). Economic development decision makers prize trophies rather than wealth (Robbins and Miller, 2000).

Consider the findings as they relate to the interpretive model specifications (see Table 5.2). Finding ambiguity in the ends and means of cash investment, capital budgeting, and budget balancing, finance decision makers interpreted the problems in a rational way. In cash investment, they interpreted the goal of cash investment as reducing losses; in capital budgeting, as a debt restructuring that lengthened the repayment period for existing debt; and in budget balancing, effort that increased the use of a tax incentive to favor a positively viewed group of taxpayers.

The finance decision makers varied. Those interpreting the cash management situation, finance officials, used their own fiduciary role definition to guide cash investment, an activity to which most others with a stake in the decision would defer. Capital budgeting decision makers deferred to outside experts, although these outside experts stood to gain by the advice, in restructuring debt for a source of funds to finance the capital program. In the budget balancing case of social welfare policy, finance officials designed a means suitable to an end leaders wanted by deferring to the leaders' social construction of target groups.

The finance officials communicated the interpretation in novel ways. In the case of cash investment, the interpretation rested on a narrative relating derivative use to gambling with public funds, hiding the insurance function derivatives provide, and muting the public perception of public officials' susceptibility to temptation. The default in the narrative created an image of the public official as a fiduciary, an image consistent with a managerial norm for finance official behavior and decision making.

In the capital budgeting and debt restructuring case, the myth of the ever-wise market prevailed. Where could expertise–wisdom–in financing come from most assuredly but from the financiers themselves, who were willing to put their money at risk to underwrite a public improvement? In a subordinate sense, the choice to borrow, rather than increase costs for transit riders, was a relatively easy one to make; borrowing would slow the rate of change in the burden transit riders bore, all transit riders would bear the burden of the improvements over the improvements' useful life, and general taxpayers would not bear any burden at all.

Table 5.2
Case Study Findings and Interpretive Model Specifications

Model Specification	Cash Investment Case	Debt Networks Case	Budgeting Trade-offs Case
Ambiguity	Insurance or speculation or guarding investment against loss	Net present value savings, additional revenue, or matching debt repayment to asset useful life	Income maintenance or employment incentive or short run budget balancing
Interpretation	Preventing losses	Additional revenue	Employment incentive and short run budget balancing
Who interprets	Finance officials based on professional knowledge and fiduciary role	Important stakeholders with authoritative decision makers refusing other means	Authoritative decision makers and finance officials own technical and professional knowledge
How interpretation constructed	Professional norms; unwillingness to take risks	Deference to important stakeholders	Dominant fiscal illusion or "it doesn't cost anything," particular place in cycles of history; fiscal socialism; construction of good policy arguments
How interpretation communicated	Narrative of gambling with the public's money	Narrative of saving the capital program	Narrative of encouraging self-reliance
How interpretation enforced	Investment policy	Debt restructuring	Tax expenditures: refundable tax credits

In the social welfare budgeting case, the decision came across as a symbolic attempt to bolster fundamental civic values. The reliance on a tax incentive, rather than direct payments to the poor, impressed the public with their leaders' fidelity to the principle of self-reliance; the poor must work to collect the refundable tax credit. The decision implicitly forbade shirking and stimulated productivity.

Finally, the enforcement of the interpretations relied on methods that countered a textbook view of policy tools and their application. The cash investment case reveals reluctance to use investments that hedge risk when finance officials publicly espoused safety and loss avoidance. The case could also suggest that the cash investment follows a risky strategy in avoiding loss.

The MTA managers implemented the capital investment financing plan through a debt restructuring, lengthening the repayment period for existing debt and producing no net present value savings. The debt restructuring appears to violate the optimizing assumption of such debt management plans. On the other hand, the restructuring may have placed the burden of paying for improvements fairly by limiting the burden largely to transit users and spreading the burden over all users through time.

The social welfare budgeting case suggests a combination of forthright work incentives and fiscal illusion. The tax incentive to work neutralized the arguments of those who see paltry job advancement opportunities and stagnant incomes for the poor. The incentive taught bargaining: government financial support could be traded for the willingness of poor people to work. In both the short and long term, the argument that tax incentives and elimination of income maintenance served budget balancing goals was illusory. Federal budget control rules forced the tax incentives into the determination of balance, but they failed to force accurate projections of the earned income tax credit's budgetary impact. By 1996, the financial consequence of the tax credit exceeded the previous most severe impact of the income maintenance policy pursued in the Aid to Families with Dependent Children (Miller and Illiash, 2001).

The model of interpretation has meaning as a description of the process that can occur among finance officials. The case study approach suggests that the model has validity. The lingering questions revolve around its counterintuitive implications. That is, can we infer from these findings that finance officials routinely disregard the optimizing logic that many expect to govern their decisions? The implications, we argue, do not suggest the primacy of any simple logic, but a complex perception finance officials have for the context in which they decide courses of action.

Consider first the implicit test for theory with which we began. What practical guide for management lies at the heart of this public profession? Is there a rational actor at the heart of the practice of public financial management, this most business-like of fields in public administration? What norms guide this rational actor? From the findings about practice, we can conclude that many rationalities exist. In the situations we examined, a rational actor exists, an actor who optimizes expected utility in the many senses of utility one could generalize from these findings. However, in the orthodox sense of a rational actor we found the financial manager behaving quite differently.

Conclusion: Summarizing Practice as Interpretation

Financial issues loom large in policy deliberation. Leaders look to the institutionalized expertise of finance officials for help. Finance officials have "fiscal values" with which they approach ambiguous phenomena. These values represent subjective views or interpretations of the ends and means connections that form policy goals and designs. The argument in this chapter holds that their institutional survival interests motivate finance officials to push or transform ambiguous events into categories in which there is some degree of agreement, whether about ends, means, or both. If the transformation succeeds in creating an objective view of both ends and means, finance officials may simply compute the answer to the problem. If less successful in gaining consensus, the result may call for bargaining or learning.

To illustrate, we discussed three cases of fiscal policy ambiguity in the chapter. In the cash investment case, we concluded that finance officials had gained consensus about ends and means. The end seemed to be "take no risks; lose no taxpayer dollars through investments." The means were investments that earned more than simply locking cash in a vault, but were nearly risk-free. The case leads to the conclusion that the optimizing or computational solution to a cash investment dilemma is one most closely related to textbook lessons on liquidity.

In the welfare financing case, we found agreement about means and no agreement about ends. The case revealed that political leaders agreed on finding a means to "help the poor help themselves." The various ends in which welfare financing became intertwined had some relationship with eliminating entitlements or outright grants of money to people sooner or later (as in eliminating welfare "as we know it"), reducing overall budget deficits, punishing shirkers, and providing incentives for gaining and holding jobs. In such cases, we should find a bargaining solution. Finance officials gave the bargainers the refundable tax credit called the Earned Income Tax Credit. The EITC seemed agreeable as an almost all-purpose solution to all the bargainers' goals. In reality, the finance officials gave bargainers what they needed to get what they wanted.

In the debt restructuring case, we found agreement about ends in the effort to preserve the New York Metropolitan Transportation Authority's capital program. The problem lay in finding the means to do so. The alternatives were state aid, city aid, and fare increases, and none were viewed as possible or preferable. Resorting to important stakeholders, or receiving unsolicited advice, the MTA's finance officials got another alternative that required wholesale debt restructuring. That debt restructuring led to stretching debt service over a longer period, at no savings, and an increase in debt capacity for financing the capital program. The stakeholders producing the solution had profits to make, but the solution helped solve the capital plan funding problem. The solution can illustrate the Latin proverb "no gain is so certain as the economical use of what you already have" and the CFO's command to do "everything possible, with as little help from the taxpayer as necessary, to give citizens what they want." Managerialism must be stretched to its limits to associate the debt restructuring idea with efficiency. However, the MTA finance officials could argue that the lengthened debt repayment period still fell within the useful life of the MTA assets, freeing financial operations from constricting debt covenants and making reserves available for other financing uses. Surely officials could argue that they had analyzed the alternatives and chosen the debt restructuring as a rational solution.

Summarizing the institutional and interpretive meanings we find in the cases, behavior of finance officials to transform ambiguous events to manageable ones can be reasonable. To control critical contingencies, whether money or knowledge about how to get and use it, finance officials made shrewd suggestions or took sensible action to conform to the expectations of leaders and important stakeholders. Recognizing the variety of interpretations possible in ambiguous circumstances, finance officials were able to leverage their expertise and gain consensus, transforming the subjective into the objective. Fiscal values may include the willingness to say no to profligacy, but they also inspire creativity and strengthened institutions. If we can generalize from these cases and the arguments here, public financial management theory grows stronger when we link practice to interpretation tightly.

References

Alexander, Jennifer. 1999. "A New Ethics of the Budgetary Process." *Administration and Society*, 34, no. 4: 542–565.

Astley, W. Graham. 1985. "Administrative Science as Socially Constructed Truth." *Administrative Science Quarterly*, 30: 497–513.

Berger, Peter L., and Thomas Luckmann. 1966. *The Social Construction of Reality: A Treatise in the Sociology of Knowledge*. New York: Doubleday.

Buchanan, James M. 1977. "Why Does Government Grow?" In *Budgets and Bureaucrats: The Sources of Government Growth,* ed. Thomas E. Borcherding, 3–18. Raleigh, NC: Duke University Press.

Burchell, Stuart, Colin Clubb, Anthony Hopwood, John Hughes, and Janine Nahapiet. 1980. "The Roles of Accounting in Organizations and Society." *Accounting, Organizations and Society,* 5, no. 1: 5–27.

Czarniawska, Barbara, and Pasquale Gagliardi. 2003. *Narratives We Organize By.* Philadelphia: John Benjamins.

Denison, Dwight V. 2002. "How Conservative Are Municipal Investment Practices in Large U.S. Cities?" *Municipal Finance Journal,* 23, no. 1: 35–51.

DeParle, Jason, and Steven A. Holmes. 2000. "A War on Poverty Subtly Linked to Race." *New York Times,* December 26, A1, A17.

Downs, Anthony. 1959-1960. "Why the Government Budget Is Too Small in a Democracy." *World Politics,* 12: 541–563.

"Lexington: The Age of Fiscal Socialism." 2000. *Economist,* 355, no. 8166 (April 15): 30.

Edwards, J. David. 2001. "Managerial Influences in Public Administration." Unpublished paper available online at http://www.utc.edu/~mpa/managerialism.htm (accessed June 30, 2001).

Forrester, John P., and Guy B. Adams. 1997. "Budgetary Reform Through Organizational Learning: Toward an Organizational Theory of Budgeting." *Administration and Society,* 28, no. 4: 466–488.

Gist, John R. 1998. "Decision Making in Public Administration." In *Handbook of Public Administration,* Jack Rabin, W. Bartley Hildreth, and Gerald J. Miller, eds., 2nd. ed., 265–291. New York: Dekker.

Golembiewski, Robert T. 1999. "Shortfalls of Public Administration as Empirical Science." *Public Administration Quarterly,* 23, no. 1 (spring): 3–17.

Jones, Bryan D., Tracy Sulkin, and Heather A. Larsen. 2003. "Policy Punctuations in American Political Institutions." *American Political Science Review,* 97, no. 1: 151–169.

Jordan, Meagan M. 2003. "Punctuations and Agendas: A New Look at Local Government Budget Expenditures." *Journal of Policy Analysis and Management,* 22, no. 3: 345–360.

Kant, Immanuel. 1992. *Perpetual Peace: A Philosophical Essay,* translation by M. Campbell Smith. Bristol, England: Thoemmes Press.

Kruger, D. 1998. "Salomon Is Big Winner of MTA Swaption." *Bond Buyer* (August 13): 32.

Lehan, Edward Anthony. 1991. "Organization of the Finance Function." In *Local Government Finance: Concepts and Practices,* John E. Petersen and Dennis R. Strachota, eds., 29–43. Chicago: Government Finance Officers Association.

Lowery, David, and Lee Sigelman. 1981. "Understanding the Tax Revolt: Eight Explanations." *American Political Science Review,* 75 (December): 963–974.

March, James G. 1994. *A Primer on Decision Making: How Decisions Happen.* New York: Free Press.

March, James G, and Johan P. Olsen. 1976. *Ambiguity and Choice in Organizations.* Bergen, Norway: Universitetsforlaget.

Martin, Rex. 2002. "Right Answers: Dworkin's Jurisprudence." In *Is There a Single Right Interpretation?* Michael Krausz, ed., 251–263. University Park: Pennsylvania State University Press.

Martinez-Vazques, Jorge. 2001. *The Impact of Budgets on the Poor: Tax and Benefit Incidence.* Working paper 01-10. Atlanta, GA: Andrew Young School of Policy Studies, Georgia State University.

Mattson, Kyle, Merl Hackbart, and James Ramsey. 1990. "State and Corporate Cash Management: A Comparison. *Public Budgeting and Finance,* 10, no. 4 (winter): 18–27.

McCamy, J. 2001. "Analysis of the Process of Decision Making." *Public Administration Review,* 7 (1947): 41–48.McCaffery, Jerry L., and L. R. Jones. *Budgeting and Financial Management in the Federal Government.* Greenwich, CT: Information Age Publishing.

McCue, Clifford P. 2000. "The Risk-Return Paradox in Local Government Investing." *Public Budgeting and Finance* 20, no. 3: 80–101.

Merton, Robert K. 1936. "The Unanticipated Consequences of Purposive Social Action." *American Sociological Review,* 1: 894–904.

Merton, Robert K. 1957. "Bureaucratic Structure and Personality" In *Social Theory and Social Structure,* Robert K. Merton, ed. 2nd ed., 195–206. Glencoe, IL: Free Press.

Metropolitan Transportation Authority (State of New York). 2003. "MTA Board Approves Fare and Toll Plan." Press release/statement, March 6. Available online at http://www.mta.nyc.ny.us/mta/news/public/proposal-statement0306.htm (accessed October 6, 2003).

Meyers, Roy T. 1994. *Strategic Budgeting.* Ann Arbor, MI: University of Michigan Press.

Miller, Gerald J. 1991. *Government Financial Management Theory.* New York: Dekker.

Miller, Gerald J. 1998. "Accreditation of Budget and Finance Offices in New Jersey." Paper delivered at the annual meeting of the Association for Public Budgeting and Financial Management, Washington, DC.

Miller, Gerald J., and Iryna Illiash. 2001. "Budgeting Interpretations." Unpublished manuscript, Department of Public Administration, Rutgers University, Newark, NJ.

Miller, Gerald J., and Jonathan B. Justice. 2002. "Managing Principals and Interests at New York's Metropolitan Transportation Authority." Paper presented to the Association for Budgeting and Financial Management, Annual Conference, Washington, DC, January 18.

Miller, Gerald J., and Lyn Evers. 2002. "Budget Structures and Citizen Participation." *Journal of Public Budgeting, Accounting and Financial Management,* 14, no. 2: 205–246.

Miller, Gerald J., W. Bartley Hildreth and Jack Rabin. 2001. *Performance-Based Budgeting.* Boulder, CO: Westview.

Olsen, Johan P. 2003. "Citizens, Public Administration and the Search for Theoretical Foundations." 17th Annual John Gaus Lecture, American Political Science Association, Philadelphia, PA, excerpted in *APSA Public Administration Section's Electronic Newsletter,* 2, no. 2 (fall) 1–4. Available online at http://www.h-net.org/~pubadmin/ (accessed October 7, 2003).

Pérez-Peña, R., and Kennedy, R. 2000. "Private Promoter for Transit Debt." *New York Times,* May 1, A1, B6.

Phillips, Kevin. 1990. *The Politics of Rich and Poor.* New York: Random House.

Robbins, Donijo, and Gerald J. Miller. 2000. "Public Economic Development Competition and the Winner's Curse." Paper presented at the Annual Conference of the Association for Budgeting and Financial Management, Kansas City, MO, October 5–7.

Roe, Emery. 1994. *Narrative Policy Analysis.* Durham, NC: Duke University Press.

Rubin, Irene S. 1998. *Class, Tax And Power.* Chatham, NJ: Chatham House.

Saaty, Thomas L. 1980. *The Analytic Hierarchy Process. Planning, Priority Setting, Resource Allocation.* New York: McGraw Hill.

Schneider, Anne Larson, and Helen Ingram. 1997. *Policy Design for Democracy.* Lawrence, KS: University of Kansas Press.

Scott, W. Richard. 2001. *Institutions and Organizations.* 2nd ed. Thousand Oaks, CA: Sage Publications.

Searle, John R. 1995. *The Construction of Social Reality.* New York: Free Press.

Selznick, Philip. 1957. *Leadership In Administration.* New York: Harper & Row.

Sherif, Muzafer. 1935. "A Study of Some Social Factors in Perception." *Archives of Psychology,* 23, monograph no. 187.

Sherman, L. 1998. "N.Y. MTA Board To Consider Entering into the World of Swaptions to Save on Debt." *Bond Buyer* (June 29): 38.

Silverman, David. 1971. *The Theory of Organizations.* New York: Basic Books.

Simon, Herbert A. 1947. *Administrative Behavior.* New York: Free Press.

Smith, Adam. 1991. *The Wealth of Nations* New York: Knopf/Random House/Everyman's Library.

Thompson, Fred, and L. R. Jones. 1986. "Controllership in the Public Sector." *Journal of Policy Analysis and Management,* 5, no. 3: 547–571.

Thompson, James D. 1967. *Organizations in Action.* New York: McGraw-Hill.

Thompson, James D., and Arthur Tuden. 1959. "Strategies, Structures and Processes of Organizational Decision." In *Comparative Studies in Administration,* James D. Thompson, Peter B. Hammond, Robert W. Hawkes, Buford H. Junker, and Arthur Tuden, eds., 195–216. Pittsburgh: University of Pittsburgh Press.

Thurmaier, Kurt M., and Katherine G. Willoughby. 2001. *Policy and Politics in State Budgeting.* Armonk, NY: M. E. Sharpe.

Tversky, Amos, and Daniel Kahneman. 2000. "Rational Choice and the Framing of Decisions." In *Choices, Values, and Frames*, Daniel Kahneman and Amos Tversky, eds., 209–223. Cambridge: Cambridge University Press.

Ventry, Dennis J. 2000. "The Collision of Tax and Wefare Politics: The Political History of the Earned Income Tax Credit, 1969–1999." *National Tax Journal* (June): 983–1026.

Wildavsky, Aaron. 1964. *The Politics of the Budgetary Process.* New York: Little, Brown.

Wildavsky, Aaron. 2001. "The Budget as a New Social Contract." In *Budgeting and Governing: Aaron Wildavsky*, Brendon Swedlow, ed., 259–275. Piscataway, NJ: Transaction.

Zucker, Lynne G. 1991. "Institutionalization and Cultural Persistence." In *The New Institutionalism in Organizational Analysis*, Walter W. Powell and Paul J. DiMaggio, eds., 83–1-7. Chicago: University of Chicago Press.

CHAPTER 6

Should Financial Reporting by Government Encompass Performance Reporting?
Origins and Implications of the GFOA-GASB Conflict

William Earle Klay, Sam M. McCall, and Curtis E. Baynes

In the United States, the Governmental Accounting Standards Board (GASB) establishes "generally accepted accounting principles" (GAAP) for state and local governments. GASB's standards authoritatively guide the preparation and external reporting of financial information, especially that which is presented in a government's Comprehensive Annual Financial Report (CAFR). Since its founding in 1984, GASB has been concerned that governments' financial reports do not fully and adequately describe their service efforts and accomplishments (SEA).

The term "service efforts" refers to the costs, the resources, consumed by governments to provide services. "Service accomplishments" refers to the performance of governments with respect to program outputs and outcomes. Since the mid-1980s, GASB has been conducting research on ways to develop and report SEA information. GASB's apparent desire to eventually require that governments' financial reports include SEA information has spurred an extraordinary conflict with the Governmental Finance Officers Association (GFOA), the leading organization of financial managers in local government.

The GFOA has also initiated research to enhance the development and dissemination of information about governments' performance. The GFOA, however, has declared in a formally adopted policy statement that GASB has exceeded its authority in moving toward SEA reporting and that GASB should immediately cease further research and deliberations on the topic (GFOA, 2002a). GFOA's position is that SEA information should be used in governments' budgeting processes, but governments should not be required to report on SEA in their external financial reports. At the time this chapter was written, GASB and GFOA were at a standoff. The resolution of the standoff will affect the theory and practice of public financial management for decades to come.

In the following pages, we look at this conflict from the perspective of critical theory, which requires that attention be given to social environments, historical contexts, and the ways in which humans make sense of things. The leading proponent of applying critical theory to the study of public financial management is Gerald Miller. His "alternative theory" perspective, focused as it is upon "sense making" within the social and historical contexts of public financial administration, is the framework for our inquiry. Our efforts at sense-making are undoubtedly affected by our own backgrounds; two of us took baccalaureate degrees in accounting, all three have taken degrees in public administration, each author has practitioner experience, and each holds one or more professional certifications related to public financial administration.

This chapter will address how the GFOA and GASB represent different "realities"–different ways of viewing the nature of public financial management. The GASB perspective looks toward greater integration between governmental accounting and the other disciplines of public financial management. The GFOA viewpoint seeks a clearly delineated division of labor between governmental accountants and other specialists in public financial management. The chapter presents a chronology of the events that have preceded the current standoff, followed by a look at the theoretical and historical underpinnings of the two points of view.

Our analysis sheds light on why the GASB's actions have engendered strong emotions. Two of the three authors are members of the GFOA, and our interactions with colleagues have heightened our awareness of the depth of feelings involved. These emotions constitute a reality that, if ignored by GASB's standards setters, could cause multiple adverse consequences in the practice of public financial administration. Moreover, the GFOA has raised important points, most notably the need to protect the policy-making prerogatives of elected officials.

Our analysis leads us to conclude that the processes of discourse associated with the GASB initiative could lead to a better fulfillment of governments' reporting obligations to their citizens. The GASB initiative could also promote greater multidisciplinary synthesis within public financial management theory, especially between the disciplinary perspectives of accounting and those of other fields such as public administration. Consequently, we look at ways to resolve the standoff by acknowledging the importance of trying to encompass SEA information within government financial reporting while also acknowledging and responding to GFOA's objections.

Chronology of the Conflict

The GASB

Organized in 1984, the Governmental Accounting Standards Board consists of seven members from state and local governments, public accounting firms, academia, and citizen organizations. GASB's mission is to establish and improve standards of state and local governmental accounting and financial reporting that will (1) result in useful information for users of financial reports and (2) guide and educate the public, including issuers, auditors, and report users. The Financial Accounting Foundation (FAF) appoints members of GASB as well as members of the Financial Accounting Standards Board (FASB), which establishes GAAP for private for-profit and nonprofit organizations. The FAF, FASB, and GASB are private, nonprofit organizations. The American Institute of Certified Public Accountants recognizes GASB and FASB pronouncements as authoritative.

GASB follows a due process procedure to encourage research and open deliberation of financial accounting and reporting issues. GASB's process includes task forces, discussion memorandums, preliminary views documents, public hearings, and exposure drafts. All meetings are open to public observation. Written comments and hearing transcripts become a part of the public record, and the comment period is generally 60 days or more. A majority vote of the board is required for adoption of a pronouncement. It is not uncommon for many years to pass between GASB's initiation of due process on an issue and the issuance of an authoritative statement.

GASB's Performance Measurement Initiatives

In 1985, GASB adopted a resolution encouraging governments to experiment with performance measures. In 1987, GASB issued Concepts Statement No.1, "Objectives of Financial Reporting." (Unlike statements of governmental accounting standards, statements of governmental accounting concepts do not establish new standards. Concepts statements provide guidance in solving problems of long-range importance.) Concepts Statement No. 1 put forth the idea that information from transaction-based accounting needs to be combined with information from other sources to enable users to assess the economy, efficiency, and effectiveness of government. In 1990, GASB began to publish a series of research reports, the first of which was titled "Service Efforts and Accomplishments: Its Time Has Come" (Hatry et al., 1990). This series addressed twelve service areas, including colleges and universities, elementary and secondary education, fire and police programs, mass transit, road maintenance, and others. Each report served as a starting point for those governments that wanted to do performance measurements.

In 1994, GASB issued Concepts Statement No.2, "Service Efforts and Accomplishments Reporting," which stated GASB's view that general purpose external financial reporting needs to include service efforts and accomplishments information. In 1997, the Alfred P. Sloan Foundation provided GASB a grant to address the needs of state and local governments in trying to develop performance measures. GASB's intent in sponsoring this research has been to develop a knowledge base for establishing guidelines for reporting SEA information as part of general purpose financial reporting. In 2000, the Sloan Foundation extended the grant for an additional three years.

Nineteen different citizen discussion groups involving 133 individual participants were conducted to learn about citizen's beliefs and expectations regarding SEA (GASB, 2002b). They believe that performance measurement and reporting increases citizen engagement and governmental accountability. The citizens indicated they want to be involved in selecting performance measures, and they want information about costs, outputs, and customer perceptions related to a variety of different services and issues. They want information reported in comparative contexts, accompanied by explanatory information, and disaggregated according to geography and demographics. Multiple communication modes, ranging from printed reports and the Internet to the press, should be used to enable citizens to evaluate the performance of their governments and hold leaders accountable. The group participants also indicated that they want performance information to be independently verified.

The GFOA

Founded in 1906, the Government Finance Officers Association (GFOA) serves nearly 15,000 members in the United States and Canada. GFOA has long been involved in matters related to governmental accounting and financial reporting. Its "Blue Book" titled "Governmental Accounting, Auditing, and Financial Reporting" has been the primary guide in these matters since the first edition was published in 1934. Its "Certificate of Achievement for Excellence in Financial Reporting" program was established in 1945 to recognize and encourage excellence in financial reporting. Over 70 percent of all American cities, 43 percent of all counties with populations in excess of 50,000, and 40 state governments participate in the program. GFOA promoted the establishment of GASB and GFOA members serve on that board.

GFOA Response to GASB Initiatives

GASB's explorations into SEA reporting have caused increasing consternation within the GFOA. The GFOA has persistently argued that SEA information falls outside the parameters of general purpose external financial reports (GPEFR). Believing that the authority of GASB is limited to the promulgation of accounting and financial reporting standards as these have been traditionally defined, the GFOA concludes that GASB lacks the jurisdictional authority and technical expertise to require that SEA information be included in external financial reporting.

In June 1993, GFOA formally asked GASB to define the scope and direction of its future SEA research and standard setting activity. GFOA's request argued the following points:

- GASB members are selected for their expertise in accounting and financial reporting. Accordingly, GASB enjoys the GFOA's full confidence and support when issuing standards involving accounting and financial reporting (authors' note: insofar as "financial reporting" has been traditionally defined to not include an SEA requirement).
- Many SEA measures, particularly those involving non-financial measures of service quality (i.e., "outcome" measures), transcend accounting and financial reporting.
- Ultimate decisions on quality of service or "outcome" measures need to be made by professionals with specialized expertise in the services under consideration, not by accountants.
- GASB would be exceeding its mandate if it attempts to use generally accepted accounting principles (GAAP), either directly or indirectly, to

require the presentation of non-financial measures of service quality as part of general purpose external financial reporting.

The GFOA has formally recommended that governments do performance measurement and calculate the full costs of services. Its recommended practice for performance measurement calls for program and service performance measures to "be developed and used as an important component of long term strategic planning and decision making which should be linked to governmental budgeting" (GFOA, 2002). GFOA has sponsored training sessions, published reference materials, and worked with other professional organizations to encourage the use and standardization of performance indicators.

What the GFOA adamantly opposes is the possibility that GASB might redefine generally accepted accounting principles (GAAP) to include a requirement that SEA information be included in the general purpose external financial reports. GFOA documents indicate that its leaders believe that the GASB board is predisposed toward SEA reporting and is, therefore, not a neutral judge of the pros and cons of the issue. At the heart of the controversy are differing views about the distinction between accounting and financial reporting. The GFOA position is that information derived from financial transactions that sheds light on the financial performance of governments (e.g. changes in net assets over time) should be included in required external financial reports, but information about service accomplishments that is derived from sources other than financial transactions should not be included. In short, the GFOA view is that the definition of financial reporting, insofar as the authority of GASB is concerned, is essentially limited to promulgations related to the reporting of information derived substantially from financial transactions. The GASB position seems to be that its authority extends to pronouncements regarding accounting *and* financial reporting, the latter being distinctive from the former in that it encompasses both the reporting of information derived from financial transactions and the reporting of other information essential to ascertaining what services governments have accomplished relative to financial costs.

The GFOA worries that requiring SEA information in GPEFR would create an unacceptable level of ambiguity and costs in auditing. Specifically, the GFOA has expressed reservations about such things as indicator neutrality, subjectivity in measurement of performance, reliability of performance measures, and the auditability of performance information. As currently defined, the GAAP for state and local governments do not require the inclusion of information in the GPEFR that lies beyond the expertise of certified public accountants to audit. Accountants, though, are not trained to ascertain service accomplishments, nor are they trained to audit the processes inherent to performance measurement. Extension of GAAP to include an SEA reporting requirement, therefore, would amount to a mandate to include information in the GPEFR that lies beyond the expertise of auditors who are trained solely in accounting.

The GFOA is concerned that a GASB requirement to report SEA information would necessarily involve independent auditors to some degree. Audit costs would increase, and the ambiguities introduced might cause auditors to issue qualifications to their opinions. The GFOA position, therefore, is that SEA information should not be included in the GPEFR and that it should be verified by internal auditors rather than by external auditors.

On June 18, 2002, the GFOA adopted a policy statement opposing any involvement of the GASB with SEA reporting (GFOA, 2002). In a letter dated September 4, 2001, to the chairperson of GASB, the president and the executive director of the GFOA wrote, "The real issue is GASB's legitimate jurisdiction. Governments created GASB as an independent body to set standards of accounting and financial reporting. GASB's legitimacy ultimately rests upon this delegation of authority by state and local governments" (Grewe and Esser, 2001).

In 1989, GFOA made clear its belief that the authority of GASB is derived from governments and is not inherent in the Financial Accounting Foundation (FAF) structure. A question arose then as to whether the FAF had the authority to remove some governmental entities from the jurisdiction of GASB and shift them to FASB. GFOA adopted a policy statement on June 6, 1989, stating that if the FAF reduced GASB's jurisdiction, the "GFOA would have no option but to provide its membership with an alternative standard-setting mechanism that they would find acceptable (GFOA, 2002)." It would be ironic if GASB's initiatives in SEA reporting endanger its legitimacy. The federal government seems to be moving toward the inclusion of SEA measures as part of GAAP for its own agencies. Also, the Financial Accounting Standards Board (FASB) is exploring the use of SEA for the financial reporting of non-profit private organizations.

The SEA Initiatives of FASB and FASAB

Though most of its efforts are directed at for-profit organizations, the FASB also pronounces the accounting and financial reporting standards for nonprofit organizations. FASB has indicated concern about the shortcomings of financial reporting for nonprofit organizations. The financial statements of charitable organizations do not indicate whether their revenues have been put to effective use. FASB (1980) has accordingly indicated its intent to encourage the development of performance reporting for nonprofit organizations.

Established in 1990, the Federal Accounting Standards Advisory Board (FASAB) establishes GAAP for the federal government. FASAB consists of nine members appointed by the Secretary of the Treasury, the Director of the Office of Management and Budget, and the Comptroller General of the United States. Admonitions that the federal government should do performance measurement and use it to guide policy making go back more than a half century to the Hoover Commissions. The Government Performance and Results Act of 1993 (GPRA) requires every federal agency to measure performance and report its service accomplishments. FASAB's Statement of Federal Financial Accounting Concepts No. 1, issued in 1993, states that performance reporting should assist report users in evaluating the costs of providing specific activities and programs, the efforts and accomplishments associated with the federal programs, and the efficiency and effectiveness of the government's management of its assets and liabilities. To date, however, FASAB has not issued a standard to require external financial reporting and auditing of performance measures.

Truncating Discourse

For more than a century, the accounting profession has engaged in a process of authoritative rule making that is based upon elaborate formal processes of discourse known as "due process." Both FASB and GASB are required by the Financial Accounting Foundation (FAF) to follow due process in establishing accounting standards. Due process requires extensive research and deliberation, including public input both orally and in writing. The due process proceedings utilized by FASB and GASB typically extend for several years prior to the issuing of authoritative changes in accounting standards. GASB's inquiries into SEA extend back as far as 1984. The GFOA's demand that the GASB cease further inquiry and deliberations about SEA reporting is extraordinary.

Discourse—open deliberation among those who are likely to be affected by decisions—has long been viewed as fundamental to democratic decision making. In philosophy, the concept that wisdom is best sought in the context of open questioning and deliberation dates back as far as Socrates. The importance of open discourse in decision-making has also been asserted by important modern philosophers. Jurgen Habermas (1975) explained that failure to critically engage stakeholders in open discourse in the making of decisions that affect the operations of governments can endanger the legitimacy of government itself. Habermas especially cautioned about the tendencies of scientific and professional bodies to limit discourse in ways that might exclude the "knowledge and conscience of its citizens" (1973, p. 256). In other words, professional organizations can tend to ignore the perspectives and well-being of citizens if the professions' discourse is not conducted in a broadly inclusive, self-critical manner.

An underlying assumption of public financial management theory (and of general public administration theory) is that the information that is reported by governments can affect the views of stakeholders toward them. If this assumption were not valid, then the issuing of financial and other reports by governments would be little more than shallow ritual. If GASB issues, and governments accept, the concept that financial reporting should include SEA information, stakeholders' opinions toward government are likely to be affected. Truncating discussion about reporting SEA information could, therefore, alter future perceptions of those governments.

There is no way of knowing what the future effects on stakeholders' perceptions of governments would be if SEA reporting becomes the norm. Proponents of SEA reporting believe that governments might perform better and that stakeholders' opinions of governments might improve. Opponents seem to believe that SEA reporting will lessen the credibility accorded to financial reports and diminish the legitimacy of governments as well as that of the accounting profession as it is practiced in government. One thing is knowable at present: the stakes are high. What is at issue is the defining of responsibility and accountability—for governments, for policy makers, for administrators, and for financial managers. If discourse is fundamental to democratic processes, and to the accounting profession in establishing its own professional standards, why does the GFOA seek to truncate discourse over SEA?

Alternate Theory

Public financial management theory has often neglected the importance of ambiguity and its effects on the behaviors of financial managers. Yet, as Gerald J. Miller (1991) has demonstrated in his pioneering book *Government Financial Management Theory*, the practice of public financial management is replete with ambiguity. Ambiguity, for example, exists in budgetary forecasting, issuing bonds, deciding a depreciation rate, choosing among bidders for a contract, determining the materiality of a possible (though not certain) future liability, and so forth. Miller, therefore, proposes a theoretical framework called "alternate theory" for public financial management. "This approach searches for description and explanation of what does happen in ambiguous circumstances, especially as the guideposts in procedure or even in consensus move toward randomness" (Miller, 1991, p. 8).

Alternative theory requires that financial management be studied from the perspective of the social sciences, especially sociology, anthropology, and history. It requires that the behaviors of financial managers be studied in an historical context, processes relating to such things as socialization be carefully understood, and careful attention be given to discerning the multiple levels of meaning attributed to key concepts. In short, alternative theory applies the critical theory perspective pioneered by philosophers such as Habermas to the study of public financial management. Habermas' arguments regarding the importance of discourse were fashioned in the broader context of the epistemology of discovery of underlying meaning as seen from the perspective of multiple disciplines (1984, 1989).

The GFOA-GASB debate occurs in the context of the authoritative promulgation of standards for governmental accounting and financial reporting. Unlike physics, in which empirical research into the functioning of nature sets the stage for deliberations, the promulgation of accounting standards involves the social processes of defining norms of accepted behavior for practitioners of the profession. The committee of the American Institute of Certified Public Accountants (known as the "Wheat Committee") that recommended the creation of the Financial Accounting Foundation acknowledged this difference. It wrote that, "financial accounting and reporting are not grounded in natural laws as are the physical sciences, but must rest on a set of conventions and standards designed to achieve what are perceived to be the desired objectives of financial accounting and reporting" (AICPA, 1972, p. 19). Accounting standards, the norms of behavior for professionals in doing such things as preparing financial reports, are social constructs developed in the context of perceptions and collective efforts to define the "desired objectives of financial accounting and reporting."

The leaders of the GFOA and of the GASB view the responsibilities of their profession in different ways. Consequently, they arrive at different perceptions of the "desired objectives of financial accounting and reporting." They differ most strongly in their attitudes toward ambiguity. Both supporters and opponents of SEA reporting acknowledge that there are ambiguities associated with the gathering, analysis, and reporting of information related to the performance of governments. The *GFOA seeks to insulate financial reporting from those ambiguities* by defining service accomplishments information as something beyond the parameters of governmental accounting and, therefore, beyond the authority of the GASB. The GASB see SEA information as being requisite to the fulfillment of the accountability and reporting responsibilities of governments. *GASB seeks to manage the ambiguities* inherent to SEA reporting. The origins of these differences in perceptions can be traced back at least a century.

Origin of Modern Professions

In the late 19th and early 20th centuries, the United States underwent a dramatic transition from a sparsely populated agricultural nation to a large, urban, industrial nation. Progressive reformers responded by creating modern professions. Accounting was one of these professions. Professions differ from one another. Nevertheless, scholars have observed that professions share many characteristics in common. For each profession, advocates led movements to gain social and legal recognition. Autonomy and deference were sought in the belief that they would enable professionals to apply knowledge in society's best interest. Deference and legal protection also served the economic self-interest of the members of the recognized professions by limiting entry to professional practice (Larsen, 1977). Established professions generally share the following characteristics (Schein, 1973; Greenwood, 1957).

1. Certification as a professional is preceded by a long period of formal training in a systematic field of knowledge, not merely in complex skills. Possession of this knowledge allows members to claim authority over its application.
2. Professions possess cultures. They are social communities that provide important sources of identity for their members. Behavioral standards and expectations are operationalized through informal group norms as well as through formal statements of ethics and practices that can be enforced both formally and informally.
3. Professions espouse a commitment of service to society. In return, professions seek deference from society in the creation and application of their specialized knowledge.
4. Professions seek a "monopoly of judgment" in their field while upholding the autonomy of individual practitioners to design treatments for clients or to frame and conduct research. The exercise of individual members' discretion is subject to peer review. Review of professionals' performance by non-members is usually resisted.

Methods for defining the relevant knowledge base, and resolving disputes about it, are essential to the professions. For many professions, the scientific method and discourse among scholars provides the framework for defining the requisite knowledge. For example, several competing approaches to medicine existed in the 19th century, but the one that relied the most upon laboratory research, allopathic medicine, prevailed. Its claim to knowledge derived from the scientific method was accepted by legislatures and special privileges and sanctions were enacted in law to facilitate the practice of that form of medicine.

The Accounting Profession

Some professions rely upon authority, more than the scientific method, in defining their knowledge base. Lawyers, for example, look to legislatures to enact law and to judges to interpret that law. Accounting also relies primarily upon authority to define its knowledge base. In the case of law, the defining authority rests partly beyond the profession in the legislative branch where most lawmakers are not attorneys. In accounting, however, the defining authority rests almost entirely within the context of the profession itself. Almost all the board members of the Financial Accounting Foundation, and of the FASB and GASB, are accountants.

The current authority structure (FAF-FASB-GASB) in the United States emerged in response to problems encountered with financial reporting that date back to the 19th century. Accountants attained professional recognition and legal status from state legislatures in the late 19th and early 20th century. The focus of the accountants who sought recognition, and of the legislatures which bestowed it, was upon protecting the investing public (Siegel and Rigsby, 1998). In the private sector, the investing public is comprised of two groups: (1) those who invest through purchasing ownership equity, and (2) those who invest by purchasing instruments of debt issued by companies.

The collapse of the stock market in 1929 was blamed, in part, on poor financial reporting. It was felt that companies had not fully disclosed their activities in their financial reports, leading to investor overconfidence and excessive risk-taking. Federal regulation of the financial marketplace greatly expanded. The Securities and Exchange Commission was given statutory authority to establish financial accounting and reporting standards, but it chose to rely upon the accounting profession to create its own arrangements for setting standards. The American Institute of Certified Public Accountants (AICPA) established a committee (1936–1959) and then a board (1959–1973) to promulgate accounting and financial reporting standards. The AICPA was the promulgating authority until the establishment of the Financial Accounting Foundation in 1972. FASB was founded in 1973, and GASB was established under the auspices of the FAF in 1984.

As with all other professions, processes of socialization have emerged to promote predictable behaviors by members of the accounting profession. Predictability in the behaviors of professionals is essential. Physicians, for example, who digress too far from the profession's diagnostic and prescriptive norms health are subject to sanction. Studies of socialization in the accounting profession are few (Fogarty, 1992). Much of it begins in universities (Mayer-Sommer and Loeb, 1981). Membership in the accounting profession becomes a source of identity for its members. Socialization in accounting is framed around the "accounting paradigm" itself.

The accounting paradigm is built around the capturing and processing of a very specific category of information–that which emanates from financial transactions. Anyone who has taken an elementary accounting course has been taught the basics of the accounting paradigm. Students are taught at the outset to recognize events that constitute financial transactions and to record essential information about each such transaction. Once obtained, this information is manipulated, analyzed, and reported according to prescribed processes and formats. Socialization in accounting seems to produce a high degree of predictability as to how accountants will process information that is derived from financial transactions (Willingham and Carmichael, 1968). Information that is not derived from financial transactions does not readily fit the accounting paradigm. For accountants, financial reporting tends to be defined in the context of the accounting paradigm.

In seeking to halt GASB's promotion of discourse and research into SEA reporting, the GFOA is seeking to avoid the ambiguities inherent to SEA reporting by declaring that GASB's authority is limited to pronouncements related to the accounting paradigm–to reporting information generated from financial transactions. If GASB declares that the "financial reporting" responsibilities of governments extend well beyond financial transaction-generated information, the practitioners of accounting in the public sector will be confronted by many new ambiguities.

Efficient Citizenship: The Origin of the SEA Perspective

SEA information is a combination of data derived from financial transactions (primarily the cost or "efforts" measurements) and from other sources (the program performance data essential to "accomplishments" measurement). GASB's "Preliminary Views of the Governmental Accounting Standards Board on Concepts Related to Service Efforts and Accomplishments Reporting," issued in December 1993, stated that external reporting of SEA data "is essential both to assess accountability and to make informed decisions to improve the efficiency and effectiveness of governmental operations" (GASB, 1993, p.1). The belief that governmental accountability can only be assessed if accounting and performance data are combined dates at least as far back as the first decade of the 20th century.

This was a fundamental belief of the founders of the New York Bureau of Municipal Research, a nonprofit, philanthropically supported "think tank" incorporated in 1907. The bureau gave birth to the nation's first professional degree program in public administration (at Syracuse University) and to the Brookings Institution. Its three founders, one of whom was a leading accountant of the day, sought to improve and unify all aspects of governmental financial management. To these "progressive" reformers, *efficient government was achievable only if reports to citizen-voters linked information about governments' finances to other information about what they were getting for their money.* The bureau explored ways to apply new methods of performance improvement to governments. Frederick Taylor, one of the leading pioneers in the new management science, was actively associated with the bureau. The bureau especially sought to inform citizens in poorer neighborhoods about the performance of governments in their neighborhoods relative to the performance in more affluent locales.

In short, the bureau saw financial reporting as being directed to multiple stakeholders—elected officials, government administrators, businessmen, buyers of municipal debt, and especially to voter-taxpayers (Schacter, 1995). GASB's viewpoint is nearly identical to the views of the founders of the NY Bureau a century ago. It is a viewpoint that seeks symmetry between financial reporting in the government and for-profit sectors.

Return on Investment Assymetry

"ROI," meaning "return on investment," is a concept as old as capitalism itself. It is fundamental in business accounting and finance. The financial reports of for-profit businesses provide essential organizational performance information to each of their "investing publics"—shareholders and bondholders. Each group of investors needs to assess the profitability of a company. When a company is profitable, its financial position changes for the better. Changes in financial position are presented in companies' financial reports, where their success in obtaining revenues, relative to the costs incurred, is revealed. Calculations of ROI are complicated due to ambiguities about such things as valuing a company's "goodwill" or its future contingent liabilities. Helping to resolve such ambiguities, in part by making company policies transparent and fully reported, is an essential task of business accountants.

The ROI concept as applied to businesses has its limits. A business' financial reports, for example, do not encompass social benefits. The full benefits for society of a company's actions in such areas as R&D, employee training, or philanthropic endeavors are not calculable from its financial reports. Nevertheless, a fundamental responsibility of business accountants is to report the requisite information needed to calculate financial returns to investors. The apparent failure of Enron to fully report the liabilities of its subsidiaries, for example, made it impossible to accurately assess the company's financial position. Accountants and managers involved are now defending against lawsuits brought by investors who maintain that there was a failure to report all information needed to accurately assess the company's true return on investment. A substantial body of law exists that establishes the responsibility of business managers and accountants to report information in a manner that is sufficient for investors to effectively calculate businesses' returns on investment. Fulfillment of this responsibility is a fundamental tenet of the accounting profession.

Governments also have two categories of "investing publics"–those who purchase government debt and those who are the citizen-taxpayer-owners of a government. When citizens pay taxes and fees, they do so not as customers of an entity owned by others, but as investors in their own government. The managers and accountants of governments are obligated to report on returns to their investors. Governmental accounting, however, is confronted by a dilemma. The essential returns to governments' owners are services received, not profits revealed through changes in financial position. Changes in financial position do not reveal the returns provided to the owners of governments. Paradoxically, governments can "improve" their financial position by over-taxing or under-serving the public relative to the amounts of money invested in fees and taxes. Under such circumstances, financial reports that are framed solely around financial transaction based information would reveal an improvement in financial position, but the actual returns to owner-investors would have been diminished. Declines, or improvements, in a government's efficiency over time cannot be readily identified without information about service accomplishments relative to costs.

Investors who purchase governments' debt issues are well served by current reporting practices. They can ascertain from governments' financial reports much of what they need to know about the likely ability of governments to repay debt. On the other hand, under current reporting practices the owners of governments, the taxpayers, learn little about their returns, the quantity and quality of the services delivered. Government financial reports, absent SEA data, therefore, do not serve the information needs of both of governments' "investing publics." Financial reporting that omits SEA data does not, and cannot, provide information about returns to the owners of governments.

Absent SEA information, financial reporting in government is not symmetrical with that of for-profit reporting. Current GAAP for for-profit organizations provide essential information to both investing publics. Current GAAP for governments (and for nonprofit private organizations) do not. Government financial reporting today provides the essential information needed by investors who finance debt, but it does not enable taxpayer-owners to make judgments about the adequacy of returns relative to their investment. This asymmetry raises doubt that current governmental GAAP are adequate to the needs of the democratic process, predicated as it is upon the needs of voters for information about governmental performance. In democratic theory, the most basic form of accountability is that to which elected officials are subject in elections. In the private sector, stockholders informed about a company's performance can hold corporate officials accountable through the voting of shares. In government, owners are handicapped in holding officials accountable because their returns relative to their investments have not been reported.

Assessing returns for the owners of a government is vastly more complex than assessing returns for business owners where the essential question is financial profitability. No single comparable measure, no *deus ex machina*, exists with which to readily summarize the returns that governments provide to their taxpayers. The assessment of governmental performance requires numerous, multidimensional measures derived from varied data sources. Accordingly, verification of performance information is a very complex process. Governmental services are so multifaceted that performance reporting could easily overwhelm report users with quantities of information that are beyond their capacity to digest. Consequently, it seems inescapable that SEA reporting would require decisions to selectively present limited amounts of performance information. Selecting the measures to be reported introduces political implications. It is complexities such as these that prompt resistance to SEA reporting.

In summary, a debate continues that began nearly a century ago. One organization, the GFOA, sees itself as protecting the credibility of financial reporting by avoiding the ambiguity of information that is not generated through financial transactions. In doing so, it reinforces the delineation created by professional boundaries as they emerged early in the 20th century. These boundaries emphasize a distinction between government accountants and other public financial managers who are educated in disciplines such as public administration, finance, and economics. The other organization, the GASB, perpetuates the perspective begun in the NY Bureau—that stewardship and accountability responsibilities to the owners of governments can only be fulfilled if governments closely link the reporting of information derived from financial transactions with that derived from other sources to demonstrate service accomplishments.

The conflict between the GFOA and the GASB is a clash of paradigms. One is a paradigm of specialization, in which each of the several disciplines associated with public financial management—accounting, public administration, public finance, and economics—occupy distinct niches with boundaries. It is a paradigm in which economists do budgetary forecasting and revenue analyses, public administration specialists prepare and execute budgets, financing specialists manage debt and investments, and accountants manage and audit the information systems that capture and report the transaction-initiated information. The SEA paradigm requires greater integration of the specializations. The GFOA, seeking credibility for its members and their governments, fears that auditors will fail to issue unqualified audit opinions. In accounting, auditors are the enforcers of norms, and the possibility of unfavorable audits is an uncertainty to be avoided. If there is ever to be a rapprochement between the GFOA perspective and that of GASB, ways must be found to bridge the two paradigms.

Financial Reporting Options under the GFOA Paradigm

If GFOA's position prevails, accountability processes will be bifurcated. The information needed to hold public officials accountable for governments' financial performance will continue to be presented in financial statements that are subject to independent audit by qualified accountants. Neither the financial statements nor the opinions issued by the auditors would address the service performance of governments. The reporting of SEA information would become part of the budget process. Budget documents would include performance information to inform decision makers about inputs, workloads, outputs, and outcomes. By shifting the responsibility for SEA reporting to the budget process, GFOA would insulate traditional financial reporting from the ambiguities associated with the development and use of SEA information. Performance measures would be disclosed, but not in a manner that would be subject to external audit. GFOA's position, though, would not make performance reporting mandatory because no authoritative body prescribes budgeting standards for state and local governments.

GFOA's position presents significant challenges to the theory and practice of government budgeting. At its core, government budgeting is a set of processes designed to enhance elected officials' capacity to plan and decide revenue and expenditure priorities. Although some attention is given to communicating budget information to the public, the central challenge is to facilitate the resource allocation decisions that elected officials must make. Budgeting processes, therefore, are not primarily designed for reporting information to persons outside the government. They are primarily designed to facilitate the decisions of those legislative bodies that ultimately exercise the power of the purse.

Nevertheless, it is widely recognized in budget theory that budgeting processes should provide effective communication with the public. The GFOA's criteria for awarding certificates for distinguished budget presentation require that the applying governments show sufficient evidence of effective communication of budgetary information to the public. The framework for budgeting developed by the National Advisory Committee on State and Local Budgeting (NACSLB) encourages governments to effectively communicate budgetary information to the public.

If the GFOA position prevails, SEA information will become effectively reported to the public only if the communication dimension of budgeting is given far greater emphasis by budget theorists and practitioners. Unfortunately, history suggests that this might not occur. Repeated reform efforts in public budgeting over the past half century—performance budgeting, PPBS, zero-based budgeting, program budgeting, and so forth—have promoted the development and use of performance-oriented information. The use of performance information in budgeting, however, has been inconsistent and often short-lived. In spite of repeated admonitions by reformers over a span of at least seven decades, budgeting processes have not become effective conduits of SEA type information to the public. The GFOA alternative, therefore, is likely to require an unprecedented level of effort to succeed in getting SEA information to the public via the budgetary process.

One option would be to reconvene the National Advisory Committee on State and Local Budgeting to amend its recommended budgeting practices to clarify ways to communicate performance information to the public. Unfortunately, the NACSLB was strictly advisory. It ceased to exist after issuing its recommended practices. No authoritative framework exists for budgeting as there is for accounting and financial reporting. No authoritative body comparable to GASB establishes generally accepted budgeting standards. If SEA reporting is relegated to budgeting, such reporting will be done voluntarily and in the absence of an authoritative framework to guide the issuance and review of the information. In this, SEA reporting would be declared to be fundamentally different from other forms of financial reporting.

Financial Reporting Options under the GASB Paradigm

GASB's position thus far is that omitting SEA information from financial reports makes them insufficient to judge the performance of a government (GASB, 1990, p. 2). This is a seemingly incontrovertible assertion. Yet it raises a fundamental dilemma. To date, all authoritative statements issued by GASB, or by FASB, deal with transaction-based information that is subject to external independent audit by trained accountants. GFOA objects to any statements being issued on SEA because such issuance would then, in its opinion, require SEA data to be audited by independent certified public accountants. CPAs, however, are not educated to develop nor to audit program performance measurements. Proponents of both paradigms seem to agree on this.

If, as GASB is asserting, SEA information is a critical element of governmental financial reporting, then financial reporting extends beyond the competence of accounting or any other single profession involved in public financial management. To operationalize GASB's position, therefore, ways must be found to report SEA information that complement, but do not compromise, the aspects of financial reporting that are necessarily accomplished by accountants. Fortunately, financial reporting mechanisms already exist to report information that is not subject to the issuance of an opinion by external auditors. These mechanisms offer possibilities for resolving the dilemma.

Financial statements are audited by independent accountants to assure that transaction-based financial information is reported consistently with GAAP. Following their reviews, auditors then issue an opinion as to whether the statements present fairly the financial position of the audited organization. Under currently accepted auditing principles, two types of information are reported: "primary" and "secondary." Primary information is central and requisite to the issuance of the auditors' opinion. Secondary information is reported with financial statements to help the reader to better understand the statements, but it is not essential to the auditors in issuing their opinion. Secondary information is reviewed by the auditor for consistency with information presented in the basic financial statements.

The key to a compromise is to separate SEA information from the transaction-based information about which accountant-auditors issue their opinions. Requiring SEA information to be reported in the financial statements (or in the notes to the financial statements) themselves would not accomplish the requisite separation. Inclusion in financial statements would require auditors to review all steps in the collection of SEA data just as they do with information generated from financial transactions.

There are at least four other alternatives for reporting SEA information. The first three are currently recognized as part of governments' Comprehensive Annual Financial Reports (CAFRs). The fifth alternative, a required SEA report, could be made a part of a government's CAFR or it could be a separately required report. The alternatives are:

- *Management Discussion and Analysis (MD&A)* The MD&A section, a required element of a CAFR, introduces the basic financial statements and provides an analytical overview of the government's activities. Currently, MD&A sections include comparisons between the current year and the prior year's financial activities based upon currently known facts, decisions, or conditions. They should assist the user in assessing whether the financial position has improved or deteriorated as a result of the year's activities. Currently, auditors have a responsibility to look at the information and to make inquiries of management regarding the methods of measurement and the presentation of information. Auditors, however, do not audit the information nor express an opinion on the information. In practice, though, auditors have taken steps to preclude the inclusion of some information by management on the grounds that the information is too far from the scope of the auditors' audits. This fact suggests that efforts to alter the MD&A section to include SEA information would be highly controversial.

- *Required Supplementary Information (RSI, other than MD&A)* The Required Supplementary Information to the financial statements and notes to the financial statements supports and explains the data in the financial statements. The external auditor has the same responsibility for RSI as for the MD&A section of a CAFR. Inclusion of SEA information as RSI, therefore, would be as controversial as its inclusion in the MD&A section. For SEA information to be included as RSI (or in the MD&A section) within CAFRs, external auditors of financial statements would have to be specifically exempted from responsibility for reviewing the SEA information.

- *Statistical Section* The statistical section of the CAFR provides social and economic data and financial trends of the government. The auditor has no responsibility for reviewing any of this information or the systems used to collect or report the information in this section of a CAFR. The auditor expresses no opinion on the information. This makes the statistical section of the CAFR a promising alternative for reporting SEA information. If GASB issues a statement that CAFRs should include SEA information within their statistical sections, governments would be expected to provide the data but the auditors of the transaction-based financial statements would be relieved of responsibility for reviewing or issuing opinions about the SEA information.

- *Separate SEA Report from CAFR* GASB could require a SEA report as a new element in the CAFR. It might be wiser, however, to separate SEA reports from the CAFR context. To date, GASB's pronouncements regarding financial reporting have centered on transaction-based information. GASB's Statement Number 34, establishing a government-wide framework for reporting transaction-based information, was a major accomplishment. GASB's commitment to comprehensive reporting within the context of the CAFR format, however, might be a prime cause of GFOA's concerns.

GFOA's members perceive the CAFR, not incorrectly, as the purview of accountants. GASB, therefore, might chose to proclaim that governments are obligated, within the context of generally accepted accounting and financial reporting principles, to report SEA information, but that they do it in a report that is separate from the CAFR. External accountant-auditors would have no responsibility to review or issue an opinion about such a financial report that is so clearly separated from CAFRs. The separate SEA reports would be considered to be required financial reports, essential to inform citizen-owners about their returns relative to their investments in their governments, but not subject to audit by external accountant-auditors. Separating SEA information from CAFRs would make it easier for governments to create other mechanisms, such as independent citizen review boards, to review the credibility of SEA data.

Perplexing Issues of SEA Reporting: Governmental Autonomy and Auditing

Governmental Autonomy

Critics argue that mandatory SEA reporting will infringe on the autonomy of state and local governments to decide policy. They fear that GASB approved performance measures would pressure governments to alter their policies. For example, if prescribed performance measures for roads placed more emphasis on road condition than traffic handling capacity, governments might do more repaving while neglecting system expansion. Existing GAAP are designed to influence the financial policies of governments. Governments, for example, are encouraged by current GAAP to become more transparent than they otherwise might be and to become less prone to engage in such illusory practices as postponing the recording of expenses to help "balance" an annual budget. SEA measures, however, have the potential to alter governments' substantive policy decisions. Accordingly, GASB must weigh its responsibility to assure that citizens are able to ascertain their returns relative to costs against the prerogative of governments to decide substantive policy. GASB could require SEA reporting while leaving it to individual governments to decide those measures that best fit their chosen policy priorities.

Auditing

The citizen participants in the GASB discussion groups indicated that they want performance information to be independently verified. Information about service "efforts" comes primarily from cost accounting systems. Accountants can readily audit this "half" of SEA information. Auditing information about service "accomplishments," however is problematic. Most information about service accomplishments is not derived from financial transactions. Accountants, therefore, are not trained to measure or to audit information about service accomplishments.

Standards for "Performance Auditing," the auditing of accomplishments, have been enumerated by the USG.AO in its "Yellow Book," formally titled "Government Auditing Standards" (available online at http://www.gao.gov/). That publication addresses standards related to the conduct of fieldwork in performance auditing and the reporting of performance audits. It directs performance auditors to review managerial controls related to the measuring, reporting, and monitoring of program performance. Management's policies and implemented procedures should be scrutinized to "reasonably ensure that valid and reliable data are obtained, maintained, and fairly disclosed in reports" (Government Auditing Standards, 2003, section 6.41.b). The Yellow Book provides essential guidance for the verification of SEA data. If GASB does decide to require SEA reporting, the procedures specified in the Yellow Book will likely need to be addressed from several standpoints, especially from the perspective of containing the costs of performance auditing.

Training to evaluate performance is offered in some schools of public administration and policy. Many public accounting firms, however, do not have staffs of persons trained in performance auditing. In the wake of the Enron scandal, public accounting firms are being pressed to separate themselves from management consulting, even though management consultants often have the training needed to do performance auditing. It seems likely, therefore, that most public accounting firms will not have the expertise to do both financial and performance auditing.

Some internal auditors can do performance audits, but their independence when reporting externally is an issue, and many smaller governments lack internal auditing capacity. Although some public accounting firms can do performance auditing, and some internal auditors have the capacity to do credible performance auditing, neither group as a whole seems capable of extensively auditing the accomplishments of many, probably most, state and local governments. Some state auditing offices have performance auditing expertise, but they lack the capacity to audit the SEA reports of all state agencies and all local governments' in the foreseeable future.

Some management consulting firms have personnel who are trained in program evaluation, and new performance auditing firms could be established in the future, but there is no fully functioning professional framework to oversee performance auditing as now exists for financial auditing. Although there are professional organizations that encourage quality evaluation, there is no established profession of performance auditing. It is not at all clear that governments will be willing to provide the funds needed to create and implement such a professional framework. Critics cite increased auditing costs as a major reason not to require SEA reporting. If GASB requires SEA reporting and if state and local governments mandate extensive performance auditing that meets the standards of the Yellow Book, substantial increases in audit costs do seem inescapable.

Conclusion

In summary, a paradox confronts SEA reporting. Without SEA reporting, governments cannot report returns relative to costs to their citizens. With SEA reporting, governments will report information that cannot be fully audited by their financial auditors and the nation's institutional capacity to perform independent performance auditing is lacking relative to probable future demand. Creative compromise, therefore, seems essential.

A semantic dilemma underlies the GFOA-GASB debate. GASB, and its counterpart FASB, exist to define GAAP, the "Generally Accepted Accounting Principles" that define the framework of knowledge and practice of accountants. Yet GASB's mission is to define both accounting and financial reporting principles. If financial reporting is defined as being limited to the expertise of the accounting profession, then GASB's jurisdiction will be perceived as excluding non-transaction based SEA measures. Our democracy's processes of holding officials accountable at the ballot box, though, will be better served by expanding financial reporting to include SEA measures. A new acronym, therefore, is needed to define the role of GASB. Instead of promulgating "GAAP," it might better be recognized as the promulgator of "GAAFRP," "Generally Accepted Accounting and Financial Reporting Principles." The change in acronyms would recognize that, to be informed of their returns, citizens must be served by financial reporting that transcends any one disciplinary perspective.

GASB's Concepts Statement No. 2 indicated that SEA measures would need to be reviewed to ensure that they have the "requisite characteristics" of understandability, reliability, relevance, timeliness, consistency, and comparability (GASB, 1994, paragraphs 62–68). Financial auditors might look at the cost measures used in SEA to determine whether they are out of line with what is presented in the financial statements. They need not, indeed should not, be required to issue an opinion about accomplishments information. Internal auditors, where available, could offer opinions about the "requisite characteristics" of the accomplishments information presented by management. Independent performance auditors, where available (e.g., in state evaluation offices), might occasionally offer detailed reviews of accomplishments information reported.

Ultimately, however, citizens themselves might be the best judges of the veracity of reported accomplishments. The most basic form of accountability in a democracy is that to which elected officials are held during elections. Efficient citizenship, as proposed nearly a century ago, called for reporting SEA information directly to citizens to inform their electoral choices. That concept relied upon citizens to judge whether the reported accomplishments were in line with their own experiences with governments. Intermediaries such as auditors, while potentially useful, were not essential for citizens to hold officials accountable for governments' performance. We recommend that GASB and others consider the potential of local independent citizen review boards. Such citizen-led boards could review the credibility of SEA data and issue observations and conclusions to their fellow citizens about that data. Such boards could be advised by financial auditors and other professionals and are likely to be far less expensive than elaborate independent audits conducted according to full Yellow Book standards. This is an alternative that needs prompt research.

From the perspective of efficient citizenship, citizens have a right to be informed about the returns they get from their investments in government. An authoritative statement from GASB would codify that right in generally accepted accounting and financial reporting principles. GFOA's proposal to report performance information with budgets makes such reporting optional and would not authoritatively recognize the right of citizens to be informed about performance. The problems inherent to performance auditing do not negate the right of citizens to be informed about their returns. The challenge, therefore, is to discover ways to provide citizens with the best possible SEA information at reasonable costs. For that, discourse must be encouraged, not truncated.

References

American Institute for Certified Public Accountants (Wheat Committee). 1972. *Report of the Study on Establishment of Accounting Principles.* New York: AICPA, March.

Financial Accounting Standards Board (FASB). 1980. *FASB Concepts Statement No. 4: Objectives of Financial Reporting by Nonbusiness Organizations.* Norwalk, CT: Financial Accounting Foundation, December.

Fogarty, Timothy J. 1992. "Organizational Socialization in Accounting Firms: A Theoretical Framework and Agenda for Future Research." *Accounting, Organizations, and Society,* 17, no. 2 (February): 129–149.

Governmental Accounting Standards Board. 1990. *Research Report on Service Efforts and Accomplishment Reporting: Its Time Has Come.* Norwalk, CT: Financial Accounting Foundation.

Governmental Accounting Standards Board. 1993. *Preliminary Views of the Governmental Accounting Standards Board on Concepts Related to Service Efforts and Accomplishments Reporting. Governmental Accounting Standards Series No. 093-A.* Norwalk, CT: Financial Accounting Foundation, December.

Governmental Accounting Standards Board. 1994. *Concepts Statement No. 2: Service Efforts and Accomplishment Reporting.* Norwalk, CT: Financial Accounting Foundation.

Governmental Accounting Standards Board. 2002. *Report on the GASB Citizen Discussion Groups on Performance Reporting.* Norwalk, CT: Financial Accounting Foundation.

Government Auditing Standards. 2003. Comptroller General of the United States. Washington, DC: U.S. Government Printing Office. Available online: www.gao.gov

Government Finance Officers Association. 2002a. *Distinguished Budget Presentation Award.* Available online at http://www.gfoa.org/services/awards .html (accessed May 17, 2002).

Government Finance Officers Association. 2002b. *Performance Measurement and the Governmental Accounting Standards Board.* Policy statement adopted June 18, 2002. www.gfoa.org/services/policy/.

Greenwood, Ernest. 1957. "Attributes of a Profession." *Social Work,* 2, no. 3 (July): 45–55.

Grewe, Timothy, and Jeffrey L. Esser. 2001. "Letter to Mr. Tom Allen." Available online at http://www.gfoa.org (accessed September 4).

Habermas, Jurgen. 1973. *Theory and Praxis.* Boston: Beacon Press.

Habermas, Jurgen. 1975. *Legitimation Crisis.* Boston: Beacon Press.

Habermas, Jurgen. 1984/1989. *The Theory of Communicative Action.* Boston: Beacon Press, 1984 (vol. 1), 1989 (vol. 2).

Hatry, Harry P., James R. Fountain, Jr., Johnathan M. Sullivan, and Lorraine Kremer. 1990. *Service Efforts and Accomplishments: Its Time Has Come.* Norwalk, CT: Financial Accounting Foundation.

Larsen, Magali Sarfati. 1977. *The Rise of Professionalism: A Sociological Analysis.* Berkeley, CA: University of California Press.

Mayer-Sommer, Alan P., and Stephen.E. Loeb. 1981. "Fostering More Successful Professional Socialization among Accounting Students." *The Accounting Review,* 56, no. 1 (January): 125–136.

Miller, Gerald J. 1991. *Government Financial Management Theory.* New York: Marcel Dekker.

Schacter, Hindy Lauer. 1995. "Democracy, Scientific Management and Urban Reform: The Case of the Bureau of Municipal Research and the 1912 New York City School Inquiry." *Journal of Management History,* 1, no. 2: 52–64.

Schein, Edgar. 1973. *Professional Education.* New York: McGraw-Hill.

Siegel, Philip H., and John T. Rigsby. 1998. "Institutionalization and Struc-
    turing of Certified Public Accountants: An Analysis of the Development
    of Education and Experience Requirements for Certified Public Accoun-
    tants." *Journal of Management History*, 4, no. 2 (July): 81–9
Willingham, John D., and D. R. Carmichael. 1968. "The Professional Audit-
    ing Subculture." *Abacus*, 4, no. 2 (December): 153–163.

CHAPTER 7

Assessing the Likely Acceptance of Financial Management Techniques in the Public Sector
A Characteristic Approach

William G. Albrecht and Rev. Thomas D. Lynch

The body of theoretical knowledge in relation to public financial management has and continues to involve substantial amounts of intellectual capital. While the field is broad in terms of content and approach, a large portion of research efforts appears to focus on either decision making in a complex democratic setting or the development, refinement, and application of instrumental theories for achieving inherently valued outputs. There are, of course, underlying normative and positive aspects to each of these areas, and empirical "reality checks" are a constant reminder that "what is" is not always "what should be." Given the current quest to establish benchmarks or identify "best practices," public financial management theorists must stop and question if the tug of war between these two dimensions perpetuates a third, defined as "what can be." However, before one answers the query, a rather obvious positive observation remains: Despite all of the accumulated knowledge, a science of muddling through appears to be the current trend in public financial management research and practice.

That assertion is substantiated with two acknowledgements. First, benchmarking and best practice identifications are relative comparisons of public versus private sectors and managers, governments, and governmental or nongovernmental agencies.[1] Theory is typically not a major concern of these methods. Marginal change prescriptions are usually qualified or quantified according to peer level performance rather than abstract or logical deductions. Transferal of desirable activities across entities is generally assumed possible, and by design, policy and administrative recommendations are essentially incremental.

The second acknowledgment is that despite the practical and intuitive appeal of benchmarking and best practice procedures and recommendations, an apparent anomaly remains in relation to managerial acceptance. Clearly even this type of advice is not always well received by decision makers. This suggests that the muddling of researchers with a peer comparison orientation does not automatically equate with that of practitioners. Therefore, in going about financial management, the great schism between theory and practice may be more accurately portrayed as a division between research and practice.[2]

The existence of such a division within the field poses both a dilemma and a challenge for public financial management theorists. As noted by Irene Rubin (1997, p. 185), beyond stating assumptions and highlighting problems of substantive significance, "in public administration, theory has the additional responsibility of culling practical problems and suggesting solutions." The very nature of the discipline precludes a simple dismissal of public problems by theorists, no matter how tempting. To do so would define theoretical efforts as basic research rather than applied. Acknowledging the division between research and practice as a practical public administration and policy problem is best. The challenge is to understand why research-driven prescriptions are not always followed and, perhaps, to respond accordingly.

Given the above, the primary purpose of this chapter is to discuss characteristics theory as an approach for assessing the likely acceptance of financial management techniques by public financial managers that researchers deem as normatively superior. Specifically, the intent is to delineate the interaction of factors influencing choice in situations where managers have discretion over available instrumental alternatives and to exploit such information with an analytic model. While our overall query resembles prior research in attempting to understand manager behavior, our approach differs with the assumption that rational public financial managers choose to adopt financial management techniques in accordance with the expected characteristics of those techniques. We rely primarily on microeconomic principles to accomplish this objective. However, we also draw on existing explanatory financial management theories, as well as empirical studies, in order to identify an appropriate choice set.

The remainder of the chapter proceeds as follows: First, a technical overview of select instrumental theories is given. Following Bailey (1968), we define instrumental theories as empirical or theoretical research efforts that focus exclusively on the refinement of managerial techniques (Henry, 1975, p. 4) and are independent of decision-making behavior. However, in the text we acknowledge that threshold methods or "rules of thumb" are possible substitutes for some instrumental theories. Next, traditional theories of decision-maker behavior in deterministic situations are considered before presenting characteristics theory as another approach. The public financial management literature is then reviewed in order to identify potential sources of manager utility. Following this, we use indifference curve analysis to demonstrate the essential elements of characteristics theory in relation to the current research problem. After a brief discussion of fundamental results, the chapter concludes with a number of comments and policy recommendations.

Public Financial Management Theories and Studies

As suggested in the introduction, public financial management knowledge exhibits an approximate dichotomous split between decision making in a complex democratic setting and the development, refinement, and application of instrumental theories for achieving inherently valued outputs. While this general division is relatively easy to detail, an enormous amount of complexity exists within each category in relation to explanation and prediction. The most obvious complications stem from traditional disciplinary considerations, methodologies, and values. However, further intricacies develop when one considers the fact that theorists typically develop, refine, and prescribe instrumental theories that are independent of decision-making considerations. This disconnection is often a primary point of contention within debates concerning the presence, absence, or possibility of rationalism during the conduction of public financial management practices. The detachment also suggests that, in isolation, existing theories and studies, while necessary, are not sufficient for explaining why financial managers do not always accept research-driven prescriptions. The sections that follow are intended to develop a complementary perspective among these alternative views of reality.[3]

Instrumental Theories: Technical Views and Alternatives

In the aggregate, instrumental theories are referred to as such with a number of synonymous labels, including tools, principles, and techniques (Ammons, 2002; Reed and Swain, 1997; Matzer, 1984). Beyond labels, instrumental theories share a similar distinction in that each "practice" is a technology or technical process, contrived by an instrumental theorist, for conducting public financial management activities in a manner that facilitates the attainment of normative public objectives (Drucker, 1986, p. 19; Bailey, 1968 as cited in Henry, 1975, p. 4).

In this sense, every tool, principle, and technique entails a distinct form of rational problem solving involving causal reasoning. According to Sarasvathy (2001, p. 6), "Causal reasoning is based on the *logic to the extent that we can predict the future, we can control it.*" Therefore, under certain assumptions, an implied element of a particular theory is that the output of a core financial management function can be known or realized at least within the boundaries of subjective probabilities.

Despite these affinities, specific theories also differ in that any one of them can be classified as a Standard Operating Procedure (SOP), decision rule, or strategy with a unique process for execution. Within these categories, individual instrumental theories vary according to emphasis on organizational orientations such as planning, management, and control, and in overall applicability across financial management activities and functions (Reed and Swain, 1997, p. 7). Beyond these aspects, particular theories fulfill various managerial purposes in numerous ways. As a final ultimate distinction, instrumental approaches differ according to overall level of theoretical acceptance in that specific SOPs, decision rules, and strategies are deemed normatively superior according to some form of normative criterion.

Table 7.1 presents these defining features of instrumental theories along with specific examples and evidence of academic or research support for viewing a particular practice as normatively superior. The list is by no means collectively exhaustive. Selection of a theory for inclusion in the table is based solely on the need for a parsimonious explanation. Citations in relation to normative superiority are mutually exclusive in that only the public financial management literature is acknowledged. This is to (1) mitigate any concerns over the transferal of private sector principles to the public sector; and (2) facilitate a number of discussions in different contexts throughout the rest of the chapter.

Table 7.1
Selected Instrumental Theories and Associated Aspects

Theories	Activities	Orientation	Process	Purpose	Normatively Superior
SOPs					
Debt Policies Element Dependent* Decision Rules	Debt Administration	Management-Control	Written Elements	Effectiveness, Accountability, Equity	Simonsen, Robbins, and Kittredge (2001)
NPV* Payback Method	Capital Budgeting	Planning	Calculation	Evaluate Alternative Projects	Finkler (2001)
TIC* NIC	Debt Administration	Management	Calculation	Measuring Interest Cost of Municipal Bond Issuance	Simonsen and Robbins (2002)
EOQ* Thresholds	Cash Management	Management	Calculation	Optimal Cash Balances	Schwartz (1996)
Strategies					
Mean-Variance* Typical Position	Investment	Management	Optimization	Efficient Portfolios	Petersen (1996)
Hedging* Typical Position	Investment	Management	Buy, Sell	Anticipating and Offsetting Interest Rate Movements	Miller (1991)

* **Normatively Superior**

Referencing the table, Simonsen, Robbins, and Kittredge (2001) assert that constructive written debt policies should include elements related to ethics and accountability, in addition to traditional aspects such as legal compliance or obtaining the lowest interest rates possible. Their emphasis on these types of facets underscores the notion that good governance consists of propriety and fairness as well as strict financial consideration. In this capacity, academics also view instrumental theories as tools for governments to directly achieve ultimately valued outcomes, such as legitimacy in the eyes of the governed. While the term "policy" is too broad to denote a specific counter arrangement to this normatively superior practice, any policy that does not include elements associated with ethics and accountability can be considered an alternative instrumental theory within the realm of debt administration activities.[4]

Compared to SOPs the decision rules in Table 7.1 portray various calculations to fulfill planning and management orientations. For example, in capital budgeting and debt administration, the Net Present Value (NPV) method and True Interest Cost (TIC) method are usually proclaimed as normatively superior instrumental theories for evaluating alternative projects and calculating bond interest rates, respectively (Finkler, 2001, pp. 152–158; Simonsen and Robbins, 2002). These declarations are primarily based on the ability of each rule to account for a singular normative criteria—namely the Time Value of Money (TVM).[5] While the Payback and Net Interest Cost (NIC) methods are other types of decision rules for capital budgeting and debt administration activities, both ignore the TVM and are not considered normatively superior by instrumental theorists.

In a similar manner, Table 7.1 denotes the Economic Ordering Quantity (EOQ) formula as a normatively superior cash management practice for determining the optimal transaction balance and excess liquidity balance that may be held in financial securities. Cash positions are maximized when enough monies are available for timely and necessary disbursements without forgoing investment benefits through underutilized stocks of cash. The EOQ formula can assist in determining the best balance. However, threshold methods (rules of thumb), such as holding a certain number of days' expenditures as the transaction balance, are another type of instrumental theory that can be used for cash management activities (Schwartz, 1996, p. 398).[6]

As a final case in point, the general purpose of each of the strategy techniques in Table 7.1 is to maximize efficiency and insulate the principal value of funds, idle or otherwise, which are invested in volatile capital markets. For example, Miller (1991, pp. 152–156) details a number of recommended strategy techniques, including the use of hedging with futures or options to anticipate or offset movements in interest rates. Another recommended tactic includes the implementation of optimization procedures to determine efficient investment portfolios (Petersen, 1996, p. 360).[7] Efficient investment portfolios are combinations of risky assets such that an investor achieves the highest amount of expected return for a given level of assumed risk. While hedging and mean variance theories are usually declared as normatively superior investment practices by instrumental theorists, typical investment positions (rules of thumb) such as 60 percent equity and 40 percent debt are alternative and "empirically driven" instrumental theories (Ambachtsheer, 1987).

Public Financial Manager Behavior: Toward a Framework for Prediction

As illustrated above, instrumental theories are technologies or technical processes contrived by instrumental theorists for conducting financial management activities. Each theory is a product of logical thought or empirical observation and is intended to assist practitioners in achieving a public purpose. Therefore, by definition, the tools, principles, and techniques that were discussed are independent of managerial decision making as the adoption by a manager is never required nor assumed necessary during the derivation of a particular practice (Harrison, 1999, pp. 5–6).[8] However, choice is an essential element in terms of actually implementing any given instrumental theory. Consequently, assumptions underlying financial manager behavior are relevant to the current research problem.

Deterministic Situations

Traditional theories of manager behavior in deterministic situations are generally derived from tenets associated with neoclassical economics and the notion of tradeoffs. Within this school of thought, financial managers (like all managers) are assumed to act rationally or decisively in a manner that an analyst can predict through marginal analysis. Marginal methodologies typically embody the optimizing principles of maximization (i.e., output) or minimization (i.e., costs), which analysts can use in isolation or in concert with the rational concept of changes in psychic satisfaction (marginal utility). If the analysts take the latter approach, then "what [a] model predicts about managerial behavior depends in large measure on the assumption about what produces utility for managers" (Khan, 2002, p. 196).

The deterministic "what" question is of both theoretical and practical consequence. In defining the sources of psychic satisfaction, theorists, by default, characterize the essential features of any financial management objective or utility-generating bundle. To illustrate, assuming that decision makers desire more or less of certain combinations of objects while being indifferent to others, means that deterministic theorists establish the bases for preference orderings in their models. Practically, if administrative and policy prescriptions or suggestions for future research are based on deterministic conclusions, then the sources of utility are an important component of recommendations. For example, if managers acquire increases of personal utility through the power and prestige associated with larger and more wasteful budgets, then an analyst might follow one type of proposal (Niskanen, 1971). However, if program commitment, professionalism, or risk-return combinations are the sources of higher levels in personal psychic satisfaction, then other recommendations may be in order (Margolis, 1975 as cited in Khan 2002, p. 197; Downs, 1967 as cited in Khan 2002, p. 197).

Although the empirical and theoretical deterministic literature remains inconclusive as to exactly what the sources of psychic satisfaction are, there is a general consensus that bureaucrats do indeed attempt to maximize their utility (Khan, 2002, p. 197).[9] The concurrence, while desirable and perhaps necessary, is not sufficient for dealing with the current research problem. Indeed, limitations extend beyond traditional debates concerning sources of utility.

Deficiencies exist in that instrumental theories, as technologies, are at least implicitly treated as moderating variables in a function specifying the relationship between focalized inputs and maximum levels of outputs.[10] This moderating relationship is embedded in comparable economic constructs such as production possibility frontiers, which can depict any number of "guns and "butter" type of relationships. Since rational decision makers in deterministic situations are typically assumed to choose among (efficient) outputs, only the actual choices over technological inputs, in whatever form, are necessarily implied; theoretically, they are left unexamined.

For practical purposes, such as assessing the acceptance of financial management techniques by decision makers, an advantage would exist if theorists could apply deterministic models to explain, for example, why some financial managers prefer one technique, whereas others prefer another. Alternatively, theorists might wish to predict the likely acceptance of a technique by decision makers following an improvement of an instrumental theory or to foresee the vulnerability of a normatively superior technique to the emergence of a new best practice or reform fad. On the whole, a logic of prediction seems to be an appropriate direction for mitigating the current state of muddling through in financial management practice and research. Characteristics theory, as a variant of traditional theories of deterministic manager behavior, is an approach for accomplishing this objective.

Characteristics Theory

In 1966, Kelvin Lancaster introduced a new approach to analyzing consumer behavior in deterministic situations, which he subsequently expanded in 1971. This "new theory of demand," while continuing to use the marginal methodologies of neoclassical economists, departed from traditional approaches by asserting that consumers derive psychic satisfaction not from the products themselves, but from the characteristics or intrinsic properties provided by the products. Thus, according to Lancaster, "an automobile is desired not for its 'automobileness'–its physical components of nuts, bolts, steel, and plastic–but for the services it provides–transportation, comfort, convenience, prestige, security, and privacy" (Douglas, 1992, p. 85). Similarly, the willingness and ability of a consumer to pay a mortgage is not just for housing, but also for accessibility to shops and schools, clean air, peace and quiet, and so on (Pearce, 1997, p. 59). Using Lancaster's reasoning, a fundamental conclusion is that the demand for goods and services is essentially derived from the demand for various intrinsic properties. Therefore, goods and services are simply mediums for providing such characteristics.

While the consumer decision maker is certainly of a different variety than that of the public financial manager, the logic of characteristics theory appears to offer several substantive insights for analyzing the current problem. First, the approach is particularly useful for explaining choices among different alternatives (i.e., instrumental theories) on the basis of their efficiency in supplying desired attributes. Thus, characteristics theory facilitates the explanation of decision-maker behavior within groups of substitutes that share some common intrinsic property(s).

In addition, analysts can consider the introduction of new alternatives and study the effect of changes in quality. The logic of characteristics theory suggests a role for "perceptions" as well as "preferences" in deterministic situations. We already identified alternative instrumental theories in an earlier section of this chapter. The purpose of the next section is to delineate the characteristics of financial management techniques that are the ultimate sources of utility for public financial managers.

Characteristics Identification

While both instrumental and traditional theories of rational manager behavior are devoid of characteristic content, the conception of intrinsic properties permeates the public administration literature. The existence of such traits within the discipline is somewhat expected, given the political nature of the field. Politics is the primary distinction between all subdivisions of public administration and business administration. Scholars, including one of us in *Public Budgeting in America*, cite political considerations as barriers to rationalism in conducting public affairs. These barriers also dissuade public financial management researchers, theoretical and empirical, from considering manager behavior in deterministic situations in favor of nondeterministic situations that elucidate actual decision-making processes. Prediction-versus explanation-debates aside, embedded in these accounts are the intrinsic properties needed to facilitate a characteristics approach to the current research problem.

In terms of theory, public organization theorists typically assert that values or value systems are a source for public administration decisions. While any agreement may subside once scholars consider the specifics of particular values, an overall consensus is that (1) factors can range from society's mandates to personal convictions; and (2) managers must ultimately blend values, in whatever context, in making public decisions (Van Wart, 1998, pp. 3–5, xviii). Harrison (1999, p. 131), who suggests that values originate primarily at the individual level and that analysts must frequently compromise personal values to satisfy groups and organizations, notes trade-offs. Without delineating the particular aspects of any given value, a logical conclusion is that value factors are a source of managerial utility.

The public financial management theoretical literature echoes the overall sentiment of public administration in defining values as a significant determinant in decision making. Miller's (1991) seminal work developing "ambiguity theory" gives testament to this fact. However, the sub-discipline appears to have narrowed the focus in terms of identifiable intrinsic properties through investigations of actual financial management behavior.

For example, empirical research concerning the investment practices of state and local governments is virtually unanimous on two conclusions. First, investment managers are extremely risk adverse in terms of their investment decisions; that is, certainty is consistently preferred to chance in terms of investing public resources. Second, investment managers' interpretations of risk and return are more characteristic in nature than scientific.

These sentiments were recently conveyed by McCue (2000) in a study comparing prospect theory (a descriptive psychological theory) and modern portfolio theory (a deterministic model based on expected utility theory) with a sample of local government Chief Investment Officers (CIOs) from Ohio. Ironically, McCue finds that the average CIO's personal disposition towards risk (risk-seeking) differs from his or her organizational preferences (risk-averse). In his conclusion, McCue suggests that "by constraining the investment function to maximizing returns and minimizing risks, we fail to fully articulate the *multidimensional attributes* [emphasis added] of risk and return" (McCue, 2000, p. 96).

McCue's observations are similar to Miller's (1991) earlier findings in relation to cash managers. However, in the process of empirically examining "ambiguity theory", Miller goes on to show the negative views that cash managers frequently have in relation to the normatively superior instrumental theory of hedging to offset interest rate movements; though he notes that the more experience managers have with a technique, the less risk averse they become (Miller, 1991, p. 165).[11] He also develops a list of ordered cash management priorities for the average cash manager that range from the preservation of capital (highest) to simple convenience (lowest) (Miller, 1991, p. 165).

While not stated exactly as such, we can translate McCue's and Miller's overall empirical conclusions concerning the typical cash and investment manager into the characteristics model by referencing the intrinsic properties noted within their investment studies—namely safety/security and value (McCue, 2000, p. 95; Miller, 1991, p. 158). Their independent focus on describing the effects of financial manager perceptions and/or preferences also supports this statement.

Other instances of characteristic identification can be found in the debt administration literature. For example, in a study concerning how debt managers view debt policies, Simonsen, Robbins, and Kittredge (2001) find that the inclusion of an item (i.e., responsibility to taxpayers or inclusion of women and/or minority business in the bond sale process) in a debt policy increases the item's perceived importance by debt managers. They also note that these results continue to hold even when controlling for other important factors, such as type of government, manager training, and experience.

In addition, when discussing how states manage the borrowing function of debt administration, Robbins and Dungan (2001, pp. 104–105) refer to an intrinsic property in their comment that "busy debt managers may simplify the issuance process by selecting the practices that they find *easiest* [emphasis added] to administer (using the broad discretion given them)." Reflecting on Miller (1991), the notion of "expediency" as a financial management characteristic may vary across managers according to the activity that they carry out.

The examples given here are far from exhaustive. However, the literature implies that public financial managers across the field often desire these types of intrinsic properties. Furthermore, scholars reference techniques in a manner that denotes their role in providing these characteristics. A case in point is Finkler (2001, p. 157), who notes that the payback method is a risk-averse technique in terms of capital budgeting. Similarly, scholars make the claim that threshold methods or rules of thumb may offer more convenience in determining cash and security positions than the EOQ formula.

Depicting Instrumental Theories in Characteristic Space

As discussed earlier, characteristics theory begins by assuming that a decision maker derives utility from the intrinsic properties associated with some activity.[12] As originally conceived, we defined the activity as consumption by consumer decision makers. However, for the present problem, we define the activity as choice among instrumental alternatives by public financial managers. Characteristics theory continues to embody the axioms of choice as outlined by Khan (2002, p. 194) with additional assumptions given by Lancaster (1966). The reader should review these sources for technical definitions and mathematical proofs.

In order to facilitate a graphical "indifference curve" presentation, the first example given here considers only two characteristics (characteristics X and Y) and assumes that any instrumental theory supplies the decision maker with both characteristics, but in a different ratio. A public financial manager with a particular orientation rates and then chooses among three techniques (A, B, and C) so that he or she can maximize their utility. In this chapter, we ignore any outside factors or constraints

Figure 7.1
Depicting Instrumental Theories in Characteristic Space

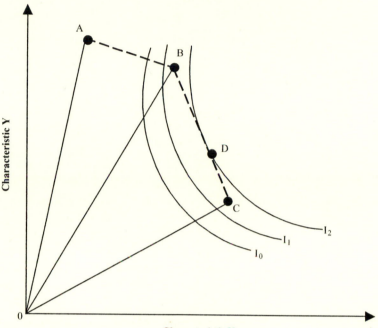

(i.e., costs or budgets) in order to focus exclusively on the essential elements of the theory. However, the approach does handle these realities and we leave this to a future discussion.

In Figure 7.1, we depict the three instrumental alternatives in characteristic space as rays from the origin. The slope of each ray is determined by the manager according to his or her "perceived" ratio of Y to X, as listed in Table 7.2.[13] If the manager decided to accept instrumental theory A, he or she would move along the steepest ray absorbing the two characteristics in the ratio of approximately 3.33:1—that is 3.33 units of characteristic Y to 1 unit of characteristic X. Similarly, if the manager decided to accept instrumental theory B, he or she would move along the middle ray, absorbing the two characteristics in the ratio of approximately 1:1, and so on. The manager is able to move out into characteristic space as far as the absolute values of the individual characteristic ratings will allow. Joining points A, B, and C with dashed line segments results in an efficiency frontier in characteristic space.

Table 7.2
Characteristics Ratings for Three Hypothetical Instrumental Theories

Instrumental Theory	Characteristic X	Characteristic Y	Ratio (Y/X)
A	3	10	10/3
B	8	8	1/1
C	10	3	3/10

For any particular combination of characteristic Y and characteristic X, the decision maker presumes to express a Marginal Rate of Substitution (MRS) between the two characteristics: That is, at any point, an extra "unit" of X will be worth giving up some amount of Y. Thus, in addition to a perception mapping, the decision maker will possess an indifference map in characteristic space expressing his or her "preferences" between the two characteristics at all levels of those characteristics. As with other deterministic models of this variety, managers prefer higher to lower curves. The curves have negative slopes throughout reflecting the economic notion of tradeoffs. In addition, the curves neither meet nor intersect as they are convex to the origin in the figure.

Again, referring to Figure 7.1, the decision maker's indifference map is superimposed in characteristic space in order to find the combination of characteristics that allows the decision maker to reach the highest attainable indifference curve. The curves' slopes indicate that the decision maker has a relatively high MRS in relation to these two characteristics. Therefore, he or she is willing to give up relatively larger amounts of characteristic Y in exchange for smaller amounts of characteristic X while retaining the same level of utility. Indifference curve I_2 through point D, which "mixes" instrumental theories B and C, is the combination of attributes that allows the decision maker to maximize his or her utility. We discuss the theoretical and practical aspects of "mixability" in the next section.

The Role of Perceptions

Obviously, the intrinsic content of an instrumental theory depends critically on the public financial manager's perception of the characteristics. Even if the technique is actually endowed with the intrinsic properties that the financial manager (and subsequently the public) desires, if he or she does not perceive their existence the characteristic is (or could become) essentially irrelevant.

For example, Figure 7.2 depicts a partial preference mapping of a financial manager confronted with two investment alternatives. The slope of the indifference curves I_0 and I_1 again indicate that the decision maker is relatively risk averse and willing to substitute a substantial amount of the characteristic "value" for the characteristic "safety." Ray OA represents the perceptions of the manager in relation to a normatively superior instrumental theory (i.e., hedging, optimization) for supplying the desired characteristics.

Ray OB represents the same for an alternative technique. The vertical direction of ray OA (essentially the vertical axis) indicates that the safety characteristic is completely absent in terms of the financial manger's perceptions. Therefore, the efficiency frontier essentially becomes dashed line segment AB. The fundamental conclusion is that while the decision maker does perceive some of the "value" characteristic in terms of investment strategy OA (the vertical distance between O and A), the choice will always be for an alternative that provides some measure of

Figure 7.2
Investment Example

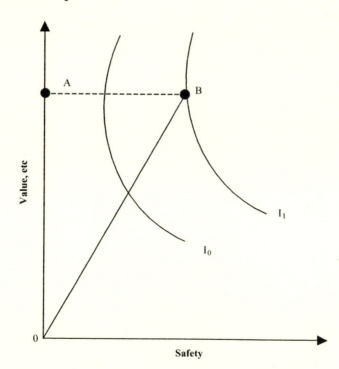

both characteristics, no matter how small, as the combination of characteristics allows him or her to attain a higher level of utility.[14]

Figure 7.2 presents an extreme condition and characteristically resembles Miller's (1991) ambiguous assessment of cash managers discussed above. As a further illustration, Figure 7.3 depicts two situations where a financial manager perceives positive but different amounts of each characteristic for two alternative instrumental theories. The examples provide a preliminary interpretation of Simonsen, Robbins, and Kittredge's (2001) study as to how debt managers view debt policies. To reiterate, their final conclusion was that the presence of a debt factor in a debt policy had a significant impact on a typical manager's perception of an items importance.

Referencing the figure, ray OA and indifference curve I_0 represent the initial state of a financial manager who desires the fulfillment of two characteristics: responsibility to taxpayers and fairness to women, minorities, and so forth. As shown, the manager has a relatively high MRS such that he or she is willing to substitute larger amounts of the fairness characteristic for smaller amounts of responsibility to taxpayers while retaining the same level of utility. The manager also perceives that the instrumental theory represented by ray OA provides more of the

Figure 7.3
Debt Administration Example

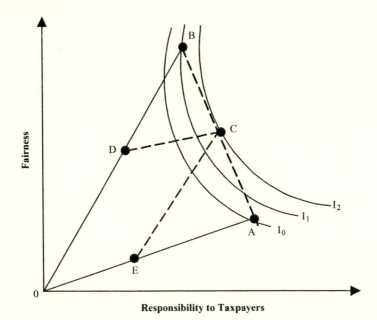

Responsibility to Taxpayers

responsibility characteristic relative to that of the fairness characteristic (denoted by the slope of OA).

If the inclusion of a debt factor causes the decision maker to believe that the characteristic content of the current debt policy changed in different proportions, then a logical conclusion is that the slope of ray OA changes in characteristic space. Assuming that the ratings of the individual characteristics are sufficiently large, and that fairness to women and minorities dominates responsibility to taxpayers, an analyst using this approach would map a ray such as OB into characteristic space. In this instance, the rational financial manager will accept the "new and improved" policy at point B as he or she is able to achieve a higher level of utility, at indifference curve I_1, by doing so.[15]

To illustrate further, if the financial manager perceives the policy with the presence of a debt factor as a distinct alternative to the original policy (that is, rays OA and OB are separate policies as opposed to the same policy), then two types of results may occur. If the financial manager cannot mix either of the policies, he or she will choose the policy represented by ray OB, as this policy affords him or her with the highest level of utility possible. However, the choice from the manager's perspective is not technically optimal, as he or she would prefer a mix of the two policies rather than either of the policies separately. The result is shown by noting that indifference curve I_1 lies beneath dashed line segment BA.

If particular aspects of the policies are mixable, the decision maker may decide to maximize utility in one of two ways. Specifically, the financial manager could choose to travel out along ray OB, to point D, and then switch to the alternative policy in order to accumulate the remaining units of the attributes in the ratio required to reach indifference curve I_2 at point C. In a similar fashion, the manager could decide to travel out along ray OA to point E and then switch to the alternative policy. We reflect the changes in the fact that (1) dashed line segment DC is parallel to ray OA, and (2) dashed line segment EC is parallel to ray OB. Parallelogram ODCE underscores the notion that the two paths to maximum utility, ODC and OEC, are equivalent channels for the financial manager to achieve maximum utility.

The Role of Preferences

The discussion above focused primarily on the role of perceptions while holding preferences constant. As demonstrated, a rational financial manager's perception of intrinsic properties supplied by an instrumental theory essentially determines the position of an efficiency frontier in characteristic space. Correspondingly, changes in perceptions shift the instrumental rays and may cause a shift in the efficiency frontier. By comparison, shifts in indifference curves occur through changes in marginal utilities that are involved in the MRS. Graphically, we can portray this as a change in the slope of the indifference curves.

Figure 7.4 is an illustration of how this might occur in capital budgeting. Here the financial manager derives utility from two characteristics: safety and a composite characteristic representing any other intrinsic properties. The alternative instrumental theories are the NPV rule (ray OA) and the payback method (ray OB) for evaluating capital acquisitions. Note that (1) time increases uncertainty; and (2) that the payback method is a risk-adverse technique (Finkler, 2001). With these understandings, we might predict that the preferences of a financial manager will change over time without any alteration in perceptions. This is depicted in Figure 7.4 by the increasedslope of I_1 compared to I_0. Note

Figure 7.4
Capital Budgeting Example

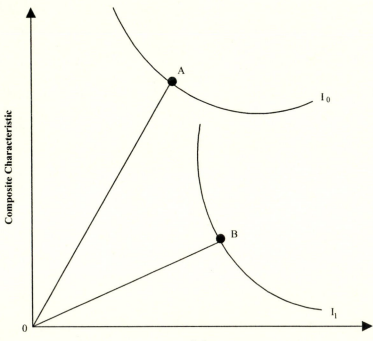

that the perception ratios have visually not changed. Consequently, neither does the efficiency frontier.

Discussion

Disaggregating perceptions and preferences has important implications for assessing the likely acceptance of financial management techniques in the public sector. Specifically, the concept suggests that financial managers can be segmented into groups with similar preferences and who tend to accept similar, if not identical, techniques.[16] Therefore, decision makers with comparable MRS, at a particular combination of characteristics, will tend to find their highest attainable indifference curve tangent to the efficiency frontier at similar points. For instance, financial managers with relatively low MRS between the characteristics will tend to accept instrumental theories with relatively high characteristics ratios. Conversely, financial managers with relatively high MRS between the characteristics will tend to accept instrumental theories with relatively low characteristics ratios.

Conclusion

The characteristic approach to decision-making behavior depicted here gives several valuable insights that are not readily apparent in the current literature. By allowing alternative instrumental theories to be portrayed on the same graph, the theory is able to clearly explain why a rational financial manager accepts one type of financial management technique in preference to the other available principles, tools, and techniques that are available. Simply put, the preferred technique offers the manager the greatest amount of the preferred characteristic mix.

Beyond this aspect, characteristics theory also helps to explain why a financial management decision maker will employ combinations of alternative techniques. Doing so allows him or her to obtain their desired characteristic ratio when there is no technique available for fulfilling that ratio. While the introduction of a new technique is not explicitly discussed, the analysis adapts easily to such an event. As managers perceive instrumental theories, they are simply added into the existing perception map.

In terms of policy and administrative recommendations, the model suggests that professional organizations, such as the Government Finance Officers Association (GFOA), reconsider their tactics if they wish their recommendations to be accepted by professionals in the field.

For example, published guidelines concerning debt policies are likely to exert little influence towards acceptance by financial managers if they are not perceived in the proper way. This may be true even if manager preferences are exactly in line with what is being espoused by policy makers, academics, or instrumental theorists.

Furthermore, any attempts to rationalize financial management need to keep in mind whether reformers are directing their efforts at influencing perceptions or preferences. If change is desired, perceptions are, in all likelihood, easier to modify than preferences. Sociologists often refer to the primacy principle to describe how what is learned first is usually what is most firmly lodged in a person's mind in terms of political preferences (Patterson, 2002, p. 165). The same kind of logic applies here.

Notes

1. Nontheoretical best practices can and should be distinguished from theoretical best practices. For example, an executive guide published by the General Accounting Office (GAO) titled *Creating Value Through World-Class Financial Management* "studies the financial management practices of nine leading private and public sector organizations to identify the success factors, practices, and outcomes associated with world-class financial management" (GAO, 2000, p. 6). The inquiry is not based on any theoretical foundation, nor are findings communicated as such. However, the conclusions could possibly be used to develop a theoretical perspective.

2. A third acknowledgment might be the suboptimal state of financial management, particularly at the federal level. For example, on March 29, 2002, the Treasury Department released the *2001 Financial Report of the United States Government*, in which the comptroller general of the United States declared that the inadequate financial practices in the federal government (1) hampered the government's ability to accurately report on significant portions of its assets, liabilities, and costs; (2) affected the government's ability to measure accurately the full cost and financial performance of certain programs and lessened the effective management of those related operations; and (3) impaired significantly the government's ability to safeguard adequately significant assets and properly record various transactions correctly (GAO, 2001, p. 25).

3. In discussing management theory and training Lee (1990, p. 245) states that "Because management theories are viewed as mutually exclusive (rather than as complementary but alternative views of reality), when theories appear to contradict each other, there is a tendency [among trainees] to believe that the competing views have canceled each other out." This statement could be extended to trainers and theorists as well.

4. In addition, policies with a different "blending" of ethics and accountability can be considered as alternative arrangements.

5. In addition, the NPV method is judged as normatively superior, in that the technology accounts for additional revenue generation from capital asset acquisitions.

6. Actually, the threshold method may be most useful for small governments and, in fact, normatively superior. However, we ignore size differences in order to facilitate a consistent discussion.

7. Optimization procedures are based on modern portfolio theory.

8. A decision among normative criteria may be needed in deriving an instrumental theory. However, from the practitioner point of view such a decision is already made. For example, NPV and TIC technologies exist based on known criteria.

9. For example, Dolan (2002) empirically finds evidence of a budget-minimizing bureaucrat rather than a budget-maximizing bureaucrat. Theoretically, Khan (2002) proposes a model in which budget decision makers maximize their utility according to a risk-return combination.

10. Actually, Porter (1996) suggests that a productivity frontier constituting the sum of all existing best practices exists at any given time. He defines the frontier as the maximum value that an organization delivering a product or service can create at a given cost, using the best technologies, skills, management techniques and purchased inputs.

11. Miller's discussions focuses on cash managers who would know about investment and hedging.

12. The depiction given here was inspired by Douglas (1992, pp. 83–99).

13. The idea is to imagine the decision maker rating each instrumental theory on an arbitrary scale, say from 1 to 10.

14. For example, one could imagine a situation where a decision maker rates a given technique such that the value characteristic receives a perfect score of "10" and the safety characteristic receives a score of "0." An alternative may receive a rating of only "1" on each of these measures. The rational decision maker will always choose the alternative technique.

15. This result would not occur if the individual characteristic ratings were not of sufficient magnitude, as the ray would not extend out beyond the original indifference curve I_0.

16. The identification of market segments is of a primary concern in business. Douglas (1992) discusses this at length.

References

Ambachtsheer, K. P. 1987. "Pension Fund Asset Allocation: In Defense of a 60/40 Equity/Debt Asset Mix." *Financial Analysts Journal* (Sept.–Oct.): 14–24.

Ammons, D. N. 2002. *Tools for Decision Making: A Practical Guide for Local Government.* Washington, DC: Congressional Quarterly Press.

Bailey, S. K. 1968. "Objectives of the Theory of Public Administration." In *Theory and Practice of Public Administration: Scope, Objectives, and Methods,* ed. J. C. Charlesworth, 128–139. Philadelphia.

Dolan, J. 2002. "The Budget Minimizing Bureaucrat? Empirical Evidence from the Senior Executive Service." *Public Administration Review,* 62 (January/ February): 42–50.

Douglas, E. J. 1992. *Managerial Economics.* Englewood Cliffs, NJ: Prentice Hall.

Drucker, P. F. 1986. *The Practice of Management.* New York: Harper & Row.

Finkler, S. A. 2001. *Financial Management for Public, Health, and Not-for-Profit Organizations.* Upper Saddle River, NJ: Prentice-Hall.

Harrison, E. F. 1999. *The Managerial Decision-Making Process.* 5th ed. Boston: Houghton Mifflin Company.

Henry, N. 1975. *Public Administration and Public Affairs.* Englewood Cliffs, NJ: Prentice-Hall.

Khan, A. 2002. "Budgets as Portfolios." In *Budget Theory In the Public Sector,* A. Khan and W. Bartley Hildreth, eds., 188–210. Westport, CT: Quorum Books.

Lancaster, K. J. 1966. "A New Approach to Consumer Theory." *Journal of Political Economy,* 74: 132–157.

Lancaster, K. J. 1971. "Consumer Demand: A New Approach." New York: Columbia University Press.

Lee, D. S. 1990. "Management Theory and Training." *Public Administration Quarterly,* 14 (summer): 245–257.

Lynch, Thomas D. 1995. *Public Budgeting in America.* Englewood Cliffs, NJ: Prentice-Hall.

Matzer, J. 1984. *Practical Financial Management: New Techniques for Local Government.* Washington, DC: International City Management Association.

McCue, C. P. 2000. "The Risk-Return Paradox in Local Government Investing." *Public Budgeting and Finance,* 20 (fall): 80–101.

Miller, G. J. 1991. *Government Financial Management Theory.* New York: Marcel Dekker.

Niskanen, W. A., Jr. 1971. *Bureaucracy and Representative Government.* Chicago: Aldine-Atherton.

Patterson, T. E. 2002. *We the People: A Concise Introduction to American Politics.* New York: McGraw-Hill.

Pearce, D. W. 1997. *The MIT Dictionary of Economics.* 4th ed. Cambridge, MA: MIT Press.

Petersen, J. E. 1996. "Public Pension Funs." In *Management Policies in Local Government Finance,* J. R. Aronson and E. Schwartz, eds., 339–363. 4th ed. Washington DC: International City/County Management Association.

Porter, M. E. 1996. "What is Strategy." *Harvard Business Review,* 74 (November/December): 61–79.

Reed, B. J., and J. W. Swain. 1997. *Public Finance Administration.* 2nd ed. Thousand Oaks, CA: Sage Publications.

Robbins, M. D., and C. Dungan. 2001. "Debt Diligence: How States Manage the Borrowing Function." *Public Budgeting and Finance*, 21 (summer): 88–105.

Rubin, I. S. 1997. "Budgeting Theory and Concepts." In *Public Budgeting and Finance*, R. T. Golembiewski and J. Rabin, eds., 185–2021. 4th ed. New York: Marcel Dekker.

Sarasvathy, S. D. 2003. *What Makes Entrepreneurs Entrepreneurial?* Working paper. Available online at http://www.effectuation.org/ftp/effectua.pdf. (accessed May 30, 2003).

Schwartz, E. 1996. "Inventory and Cash Management." In *Management Policies in Local Government Finance*, J. R. Aronson and E. Schwartz, eds., 389–410. 4th ed. Washington DC: International City/County Management Association.

Simonsen, B., and M. D. Robbins. 2002. "Measuring Municipal Borrowing Costs: How Missing Cost Information Biases Interest Rate Calculations." *Public Budgeting and Finance*, 22 (spring): 46–59.

Simonsen, B., M. D. Robbins, and B. Kittredge. 2001. "Do Debt Policies Make a Difference in Financial Officers' Perceptions of the Importance of Debt Management Factors?" *Public Budgeting and Finance*, 21 (spring): 87–102.

United States General Accounting Office. 2000. "Executive Guide: Creating Value Through World-Class Financial Management." *GAO/A1MD-00-134*, (April): 1–54. Available online at www.gao.gov (accessed June 17, 2002).

United States General Accounting Office. 2002. "2001 Financial Report of the United States Government." (March) Available online at www.gao.gov (accessed June 17, 2002).

Van Wart, M. 1998. *Changing Public Sector Values*. New York: Garland Publishing.

CHAPTER 8

Fiscal Decentralization
Theory as Reform

James Edwin Kee

> The federal system was created with the intention of combining the different advantages which result from the magnitude and the littleness of nations.
>
> Alexis de Tocqueville, *Democracy in America*

When Wallace Oates began his 1977 book *The Political Economy of Fiscal Federalism,* the quote by de Tocqueville seemed an appropriate starting point (Oates, 1977). Indeed, the United States' founding fathers, in *The Federalist,* argued the advantages of a strong (but limited) federal government and independent state governments would provide the best opportunity for the protection of, and responsiveness to, the citizens in the fledgling nation (see especially Madison, No. 39).

During the period following World War II, and in particular the 1960s and 1970s, the United States, like many nations–both developed and developing–embarked upon a strong centralization of government policy and functions. Central government expenditures of 15 percent of GDP in 1960 doubled to 30 percent by 1985 (World Bank, 1997). However, in the United States, the 1980s and 1990s saw a resurgence of interest in strengthening state and local governments and restraining the growth of the national government. That pattern was repeated in other nations. By the mid-1990s, 62 of 75 developing nations with populations over 5 million were embarked on some form of fiscal decentralization (World Bank, 1997).

Fiscal decentralization also has become part of a worldwide "reform" agenda, supported by the World Bank, USAID, the Asian Development Bank, and many others, and has become an integral part of economic development and governance strategies in developing and transitional economies (Bahl, 1999a). Along with "globalization," fiscal decentralization and the desire for local discretion and devolution of power is seen by the World Bank as one of the most important forces shaping governance and development today (World Bank, 1999). My definition of fiscal decentralization is the following:

> Fiscal decentralization is the devolution by the central government to local governments (states, regions, municipalities) of specific functions with the administrative authority and fiscal revenue to perform those functions.

This chapter examines the underlying theory supporting and opposing fiscal decentralization; examines some specific issues concerning the implementation of fiscal decentralization; examines two nations, Brazil and China, that have been struggling with the issue of fiscal decentralization; and proposes a model for fiscal decentralization that attempts, as de Tocqueville argued, to take advantages of the strengths of strong national and local governments.

Why this renewed interest in fiscal decentralization as reform? There are three basic reasons:

1. Central governments increasingly are finding that it is impossible for them to meet all of the competing needs of their various constituencies, and are attempting to build local capacity by delegating responsibilities downward to their regional governments.
2. Central governments are looking to local and regional governments to assist them on national economic development strategies.
3. Regional and local political leaders are demanding more autonomy and want the taxation powers that go along with their expenditure responsibility.

Fiscal decentralization is now seen as part of a reform agenda of many nations to strengthen their regional and local governments to meet the challenges of the 21st century.

The Theoretical Framework for Fiscal Decentralization

The "proper" distribution of tax authority and expenditure responsibility is an extremely complex issue. Economists generally focus on issues of efficiency and equity, while public administration and political science scholars tend to focus on distribution of powers, responsiveness and accountability, and tax competition and coordination. Economist Richard Musgrave's framework for analyzing roles or functions is widely accepted (Musgrave, 1959, 1961; see also Oates, 1977).

The stabilization function involves the role of tax and spending policies and monetary policy in managing the overall level of economic activity. It is widely agreed that this macroeconomic function should be assigned to the national government. This suggests that the national government must have a broad-based tax suitable for this role. However, Oates's (1993) analysis of 58 countries demonstrated a positive relationship between economic growth and fiscal decentralization—suggesting some role for local governments, especially infrastructure development.

The distribution function involves the role of government in changing the distribution of income, wealth, or other indicators of economic well being to make them more equitable than would otherwise be the case. The case for assigning this function to the national government rests on two assumptions: (1) that the national government's broad taxing powers can more easily redistribute income; and (2) that the ability of taxpayers to move from one jurisdiction to another to take advantage of more attractive spending and taxation policies weakens local government's ability to "soak the rich and redistribute to the poor." The case for regional and local redistributive policies rests on the fact that subnational levels of government provide the services most used by low-income families. However, most economists view the national role as primary.

The allocation function is government's role in deciding the mix of public and private goods that are provided by the economy or by government. Each level of government may be more efficient in delivering certain governmental goods and services. The superiority of the national government in delivering national defense or national health research is obvious as is the likelihood that certain services (such as fire and police protection) are more suitable for local government. In attempting to match local revenues and expenditures in the allocation process, economists are concerned about efficiency, vertical imbalances (mismatches between revenues and expenditures), horizontal equity (fiscal capacity among regions), externalities (spillovers), and tax exportation. Additional public management concerns have to do with overlapping of taxes and roles, and responsiveness and accountability for service delivery.

This framework is most helpful in thinking about which taxes are levied at each level of government and the total tax authority of each level. A commonly cited public finance principal is "finance should follow function." If certain expenditure roles are assigned to a level of government, that level must have the resources to meet those responsibilities. Taxes are the principal source of "own-source" revenue for governments at all levels. If tax collections or fiscal capacity falls short expenditure responsibilities, then that level of government must have additional taxing authority, develop user fees, or rely on intergovernmental transfers (such as grants and shared taxes) to support its expenditures.

Arguments for Fiscal Decentralization

The theoretical case for fiscal decentralization dates from 17th and 18th century philosophers, including Rousseau, Mill, de Tocqueville, Montesquieu, and Madison. Central governments were distrusted and small, democratic governments were seen as the principal hope to preserve the liberties of free men. The modern case for decentralized government was articulated by Wolman (in Bennet, 1990). Wolman divided the proponents arguments under two headings: efficiency values and governance values.

Efficiency Values

Efficiency is an economic value seen as the "maximization" of social welfare. The public sector does not contain the same price signals as the private sector to regulate supply and demand. Public sector allocation of goods and services are inherently political; however, as nearly as possible tax and service packages should reflect "the aggregate preferences of community members" (Wolman, 1997, p. 27). However, within any political jurisdiction, some people will prefer more public services, and some less. As a result there is a "divergence between the preferences of individual community members and the tax and service packages reflecting the aggregate community preferences" (ibid). Since such divergence reduces social welfare, it is desirable to hold those to a minimum, and they will be less in smaller communities (e.g., municipalities) than in larger, more heterogeneous areas (the nation).

Governance Values

Governance values include responsiveness and accountability, diversity, and political participation (Wolman, 1997). Decentralization places allocational decision making closer to the people. This fosters greater responsiveness of local officials and greater accountability to citizens.

This is because we expect local decision makers to be more knowledge-able about the problems and needs of their local area than centralized decision makers. Further, to the extent that there is accountability through local elections, those elections are more likely driven by issues of local allocation, whereas national elections are seldom focused on local service delivery.

Diversity in public policy is a second governance argument for fiscal decentralization. It is valued because it offers citizens a greater choice in public service and tax options when they are deciding where to reside (Tiebout, 1956). In addition, it helps to create "laboratories" for innova-tion and experimentation, which sometime serve as models for later implementation by the central government or, by example, to other local governments. While there is no theoretical reason why a central government could not be diverse in its solutions, there is great pressure on the central government towards uniform policies and procedures.

Finally, fiscal decentralization is thought to enhance political partici-pation at the local level. This has the potential to enhance democratic values and political stability at the local level. It provides a forum for local debate about local priorities, and can be a proving ground for future political leaders. For example, four of the last five U.S. presidents were state governors.

Arguments Against
Fiscal Decentralization

While the international political movement towards fiscal decentrali-zation is strong, there have been some recent cautionary notes that need to be considered (Hommes, 1995; Tanzi, 1995; Prud'homme, 1995). Tanzi summarizes this critique by raising a number of situations or con-ditions, especially in developing countries, where fiscal decentralization may lead to less than an optimal result:

1. Taxpayers may have insufficient information or no political power to pressure local policymakers to make resource-efficient decisions.
2. Local politicians may be more corrupt than national politicians or at least find themselves in more corrupting situations.
3. The quality of national bureaucracies is likely to be better than local bureaucracies.
4. Technological chance and increased mobility may reduce the number of services that are truly "local" in nature.
5. Local governments often lack good public expenditure management systems to assist them in their tax and budget choices.

6. Fiscal decentralization may exacerbate a central government's ability to deal with structural fiscal imbalances.

Prud'homme (1995) finds other potential flaws in the theory of fiscal decentralization. The economic efficiency argument, he suggests, requires roughly even regional fiscal capacities—a condition not existing in developing countries. Fiscal inequities may actually increase with decentralization. In addition, localities might engage in destructive competition to attract industry. He also argues that the rationale for decentralization of revenues is not the same as expenditures, and "in many cases the problem is not so much whether a certain service should be provided by a central, regional, or local government, but rather how to organize the joint production of the of the service by the various levels" (p. 201). Finally, to the extent that local governments are viewed as agents of the central government, fiscal decentralization may limit the ability of the principal (the central government) to influence policy at the local level.

Hommes (1995) sees decentralization as "essentially a political problem" representing, in Latin America for example, a stark departure from centuries of centralism. The success of decentralization may depend upon the existence at the local level of a civic cultural tradition—informal civic institutions, such as solidarity, cooperatives, etc. With a lack of local governmental experience and riddled with patronage, local governments in Latin America tend to be held captive by the elites and political barons. Thus for Hommes, an irony of fiscal decentralization may be the need for more central government controls to protect against this danger.

Rejoinder

The concerns raised have been partially addressed by other scholars (McClure, 1995; Oates, 1995). McClure argues that Prud'homme sets up a straw man—pure decentralization of fiscal federalism—and easily details its flaws. Decentralization done badly, says McClure, will cause problems. However, no one proposes full decentralization; rather, what is proposed is decentralization of some functions. Clearly, the central government must retain sufficient revenues (and discretion) to be effective in both their stabilization and distribution roles. Furthermore, a national role in establishing uniform financial reporting requirements and in clarifying roles and responsibilities is also an important aspect of effective fiscal decentralization.

Perhaps the most important issue raised by opponents is the "local capacity" issue. However, it is not self-evident that national politicians and bureaucracies are superior to or less corrupt than their local counterparts. Political and bureaucratic skills may well flow to "the action." If political decision making is decentralized to the local level, you may see an increase in the capacities of local governments. One of the major objectives of reform *is* building the capacity of local government and local citizens to actively participate in their governmental decisions. Both Brazil and China have experienced corruption and failures at both the central government and local government level. Local corruption may be easier to uncover through central government oversight, whereas central governments may lack sufficient internal checks to monitor their own performance.

Prud'homme and Hommes are correct that a simple division of responsibilities is seldom appropriate. A good illustration of this issue is environmental protection, where national standards are appropriate, and regional or local governments may enforce, regulate, and produce (e.g., water quality). Financing could easily be a shared responsibility. Hommes suggests providing grants with strings attached to enforce local accountability.

Hommes notes the seeming paradox of decentralization is that it demands of the central government more sophisticated political control. Ultimately, however, effective decentralization requires the relinquishing of some central control. Oates (1977, p. 351) notes that, as John Stuart Mill pointed out more than a century ago, "decentralized political institutions play an important role in developing skilled public administrators by allowing more widespread and direct participation in the affairs of government." The United States' experience in decentralization was (and is) not always an "ideal success." However, even failures provide learning opportunities for local citizens and their political representatives. Local control over own-source revenues and spending decisions is at the heart of effective decentralization.

Illustrations

The following table provides a comparison of macro-tax revenue allocations in Brazil and China in comparison to some other nations. Four of the other nations (Germany, India, Russia, and the United States) are federal nations, like Brazil; the other two (Japan and Korea) are unitary nations like China. The percentage shares of tax revenues include any formal tax-sharing provisions but do not include other transfers (such as grants) made by the central government. Also excluded are social insurance revenues and non-tax revenues such as fees and charges (because of the lack of comparable data among the nations).

While Table 8.1 does not reveal which taxes are levied by each country, it does provide an overview of policy regarding the *amount* of total taxes allocated to each level. With the exception of Korea, all of the central governments' shares of revenue are within a fairly narrow range, with a high of 60 percent for Japan and a low of 45.6 percent for Brazil. Somewhat surprising, the United States appears more centralized than

Table 8.1
Tax Allocations Among Levels of Government
(Percent of total taxes collected)

Country	Federal	Region/State	Local
Brazil	45.6	47.4	7.0
China	52.1	47.9*	
Germany	50.2	37.4	12.4
India	46.6	53.4*	
Japan	60.0	40.0*	
Korea	79.0	21.0*	
Russia	46.3	53.7*	
United States	59.5	25.3	15.2

* Local tax revenues are included in the state totals
Source: Financial documents from the various countries for FY 1997
   or 1998; see references.

any of the other federal nations studied. This first glance, however, is somewhat deceptive. State and local tax revenue in the United States is all "own-source" revenue; that is, state and local governments rely on their own taxing powers to raise their tax revenue. For the other countries, a substantial percentage of the regional/state share of taxes is the result of constitutional or legislative decisions to allow regional governments to *share* national tax revenues.

From a fiscal decentralization perspective, it is not just the amount of taxes allocated to each sector, but also the composition of those taxes and the extent that regional and local governments control their own taxes. The former is important in assessing whether the specific taxes match the policy responsibilities at each level. The latter is critical in establishing accountability for local spending. Thus, at least at the margin, subnational governments should control their own-source revenues sufficient to allow some discretion in matching the needs of citizens and the taxes paid (Tiebout, 1956). A closer examination of China and Brazil reveals strikingly different revenue compositions, which are summarized in Table 8.2.

Brazil

Brazil is the largest of the Latin American countries and the sixth largest country in the world after China, the United States, Canada, Russia, and Indonesia. The Constitution of the Federative Republic of Brazil establishes three government tiers: the Federal Union, or central govern-

Table 8.2
**Percent Composition of Tax Revenue: China and Brazil
By Levels of Government, FY 1997, 1998**

Tax	China Central	China Province/ Local	Brazil Union	Brazil State/ Local
Personal Income Tax		19.9	15.8	10.5
Business IT	8.2	3.1		
Other Business	4.9	41.1	2.1	
Consumption: VAT	56.2	20.8	11.5	76.5
Cons: Sales	16.9			
Cons: Services				1.6
Customs/Duties	8.9		3.9	
Prop/Land/Agr		9.8	.1	1.6
Social Contributions			52.9	6.8
Miscellaneous	5.0	5.3	13.7	3.0

Sources: Finance Ministries of China and Brazil and calculations by the author.

ment; 26 states and the Federal District of Brasilia (which has the powers of both a state and a municipality); and 5,507 municipalities. The central government determines the boundaries of states, and the states determine the process for establishing municipalities within their borders; both require approval of the population in the proposed new jurisdiction. Industrial activity is concentrated in the southeastern region of Brazil, with approximately 50 percent of industrial production located in the state of Sao Paulo, the most populous state.

The current tax system in Brazil dates from the constitutional and tax reform of 1966 and the new Federal Constitution of 1988. A major purpose of the 1988 Constitution was to decentralize tax revenue so as to provide greater tax resources to subnational governments, Brazilian states, and municipalities. While the Union continues to collect more than two-thirds of total revenue, the constitutional fiscal decentralization has resulted in the federal government's using for national purposes (after tax sharing) less than one-half of total national taxes. In FY 1997, the federal share was 12.7 percent of GDP, state share was 13.3 percent, and municipalities accounted for about 2 percent.

Overall, direct taxes (such as income taxes) account for only 30 percent of all tax revenues, while indirect taxes (such as value-added taxes) account for the remaining 70 percent. For Brazilian governments, taxes can be broken down into two categories: own-source (collected and spent by the same level of government) and shared (collected by one level of government and distributed to lower levels). The major sources of revenue for the federal government are the Personal Income Tax and the Industrialized Products Tax (a limited value-added tax). The federal government keeps 56 percent of the revenue from those two taxes and distributes 21.5 percent to the states and 22.5 percent to municipalities, with part of the distribution providing greater funding to poorer states and municipalities.

The states' chief source of own-source revenue is the tax on Circulation of Goods and Services (a value-added tax at the state level), of which they retain 75 percent and distribute 25 percent to municipalities. States, as indicated, also share the federal government's Personal Income Tax (PIT) and the Industrial Products Tax revenue. Municipalities, in addition to sharing the federal PIT and Industrial Products taxes and the state value-added tax, levy own-source taxes on certain services and urban property. They also are increasingly relying on fees and charges to fund municipal operations.

China

With an area of 9.6 million sq. km. (3.8 million sq. mi.) and a population of about 1.3 billion, China is the fourth largest country in area and the most populous in the world. The constitution establishes three government tiers: the central government; 32 provincial authorities consisting of 23 provinces, 5 autonomous regions, and 4 metropolitan cities—Beijing, Shanghai, Tianjin, and Chongqing; and numerous municipalities and counties. Industry is concentrated in northeastern and southeastern provinces, whereas natural resources are primarily located in the northwest. Regional disparities in the level of income are large.

The current tax system in China dates from fiscal reforms in the 1980s and the 1990s (especially the 1994 tax reform). Fiscal reform has been an important part of China's macroeconomic reforms. The prior revenue remittance system, under which government was financed by the profits of state-owned enterprises, is being converted into a tax system that is generally modeled on Western systems. One purpose of fiscal reform is to decentralize fiscal management by granting the provinces and localities greater flexibility in collecting revenues and making expenditure decisions. The central government's transfers (both tax sharing and grants) to provinces are extensive (Rmb 332.2 billion in 1998), constituting more than two-thirds of provincial/local revenue.

China's taxes are divided into three categories: central government taxes, provincial taxes, and local taxes. The major sources of revenue for the central government are the VAT, Consumption Tax (both on domestic and on imported goods), Business Tax (on railroads and financial institutions), Income Tax on state-owned enterprises, and Customs Duties. Since the tax reform in 1994, the central government keeps approximately 75 percent of the revenue from VAT, which is the primary source of revenue for the central government budget, providing more than 50 percent of all central government tax revenue in 1998. Provincial governments' own-source revenues are the Income Tax on provincially and privately owned enterprises, Personal Income Tax, Business Tax (excluding railroads and financial institutions), Urban and Town Land Use Tax, and Stamp Duties. Provinces also receive from the central government approximately 25 percent of the VAT, all of the urban maintenance and construction tax, and the natural resource tax (except on offshore oil, which is retained by the central government). Local governments, in addition to sharing some tax revenue from provincial governments, may collect taxes on locally owned enterprises, agricultural products, animal slaughtering, and certain agricultural contracts.

China's system of taxation and the assignment of tax revenues are specified by its central government statutes, not by the constitution. The National People's Congress (NPC) alone has the power to make tax laws, and the State Council is responsible for enacting provisional regulations specifying the details of taxation. In 1998, the State Council issued a circular requiring subnational governments and departments to strengthen tax administration. The circular reiterates that legislative power over taxation (tax bases, taxpayers, and tax rates), including all central, provincial and local taxes, is the sole domain of the central government.

One of the major current concerns in Chinese tax policy is the growth of user fees and charges at the provincial and local government level. Virtually all of these are *extrabudgetary* (off-budget) and nearly half are considered nonsanctioned by the central government. While provincial and local taxes represent only 5–6 percent of GDP, authorized user fees and charges boast total revenue to approximately 10 percent of GDP; and when the non-sanctioned revenue is included, the estimated local spending is nearly 14 percent of GDP—more than double the central government's general revenue (6.1 percent of GDP in 1998). Many of these charges and fees are quasi-taxes in nature and do not reflect payments for benefits received.

Major Implementation Issues in Fiscal Decentralization

Both Brazil and China seem committed to their current course of fiscal decentralization. However, issues in both countries raise question regarding some of the elements of their current tax policy. Bahl (1999b) notes that while there has been significant analysis of fiscal decentralization as a policy strategy (e.g., Gramlich, 1993), far less attention has been given to implementation strategies. In fiscal decentralization, the details do matter.

How Much Fiscal Decentralization?

Policymakers in Brazil and China (and elsewhere) are asking whether the revenues available at the national level, after current decentralization efforts, are sufficient to meet the needs of the central government. In both countries, available revenues, including taxes and fees, at the regional and local levels now exceed the central government's revenues. This allocation may make it harder for these countries to eliminate their structural fiscal deficits and effectively perform other stabilization functions (Tanzi, 1995; Prud'homme, 1995).

The assignment in China of the Personal Income Tax to local government seems particularly problematic. While not a significant revenue source to date in China's transitional economy (largely due to poor enforcement and tax evasion), it likely will become a greater potential source of future revenue. Because of its revenue significance and its potential ability to act as an important macroeconomic tool, most nations assign this tax to the central government. However, Bahl (1999b) argues that personal income taxes–primarily a wage tax in developing countries–could be a good local tax. Alternatively, regional and local governments might be allowed to "piggyback" a regional/local rate on top of the national rate, while leaving the central government in control of structure–even if the tax is collected at the local level.

How Much Discretion Should the Central Government Provide Regional and Local Governments?

There are a variety of methods of assignment of taxation authority. Regional and local governments can be given authority to levy a range of taxes–perhaps with modest discretion as to methods and rates. This is the current case to a large extent in Brazil and in India and Germany. This approach might also include the "piggybacking" of subnational rates on top of the national tax. The advantage of limited discretion is more central control and uniformity across a nation; however, the limited discretion may result in reliance by regional and local governments on the central government.

A second approach is to specifically assign taxes to each level of government. This is the current case in China, where the central government has reasserted itself as the determiner of tax policy, rates, bases, and administrative procedures. Russia also has followed this model, as have most centralized systems of government, including Japan and Korea.

A third approach is to have overlapping authority, where both the central government and regional governments have plenary power to institute a broad range of taxes. This is the case in the United States and (to some extent) Brazil with respect to consumption taxes.

Finally, taxes can be shared in some fashion with one government (usually the central government) taking the lead, imposing and collecting the tax and sharing it under some constitutionally or legislatively mandated formula. Many countries use this approach to some extent, including Germany and Japan, as well as China and Brazil. While this provides the revenues to localities, it keeps the control at the central government level.

Bahl (1999b) argues that in some cases it may be wise to differentiate among local governments, with those of a certain size or maturity having more discretion. In addition, it may be necessary to handle decentralization differently in urban and rural areas. However, to achieve its theoretical gains, fiscal decentralization requires significant local taxing power and discretion to hold local official accountable for local services.

How Much Central Control Should the Central Government Exercise over Regional and Local Governments?

There are inherent tradeoffs between central government control and local flexibility. Controlling the tax base ensures standard treatment for all taxpayers, but may not fully account for local conditions. Controlling tax rates ensures uniformity but doesn't provide local flexibility to meet specific local needs. Controlling tax exemptions prevents unhealthy local competition but may limit local economic development incentives and options. On a continuum of maximum control to maximum flexibility, the United States and India are two countries toward the "liberal" end of the flexibility scale; China is toward the control end; and Brazil, somewhat in the middle. One approach is to authorize a limited range of tax rates for localities.

Whatever the level of control, Bahl (1999b) argues that the central government must maintain an ability to monitor and evaluate decentralization. This may require the imposition of a uniform system of accounts and the provision of technical assistance to local governments.

To What Extent and in What Manner Will a Nation Deal with Vertical Imbalances and Horizontal Inequities?

Some type of revenue sharing, from the central government to regional (and possibly local) governments is necessary if central policymakers are concerned about vertical imbalances and horizontal inequities. Vertical imbalances arise when regional and local governments have more expenditure responsibilities than the revenues to fund them. Horizontal inequities refer to the differing fiscal capacities of regions. Both of these issues must be dealt with at the central government level; although regional governments could play a mediating role with local governments.

Both China and Brazil deal with the vertical problem by using explicit tax-sharing arrangements. Brazil's (like Germany's) arrangement is anchored in its constitution. China's is through central government policy. Both China and Brazil rely on the VAT as their principal sharing tax. Brazil, in addition, shares the Personal Income Tax and certain minor taxes. China also shares certain natural resource taxes. Both nations also provide some of that tax sharing in a fashion to address horizontal fiscal inequities.

There are three challenges in designing an effective tax sharing system. First, it is necessary to develop a formula that deals with the problems without eliminating incentives for regional and local governments to develop their own tax resources. For example, Russia uses taxes per capita as a measure of fiscal capacity, but this formula has the effect of penalizing those regions that are developing their tax base. Second, the formula should allow the central government to raise revenues for stabilization purposes without also increasing subnational revenue. Thus, a rate "piggybacking" approach may be superior to the tax-sharing approach in use in both China and Brazil. Finally, the tax sharing needs to be fixed, providing a hard budget constraint for local governments. Otherwise, local governments will feel they can negotiate additional funding from the central government, thereby reducing local accountability—a major rationale for fiscal decentralization.

Conclusion: Toward a Model Allocation?

After examining the theory of fiscal decentralization and the practices of nations such as Brazil and China, it might seem impossible to find any common elements that could lead to a "desired" allocation of taxing powers. In addition, differing political aims may suggest alternative revenue strategies. However, there are widely agreed to principles that suggest a particular direction in fiscal decentralization reform, even if falling short of a "model" allocation system.

First: For stabilization and fiscal equalization/redistribution purposes, the central government should collect 50 percent or more of total taxes, and those taxes should be from a broad-based elastic tax bases (such as income or value-added). The three developed nations whose central share exceeds 50 percent, Germany, Japan and the United States, arguably have the strongest macroeconomic programs. In contrast, Brazil, China, India, and Russia have all experienced problems with having insufficient national revenues.

Second: For allocational efficiency and accountability, regional and local governments should have sufficient discretion on "own-source" taxes. If regional and local governments rely on sharing national revenues, there is less incentive to develop their own tax resources and more incentive to overspend with money other than their own. This discretion should be broad enough to allow local officials to develop their own-source taxes (including some discretion on rates) to fund discretionary local expenditures.

Third: For horizontal equity (among regions and states) and vertical balance (matching revenues and expenditures), the national government should have at least one tax that is shared with subnational governments on a formula basis that takes into account fiscal capacity and tax effort. While the degree of fiscal equalization is a political question, attempts at 100 percent equalization are probably not desirable. In Germany and Russia, there is little incentive for states and local governments to develop their own-source revenues because it simply results in less revenue sharing from the national government. The lack of any equalization program is often regarded as one of the defects in the U.S. federal system. Some combination of tax sharing and rate sharing (or piggybacking) could deal with the equity issues while not crippling national stabilization functions.

Fourth: Regional or state governments could play a useful intermediary role, allowing the national government to deal with national disparities and the regions to deal with local disparities and individual allocational needs. Regional oversight over local taxes may be important to ensure integrity and uniformity, especially if the local tax base is used in a formula determining fiscal capacity (e.g., assessed real property values).

A Tax Allocational Model of Fiscal Decentralization

What does this all mean for a specific allocation of taxing powers? Table 8.3 provides for a type of model tax system that would achieve the four objectives outlined above.

Table 8.3
Model Tax Allocation System

Central Government	Regional/Local Government
Income Taxes	Property Taxes
Import and Export Duties	Business Taxes
	Charges and Fees
Shared/Joint Taxes	Gaming/Lottery
Natural Resource Taxes	Income or VAT (piggybacked on national tax)
VAT	Excise Taxes

While the case for national import and export duties is obvious from an interstate/international perspective, the case for national income taxes is less obvious. Income taxes, both personal and corporate, are highly elastic and therefore excellent macroeconomic tools. In addition, issues such as tax coordination and compliance and reducing tax evasion argues that income taxes are more appropriate for the national government. However, Bahl (1999b) argues that in developing countries, personal income taxes are primarily wage taxes that can be monitored and enforced at the local level. A compromise model would have the central government the principal actor with local governments piggybacking a local rate and possibly collecting the tax.

The VAT makes a good shared tax. It can be collected at either the national or regional level. It is more stable than the income tax and thus provides a more assured revenue stream for regions and/or local governments. Sharing natural resource taxes is appropriate because in one sense, oil, gas, and coal reserves are a national resource; yet, in another sense, the exploitation of those resources imposes costs on local governments. What does not seem appropriate is windfall profits to one region at the expense of other regions.

The property tax is a good local tax. Real property is immobile and local assessment of valuation is appropriate (perhaps, as in the United States, under state or regional supervision). Business taxes, charges, and fees are often closely related to specific services provided by state or local government and thus are good from a standpoint of allocational efficiency. Some would argue against allowing state or local gaming taxes because it leads to exportation of local taxes (and hence lowers the real price for local services); however, there are governmental costs associated with this revenue source.

Regional governments might rely on a piggybacked source of revenue, such as on a national income tax or VAT, or on excise taxes (gasoline, alcohol, and tobacco, for example).

Of course, no country starts from scratch. There are existing structures of taxation and political commitments. However, change is in the air. Brazil, China, India, and Russia are all in discussions–in one degree or other–about the appropriate allocation of revenues among the central and subnational governments. Sound political and economic principles should be applied in the discussion.

Fiscal Decentralization as Reform

The theoretical case for continuing the efforts to find the right mix of tax and revenue sharing for subnational governments is the following. When regional and local governments are involved in financing their own expenditures, at least at the margin, they will be more accountable to their citizens (and the central government) for the efficient delivery of public services. In contrast, when the bulk of financing of local services comes from revenues transferred from a higher level of government, local governments are less likely to be parsimonious with those expenditures. Thus, tax sharing formulas need to be constructed in a fashion that encourages (or at least not discourages) local governments from developing their own-source revenues.

The case for local tax administration, and at least some local discretion on tax rates, is to place greater responsibility on local government to collect taxes owed and to use discretion as to tax rates to provide discretionary services or to use for economic development purposes. The goal is to provide the greatest stake in the success of local governments with the local officials and to take away the excuse that they are "bound" and therefore unfairly limited by national legislation.

Both Brazil and China have moved strongly in the direction of fiscal decentralization reform, and they both share some common problems typical of developing nations:

1. There is overlapping and confusion over expenditure responsibility in both countries. This confusion leads to *ad hoc* bargaining over central government grants and creates a disincentive for local governments to develop their own-source revenues. This is especially true if local governments are "punished" by a reduction in central government transfers.

2. There is a need–in both countries–to develop a comprehensive VAT, applying to all products uniformly, that can be shared with regions and local governments. This will eliminate any problem of "cascading" tax

increases on the product. The central government can either share revenue on a percentage basis or could allow their states/provinces to apply a regional tax as a surcharge on the national tax. This latter has some advantages because the central government can vary its VAT rates, for macroeconomic purposes, without affecting revenue raised by the state VAT portion.

3. Both countries need to develop a long-run strategy for development of a comprehensive real property tax for their localities. States and provinces might be given the task of assisting localities in this effort and ensuring common assessment practices. While developing such a system is time consuming and resource intensive, it can, over time, provide a steady source of revenue for local governments.

4. There needs to be more discussion and national agreement on the degree of fiscal equalization desired among the regions. Neither country may desire (or have the fiscal capacity) to equalize to the extent that Germany does. And total equalization, as in Germany, also may be a disincentive for localities to develop their own-source revenues. What is important is for the national government to provide a steady stream of transfers that local governments can rely on for budget purposes. The revenue-sharing formula should be transparent and create some incentives for the development of own-source revenue at the regional and local level.

There also are issues that are specific to each country. China's assignment of its personal income and certain enterprise taxes to its provinces runs counter to the common wisdom that such taxes should be national taxes—for both stabilization and redistributional purposes. Provinces could impose a surcharge and piggyback their tax on the national tax. National collection and enforcement is critical to long-run growth of this revenue source.

China needs to get better budgetary control over fees and charges levied at the provincial and local level. The central government should create a framework for appropriate user fees and charges, both to the type of allowable fees and charges and to the method of pricing. Fees for services that could be provided by the private sector and are not considered "essential" should be prohibited and/or privatized. All fees and charges should be part of the budgetary review process and not "off-budget." Finally, fees and charges that have a characteristic of a tax should be converted to taxes (for example, various transportation fees might be converted into a broad-based fuel tax).

China's recent reforms on tax administration, creating the State Administration of Taxation (SAT), are a move in the right direction. However, dual loyalty problems (created by local funding of regional

SAT offices) need to be resolved by full funding by the central government and by thorough training by the headquarters.

The constitution of Brazil contains far too much tax detail to allow the central government to make changes necessary for effective fiscal policy. It does, however, provide considerable protection for state and local government. While a major overhaul of the tax provisions in the constitution is unlikely and unnecessary, Brazilian policymakers should consider creating some more flexibility in the constitution so as to relieve the necessity of passing "emergency" legislation to deal with macroeconomic problems.

Brazil and China have taken the path of fiscal decentralization reform, and yet are struggling with implementation issues. However, if reform follows theory, greater fiscal decentralization and discretion should lead to stronger regional and local governments and greater accountability to for local taxes and expenditures. In the final analysis, fiscal decentralization is a political question and requires a combination of political will, local development and sound implementation strategies to succeed.

Acknowledgment

The research for this chapter was initially conducted as part of a larger study, "Tax Policy Management and Division of Responsibilities among Levels of Government," conducted by the author and James W. Wetzler, for the Ministry of Finance, People's Republic of China. That study was conducted under the auspices of Deloitte Touche Tohmatsu. The views in the paper are solely the authors and not those of Deloitte Touche Tohmatsu, Mr. Wetzler, or the Ministry of Finance. The author also would like to acknowledge the research assistance of Chang Jun Lee, a graduate of the Master of Public Administration degree program at George Washington University.

References

Arora, Vivek B., and John Norregaard. 1997. *Intergovernmental Fiscal Relations: The Chinese System in Perspective.* Working paper of the International Monetary Fund, Washington, DC: IMF.

Bahl, Roy. 1999a. "Fiscal Decentralization as Development Policy." *Public Budgeting and Finance,* (summer): 59–75.

Bahl, Roy. 1999b. "Implementation Rules for Fiscal Decentralization." Paper presented at the International Seminar on Land Policy and Economic Development, Land Reform Training Institute, Taiwan, November 17, 1998 (January).

Bennet, R. J. 1990. *Decentralization: Local Governments and Markets.* London: Clarendon Press.

Bird, Richard M. 1993. "Threading the Fiscal Labyrinth: Some Issues in Fiscal Decentralization." *National Tax Journal,* 42, no. 2: 207–227.

Federal Statistical Office of Germany. Economic and financial data for Germany. Available online at www.statistik-bund.de.

Georgetown University. *Brazil: Constitution, 1988 with 1996 Reforms, Title VI.* Available online at http://www.georgetown.edu/LatAmerPolitical/Constitutions/Brazil/brtitle6.html.

Gramlich, Edward M. 1993. "A Policymaker's Guide to Fiscal Decentralization." *National Tax Journal,* 46, no. 2: 229–236.

Hommes, Rudolf. 1995. "Conflicts and Dilemmas of Decentralization." *The World Bank Research Observer.* 295–316.

Indian Tax Institute. 1999. *Indian Tax Database. (1950–1998)* Delhi, India: Indian Tax Institute.

International Monetary Fund. 1998. *Government Finance Statistics Yearbook 1997.* Washington DC: IMF.

McLure, Charles E., Jr. 1995. "Comment on 'The Dangers of Decentralization' by Prud'homme." *The World Bank Observer,* 10, no. 2 (August): 221–227.

Ministry of Finance of India. *Union Budget 1998–1999.* Available online at http://www.finmin.nic.in.

Musgrave, Richard A. 1959. *The Theory of Public Finance.* New York: McGraw-Hill.

Musgrave, Richard A. 1961. "Approaches to a Fiscal Theory of Political Federalism." In *Public Finances: Needs, Sources, and Utilization,* ed. National Bureau of Economic Research. Princeton, NJ: Princeton University Press.

Oates, Wallace E. 1977. *The Political Economy of Fiscal Federalism.* Lexington, MA: Lexington Books.

Oates, Wallace E. 1993. "Fiscal Decentralization and Economic Development." *National Tax Journal,* 46, no. 2: 237–243.

Oates, Wallace E. 1995. "Comment on 'Conflicts an Dilemmas of Decentralization' by Rudolf Hommes." *The World Bank Research Observer.* 323–325.

Organization for Economic Co-operation and Development. 1998. *Revenue Statistics 1965–1997.* Paris: OECD.

Peterson, George E. 2000. "Local Tax: Case Studies and Policy Overview." Washington, DC: Deloitte Touche Tohmatsu.

Prud'homme, Remy. 1995. "The Dangers of Decentralization." *The World Bank Research Observer,* 10, no. 2: 201–220.

Tanzi, Vito. 1995. "Fiscal Federalism and Decentralization: A Review of Some Efficiency and Macroeconomic Aspects." *The World Bank Research Observer.* 295–316.

Tiebout, Charles M. 1956. "A Pure Theory of Local Expenditures." *Journal of Political Economy,* (October): 415–424.

United States Government Technical Assistance Team. 1998. *Fiscal Decentralization in the Russian Federation* (for consolidated subnational government revenue in Russia, 1997), Washington DC: World Bank.

World Bank. 1996. *Fiscal Management in Russia.* Washington, DC: World Bank Country Study.

World Bank. 1997. *World Development Report: The State in a Changing World.* New York: Oxford University Press.

World Bank. 1999. *India 1998 Macroeconomic Update.* Washington, DC: World Bank Country Study.

CHAPTER 9

Managing Structural Imbalances
Implications for Fiscal Decision Making and Policy

Merl Hackbart and James R. Ramsey

With one exception during President Johnson's administration in 1968, the federal government operated with continuous budget deficits from the 1940s to 1997. The continuous federal deficits required Congress to periodically raise the national debt ceiling as efforts to balance the federal budget failed fiscal year after fiscal year. Efforts to match federal revenue growth with expenditure growth failed, more often than not, due to the political difficulty of raising revenue and the pressures for increased federal spending.

The federal government's continued deficit spending led to public criticism of the budget process and Congress's ability to manage its fiscal affairs. Such criticism was particularly strong in the 1980s as structural deficits (deficits resulting from continuing expenditures exceeding continuing revenues) emerged, and large fiscal year financial deficits appeared to be the fiscal "norm." The concern was heightened when it became apparent that Congress was unable to take the fiscal policy actions necessary to stem the deficits and growing national debt. At the same time, economists and public financial policy analysts focused the fiscal and budgetary policy debate on a more fundamental question regarding the prevailing deficits and ever-increasing federal debt, "Do federal deficits matter?" (Caiden, 1999; Barro, 1989; True, 1995; Savage, 1994). That debate continues today.

While public debate over federal budget deficits has continued for decades, deficit spending by state and local governments has attracted limited attention (Wolkoff, 1999). Limited concerns regarding state budget deficits probably have resulted from the public's understanding that, generally, state deficits are not permitted by state constitutions or statutes. For the most part, such public perceptions are warranted since forty-eight states are required to have "financially" balanced budgets although the specific balanced budget requirements vary among the states (NASBO, 1992).

For example, the Advisory Commission for Intergovernmental Relations (ACIR) (ACIR, 1987; Levinson, 1998) indicated that there are at least five types of state balanced budget requirements. Requirements vary from those that require governors to submit balanced budgets to state requirements that mandate that legislatures must pass balanced budgets. Some states have balanced budget stipulations that states can carry deficits into the following fiscal year but must correct the deficit in the next fiscal year, while other states may not carry deficits into the next fiscal period.

While the budget balancing requirements vary for the states, the constitutional or statutory requirements focus on having a "financially" balanced budget for a fiscal year period. A financially balanced budget means that at the end of the fiscal year, "recorded" revenues for the fiscal year must equal or exceed "recorded" expenditures. While "financially" balanced budgets are required, state constitutions and state statutes are silent regarding structural balances that might pose greater financial management concerns and that may have greater policy and program impacts and implications.

The economic slowdowns of the early 1980s, the early 1990s, and the most recent recession of 2001 focused attention on the fact that cyclical and structural deficits can and do occur simultaneously. While sometimes initially hidden by economic good times, structural imbalances can emerge due to changes occurring in the economy, tax system characteristics, overly optimistic views of long-term revenue growth, and program expansion.

For example, as states began to analyze their fiscal condition in recent years, it became apparent that underlying structural imbalances were embedded with state cyclical deficits and adding to the states' fiscal stress (Hovey, 1999; Reschovsky, 2002; Jones, 2003; Conant, 2003; Lauth, 2003). The realization of the existence of structural budget imbalances, in turn, raised questions regarding the financial management policy options available to regain fiscal stability. This issue is particularly challenging for states, as they must maintain financially balanced budgets while taking corrective action to mitigate structural imbalances.

The purpose of this chapter is to consider the causes of structural budget imbalances and to assess how such structural imbalances may impact budget and financial management decisions and resource allocations. In so doing, we expand on incremental budget theory and analyze how structural imbalances may produce "punctuated solutions" (Jordan, 2002; Jones, 1994) to structural budget problems. Punctuated solutions involving nonincremental adjustments to budget patterns may replace otherwise normal, incremental budget decisions when structural imbalances emerge (particularly for state governments that face balanced budget requirements). We also suggest that state budget punctuations (or nonincremental budget adjustments period to period) may be the indirect result of budget or financial management related policy decisions, rather than external forces (such as intergovernmental policy changes or court decisions) that often have been identified as the main drivers of nonincremental state budget adjustments.

In addition, we explore budget-related financial management strategies that may provide a smoother solution to structural imbalances than more aggressive "punctuated" remedies. Such strategies are designed to be less disruptive and provide greater program continuity. In so doing, such strategies could be classified as "incremental financial management strategies" for regaining state budget structural balances.

The focus on budget structural imbalances is timely due to the number of states that are recognizing their structural deficits and are beginning to deal with the consequences (Boyd, 2002). This chapter also considers how state reactions to the structural balance problem may shed light on budget and financial management decision making under stress. As such, it may add to our understanding of how budget allocation decisions are made.

Structural Imbalances: Theoretical Issues and Concerns

As indicated, much of the public finance and public financial management theoretical debate regarding federal deficits and debt has focused on the "Do deficits matter?" issue. Much of that discourse has focused on the theoretical impacts of government deficits on interest rates and investment (the Neo-Keynesians) and the intergenerational impacts and transparency issues raised by the "Ricardian equivalence theorem" view of deficits by Barro and others (Barro, 1989, McCallum, 1984; Buchanan, 1976). The conceptual and theoretical concerns emphasized in this chapter do not further the "Do deficits matter?" debate. Rather, we focus on how structural deficits may alter or disrupt the incremental public budget and financial management decision making processes described by Wildavsky, Lindblom, and others (Wildavsky, 1964, 1975; Lindblom, 1959).

Because structural deficits are principally policy-driven, policy decisions have to be part of the structural "imbalance" solution (Conant, 2003; Lauth, 2003; Wolkoff, 1999). Such policy solutions may involve both revenue and expenditure adjustments, which often include nonincremental budget decisions. Consequently, budget allocation decisions associated with structural balance mitigating strategies tend to differ from traditional incremental budget allocation changes.

While nonincremental allocation outcomes may result from structural imbalances, policy makers may decide that short-term nonincremental budget decisions (or punctuated changes) are too disruptive to the budgetary stasis, and a preferable financial management strategy might be to gradually bring continuing revenues and expenditures back into line. The budget policy chosen (nonincremental, punctuated, or incremental revenue and expenditure adjustments) can have major impacts on state budget allocations. In other words, the emergence of structural imbalances adds to the list of factors that determine the "X vs. Y" question posed by V. O. Key many years ago (Key, 1940).

Structural Balances: Causes and Effects

As suggested, a structurally balanced budget implies that a government's expected recurring revenues are matched with projected recurring expenditures (Proctor, 1992; Wolkoff, 1999), absent major policy initiatives, unanticipated events, or punctuations. That is, for the expenditure side of the budget, growth is normally accounted for by: (1) program cost increases from one year to the next, as proxied by the Consumer Price Index or another index sometimes referred to as the current services base budget; and (2) increases in program activity due to growth in the population served by the program or program demand (e.g., Medicaid, prison population, daily attendance in K–12 schools, and the like).

To maintain a structurally balanced budget, increased "continuing" program expenditures must be accompanied by recurring revenue growth equal to the anticipated expenditure growth. When recurring revenue/expenditure mismatches occur, either structural surpluses or deficits can emerge. For example, if recurring revenue growth exceeds recurring expenditure growth, governments will accumulate surpluses (as was commonly the case with state governments throughout the

1990s); add new or expand current program initiatives; and/or reduce taxes to balance anticipated long-term revenues and expenditures to achieve a structural balance (NCSL, 2002; NASBO, 2001).

When current and continuing expenditure growth rates exceed projected revenue, governments can either modify the scope and content of programs to reduce current and future expenditures or raise revenues to ensure a structurally balanced budget. Actions to deal with either condition (structural surpluses or deficits) require revenue or expenditure policy decisions–hence further evidence of the policy-driven nature of structural balances.

As indicated, if state governments delay revenue or expenditure decisions needed to rectify structural imbalances and focus, instead, on the more immediate need to meet their fiscal year "financially balanced" budget requirements, structural imbalances can be exacerbated, and the magnitude (or punctuation) of future revenue and expenditure policy decisions may be magnified.

The emergence of a state's budget structural imbalance is shown in Figures 9.1 and 9.2. In Figure 9.1, long-term revenue growth and expenditure expansion is shown for a representative state (Kentucky) as of December 2001. The figure displays estimated "continuing" revenues and expenditures for FY94 through FY01 based on an analysis of revenue and expenditure patterns. The revenue and expenditure patterns for FY02, FY03, and FY04 reflect estimated revenues for the three fiscal years, actual appropriations for FY02, and the executive branch budget recommendations for FY03 and FY04.

The "out year" revenue and expenditure patterns were based on extrapolations of anticipated FY04 revenues and expenditures. Given the economic conditions in December 2001, and anticipated revenues and expenditures, there was some evidence of an emerging, temporary structural imbalance in FY01, but projections indicated that the combination of anticipated revenue growth and controlled expenditure growth would produce a structurally balanced for the long-term future (five years).

State appropriations for FY02 were based on projected revenues for FY02 that were not realized due to the recession and associated lower state revenues. "One-time" receipts and "rainy day" funds were used to financially balance the FY02 budget. Hence, as a result of the policy decisions to maintain expenditures at the original appropriation level while not adjusting the revenue base (through tax or revenue policy changes), a structural imbalance emerged.

Figure 9.2 displays the December 2002 adjustments to the state's long-term revenue and expenditure outlook. The revenue forecasts were revised from December 2001 and reflect revenue reductions associated

Figure 9.1
December 2001 Estimates and Projections of Kentucky General Fund
Continuing Revenues and Expenditures

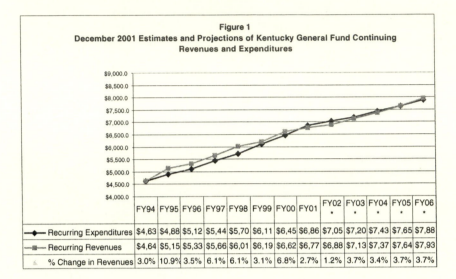

Figure 1
December 2001 Estimates and Projections of Kentucky General Fund Continuing
Revenues and Expenditures

	FY94	FY95	FY96	FY97	FY98	FY99	FY00	FY01	FY02 *	FY03 *	FY04 *	FY05 *	FY06 *
◆ Recurring Expenditures	$4,63	$4,88	$5,12	$5,44	$5,70	$6,11	$6,45	$6,86	$7,05	$7,20	$7,43	$7,65	$7,88
▩ Recurring Revenues	$4,64	$5,15	$5,33	$5,66	$6,01	$6,19	$6,62	$6,77	$6,88	$7,13	$7,37	$7,64	$7,93
% Change in Revenues	3.0%	10.9%	3.5%	6.1%	6.1%	3.1%	6.8%	2.7%	1.2%	3.7%	3.4%	3.7%	3.7%

with the economic downturn. As shown, the December 2002 revenue and expenditure outlook (in contrast to the analysis of a year earlier) suggests a prolonged structural balance problem as continuing revenues were projected to be below expected expenditures, at least through FY06. Projected out-year expenditure patterns reflect expenditure trends that are principally driven by entitlement programs, such as Medicaid, and other high priority state programs, such as education and corrections. Kentucky's structural budget imbalance problem has origins similar to those of many other states. Therefore, it is likely that other states that delayed adopting structural imbalance policy remedies face similar budgetary futures.

In fact, recent economic realities and state revenue and expenditure decisions have produced budget stress (and probable structural balance problems) in nearly every state (NCSL, 2002). The National Association of State Budget Officers, the National Conference of State Legislators, and the American Legislative Exchange Council conducted surveys to identify actions taken by states to ensure financially balanced budgets. Budget balancing actions include the use of Budget Reserve Trust Funds (or Rainy Day Funds), and other one-time sources of cash. The utilization of one-time monies to balance current state budgets has worsened the state structural balance problem that was already emerging due to eroding state tax bases (particularly, the sales tax base due to economic

Figure 9.2

December 2001 Estimates and Projections of Kentucky General Fund Continuing Revenues and Expenditures

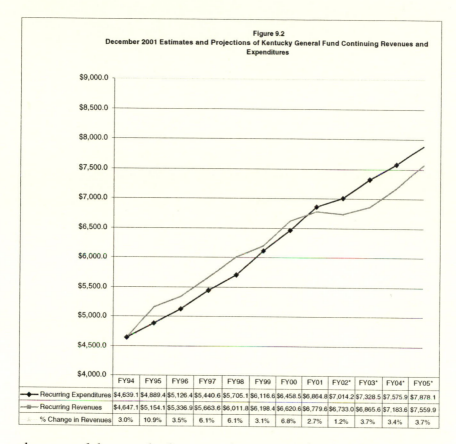

Figure 9.2
December 2001 Estimates and Projections of Kentucky General Fund Continuing Revenues and Expenditures

	FY94	FY95	FY96	FY97	FY98	FY99	FY00	FY01	FY02*	FY03*	FY04*	FY05*
Recurring Expenditures	$4,639.1	$4,889.4	$5,126.4	$5,440.6	$5,705.1	$6,116.6	$6,458.5	$6,864.8	$7,014.2	$7,328.5	$7,575.9	$7,878.1
Recurring Revenues	$4,647.1	$5,154.1	$5,336.9	$5,663.6	$6,011.8	$6,198.4	$6,620.6	$6,779.6	$6,733.0	$6,865.6	$7,183.6	$7,559.9
% Change in Revenues	3.0%	10.9%	3.5%	6.1%	6.1%	3.1%	6.8%	2.7%	1.2%	3.7%	3.4%	3.7%

changes and the growth of non-taxed remote sales) and increased expenditure demand for entitlements and priority programs (Conant, 2003; Lauth, 2003).

Structural Deficits: A Federal Retrospective

The failure of the federal government to match major tax cuts with expenditure reductions produced structural deficits as well as record overall deficit levels in the 1980s. The continuing revenue/expenditure mismatches of the federal budget under the Reagan administration produced major structural deficits and exacerbated the cyclical deficits produced by slow economic growth of the early 1980s. The structural deficits that emerged during that period represented a relatively new budget phenomenon. Business cycle driven "cyclical deficits" are common in market economies and emerge and disappear with economic change. However, the federal structural deficits, principally resulting from policy decisions, did not disappear with economic recovery.

The federal structural balance issue emerged as a national policy concern in 1983 as the Reagan tax cuts began to impact federal revenues and the structural deficit doubled from $64 billion to over $126 billion (CBO, 1996). The structural deficit averaged $176 billion from FY83 to FY96, which was equivalent to 3.3 percent of the Gross Domestic Product for that period, according to CBO estimates (CBO, 1996). The structural and cyclical deficits produced an average combined financial deficit of $202 billion per fiscal year for the period.

The federal deficits for the period increased the national debt outstanding from the equivalent of 25.8 percent of the GDP to 50.2 percent by 1995. It is noted that the structural deficit was not only the result of federal tax policy, but also partially resulted from a failure to adjust continuing expenditures, as Congress and the president were reluctant to reduce federal programs. The combination of an active revenue reducing policy (tax cuts) and a passive expenditure policy (the failure to simultaneously reduce expenditures) produced structural deficits that prevailed for a decade and a half. In other words, the major or "punctuated" revenue base reductions were matched with "incremental" expenditures changes—a classic combination of policies that can create a structurally imbalanced budget.

Aware of the origin of the persistent structural deficits and pushed by public concerns regarding continuing federal deficits and growing federal debt levels, Congress responded to the ballooning federal debt by passing a series of deficit reduction legislative acts in the 1980s and 1990s, including Gramm, Rudman, Hollings I; Gramm, Rudman, Hollings II in 1985 and 1987; the Budget Enforcement Act (BEA) of 1990; and subsequent similar legislative initiatives, such as the Omnibus Budget Reconciliation Act (OBRA) of 1993.

These initiatives, particularly the BEA, placed even greater emphasis on Congressional budget discipline. BEA divided the discretionary portion of the federal budget into three groups or categories and established spending caps for each (defense, domestic programs, and foreign spending). The budget walls created by BEA and OBRA prevented the movement of funds from one discretionary category to another (Doyle and McCaffrey, 1993; Joyce and Meyers, 2001). These new, more effective federal expenditure control measures, in combination with the Bush (1990) and Clinton (1993) tax increases accompanied by accommodating monetary policy, produced stronger than expected revenue growth through the 1990s and accomplished the unthinkable—the elimination of the federal deficit in 1997 and the appearance of a federal surplus (Joyce and Meyers, 2001; Kee and Nystrom, 1991). The federal budgetary experience of the 1980s and 1990s established that structural deficits, unlike their cousins–cyclical deficits–can be managed by policy adjustments, incremental or punctuated, if the will exists.

It is interesting to note that some have argued that the creation of the federal structural deficit in the 1980s was a deliberate effort by the Reagan administration to reduce the size of government or to produce a punctuated reduction in federal programs. Given the difficulty of increasing taxes to restore the federal government's revenue base and the reluctance of Congress and President Reagan to make hard, punctuated budget balancing choices, the only option available to eliminate the structural deficit was either to reduce continuing expenditures or increase revenues, incrementally, over an extended period of time. Because of the federal government's ability to operate with a continuing deficit, unlike the states, a longer-term "incremental" approach was feasible.

So if the Reagan administration's goal was to use a structural deficit to reduce the size of the federal government and its programs, it worked reasonably well. The continuing deficits (part cyclical and part structural) of the 1980s and 1990s brought legislative budget process changes (GRH1, GRH2, BEA, and OBRA) that, in turn, incrementally reduced federal expenditures, or at least modified the growth of federal expenditures.

Unfortunately, 2001 tax cuts, combined with increased expenditures for the war on terrorism and homeland security and a dramatically slowed economy, have recreated a dual federal structural and cyclical deficit problem. Consequently, current federal budget policy debate is focused on whether enacted revenue and likely expenditure policies will produce continuous federal structural imbalances and deficits over the next decade, or whether structural deficits are a short-term phenomenon and can be overcome and, perhaps, replaced by surplus. If the economy recovers and budget policy is adjusted (revenue, expenditure, or both), surpluses may indeed reappear. On the other hand, economic recovery alone (which mainly impacts the cyclical deficit) will probably not be sufficient to overcome the nagging federal structural deficit issue.

Structural Deficits: A State Retrospective

Like the federal structural deficits of the 1980s, 1990s, and the re-emerging deficits of the current decade, state structural deficits have resulted principally from state revenue and expenditure policy decisions. On the revenue side, decisions to enact special tax exemptions and tax cuts during the good economic times of the 1990s, combined with the failure of the states to modernize tax structures to reflect changes occurring in the economy, reduced continuing state revenue. The impact of those policy decisions, combined with the erosion of sales tax bases due to increased untaxed remote sales, gradually reduced the elasticity of state revenue systems as well. As a consequence, state recurring revenues have failed to keep up with recurring demand for state resources. Likewise, buoyed by the temporary robust economic conditions of the late 1990s, state policy makers expanded programs in a manner that added to the emerging structural problems. Still other structural deficits resulted from a lack of policy action to meet the financial demands imposed by unanticipated population and social program growth.

Several studies have been undertaken to estimate state structural imbalances and determine structural deficit causal factors. For example, during the FY91–92 period, Savage (1992) estimated that California incurred a $4–6 billion structural deficit along with a $8–10 billion cyclical deficit. In his analysis, Savage suggests that the structural deficit of that period was partially the result of population expansion and associated uncontrollable school and social service cost growth, and partially the result of "ballot box budgeting" (tax relief and tax ear-marking voter initiatives). New York structural deficits for the same period were driven by an expanding expenditure base, or expenditures necessitated by social welfare programs, amidst a declining revenue base (Brecher, Horton, and Mead, 1994).

In another study of state structural deficits (State Policy Research, 1998), it was estimated that only 11 states would have structurally balanced budgets by FY06. The study, which preceded the state tax cuts of the late 1990s and the slower economic growth and diminishing state revenue elasticities recently realized by the states, developed estimates of FY06 structural balances by analyzing probable state program expenditure and revenue growth compared to projected long-term income growth. The latter projection, coupled with revenue elasticity estimates, provided estimates of future baseline state revenues, and a similar methodology provided estimates of state-by-state expenditure growth for eight years into the future.

Given recent state trends, state expenditure growth estimates tend to exceed state income or revenue growth overall–hence the negative outlook for structurally balanced state budgets. In previous research by the same organization (State Policy Reports, 1998), state revenues were projected to grow faster than income in only 13 states. In other words, only 13 states were identified as having elastic revenue structures. Meanwhile, their study indicated that 22 states had projected revenue growth of 9.5 percent for every 10 percent increase in personal income, while their projections suggested that, due to declining revenue elasticities, 7 states would have revenue growth of less than 9 percent for every 10 percent increase in personal income. If this study accurately describes the future financial condition of the states, state tax or expenditure policy action will be needed in order for the states to meet their balanced budget requirements and to manage the structure balance problems currently envisioned.

Managing Structural Budget Imbalances: State Actions

The concept of a balanced budget is ingrained within the legal structures of state governments. As noted earlier, most states have constitutional and/or statutory balanced budgets requirements. As also previously indicated, the concept of a balanced budget for state governments is complicated by the fact that in some states, a balanced budget may mean balanced at the time of presentation by the governor; in other states, a balanced budget may mean balanced upon enactment by the legislature; in other cases, a balanced budget may mean balanced at the end of the fiscal year; and finally, in some cases, a balanced budget may mean a combination of some or all of the previously cited examples. Still, with only minor exceptions, attaining and maintaining balanced budgets are financial management requirements that state governments, unlike the federal government, have dealt with for many years.

State concerns over structural imbalances have emerged from internal analysis and external pressures. Internally, states have begun to visualize their structural imbalances as they develop long-term projections of expenditure needs and anticipated future revenues. Concerns over the ability of the states to manage their structural imbalances have also been raised by external third parties such as the rating agencies. The rating agencies observe and analyze the fiscal condition of the states and their ability to meet long-term debt service commitments.

Bond rating agencies have recently expressed concern over the emergence of state structural deficits (Moody's, 2002). The rating agencies' concerns arise from the potential state financial instability that recurring expenditures in excess of recurring revenues may pose for the states. More specifically, the rating agencies understand that continuing structural deficits will create budgetary pressures as state governments attempt to meet their statutory or constitutional requirements for a financially balanced budget. As a result, states may be tempted to take extreme actions, such as deferring debt service payments, in order to balance their budgets while attempting to meet other high priority obligations, such as education, health care, and public safety. Budget actions that threaten to impact the ability of a state to meet its debt obligations could undermine its perceived credit quality and lead to bond rating reductions. Therefore, for these and other reasons, state budget and financial management policy debate has begun to focus on the necessity of ensuring not only financially balanced budgets, but structurally balanced budgets as well.

As indicated, bond rating companies are concerned with both financial and structural balances and actions taken to attain and maintain both of them. For example, a special credit report published by Moody's Investors Service in October 2002 (Moody's, 2002) included the following views of state actions taken to deal with the continued national economic weakness and associated state fiscal challenges:

> 2002 legislative sessions produced a range of responses among the states to the steepest drop in tax revenues in over a decade. Some states took swift budgetary steps to prevent a larger problem from developing; others used non-recurring revenue or expenditure fixes to plug the budget gaps. With economic recovery tepid at best, it is doubtful that states will grow out of this fiscal stress in the coming years. Those that did not seek permanent solutions will likely face a similar, if not worse, situation next year.

While not specifically citing structural imbalances as their major concern, Moody's did cite the non-recurring, temporary budget balancing actions of the states in the group of 15 that were included in their "negative outlook" list. Among the actions taken by the 15 states assigned to their "negative outlook" group were: (1) the use of tobacco securitization to address a mounting budgetary gap (Missouri, Wisconsin, New Jersey, Washington, Rhode Island, California); and (2) the use of Rainy Day Fund as a source of "one-time" cash (Indiana, Connecticut, Michigan, North Carolina, Kansas, New York). Moody's further noted that more permanent measures would have to be taken to manage the structural balance issue when they stated in the same report:

> The use of reserves proves how valuable such funds can be and how better prepared many states were compared to the early 1990s recession when most did not have a stop-gap measure that states can take before taking more permanent action to be in structural balance.

While state policy actions to cut taxes or expand programs during the strong economic and fiscal period of the 1990s were major factors in creating the structural imbalances experienced by the states, state financial management policy responses to the structural problem involved both incremental and punctuated actions. For example, as noted by Moody's, the National Conference of State Legislators, the National Association of State Budget Officers, and the American Legislative Exchange Council, many states made both temporary adjustments (use of one-time moneys) as well as budget adjustments that could be considered more of a permanent nature to address recent budget shortfalls.

The more permanent budget policy decisions included: (1) tax increases or revenue adjustments; (2) programmatic or expenditure cuts; (3) enhanced efficiency processes such as re-engineering efforts to produce recurring savings and efficiencies; and (4) a combination of the above. These survey analyses of state actions showed that in states where recurring expenditures were cut, significant programmatic impacts were often felt in critical program areas such as education, corrections, Medicaid, and the like. Many of the permanent budget adjustments could be considered budget punctuations (tax increases, program cuts and major re-engineering efforts). Nonincremental or punctuated budget adjustments would include budget decisions to apply program cuts selectively and/or to increase some taxes while retaining other tax structures unchanged. By contrast, incremental policy decisions would rely on an across-the-board strategy to achieve overall budget expenditure base reductions.

As noted, to avoid immediate programmatic cuts, policymakers in several states relied upon one-time or nonrecurring fixes to avoid program adjustments that would be viewed as detrimental to the attainment of the state's long-term social goals (i.e., cuts in educational expenditures). Apparently, policymakers in those states did so based upon a longer-term analysis that revenue growth in the future would incrementally catch up with recurring expenditures and permit the structural balance to be achieved in the long term.

For most states throughout the 1990s, revenue growth exceeded historical growth rates and estimates used to prepare state budgets. This strong revenue growth pattern resulted in surpluses with revenues exceeding state expenditures. The surpluses allowed a variety of public policy initiatives to be pursued. Such public policy initiatives included (1) tax cuts, (2) expansion of program and policy initiatives, and (3) enhanced budget reserve trust funds. However, beginning in late 2000, a dramatic slowdown in economic activity was realized; first by the manufacturing states in the Midwest and Southeast, and then later by practically every state. As a result, fiscal years 2001 and 2002 were periods of slow revenue growth. In many states, revenue growth was less than originally forecasted for budgetary purposes. In other cases, states actually experienced declining revenues from prior year collections. In either case, policy decisions had to be made to meet balanced budget requirements.

To illustrate the financial management implications of structural imbalances, consider a hypothetical state, "State A," which has a $10 million budget and which experienced an average revenue growth throughout the 1990s of 6 percent per year. Assume the state's expenditure budgets for FY01 and FY02 were originally based upon a conservative 5 percent revenue growth rate, and their enacted budgets for both FY01 and FY02 were projected to be structurally balanced. Further assume that our hypothetical state had prudently built up its budget reserve trust fund to a targeted 5 percent level (5 percent of its General Fund budget) and entered this period of economic downturn with a budget reserve trust fund of $500,000.

In addition, assume that FY01 revenue growth did not meet the projected 5 percent rate, but grew at a 3 percent rate. This revenue growth slowdown resulted in a $200,000 budget revenue shortfall, requiring the state to take policy actions to produce a financially balanced budget. Assume further that our hypothetical state adjusted its FY01 budget plan on both the revenue and expenditure sides of the budget by $100,000 to manage the $200,000 revenue shortfall with the revenue "enhancement" adjustment involving the use of one-time, non-recurring funds drawn from the budget reserve trust fund (which had held $500,000). The $100,000 of expenditure adjustments (which reduced the expenditure growth rate for FY01 to 4 percent) resulted from savings initiatives that were put in place with minimal programmatic impacts (expenditure adjustments such as reduced travel, hiring freezes for non-critical positions, reduced overtime, and the like).

For FY02, our hypothetical state rebuilt its budget on a revised 3 percent revenue growth estimate (matching the revised economic and revenue outlook) matched by expenditure growth of 3 percent. However, our state needed a 4 percent revenue growth rate to balance its budget (financially and structurally), since its FY01 expenditure adjustments only reduced spending from the original budgeted 5 percent to a 4 percent level. While revised revenue estimates for FY02 anticipated a 3 percent growth rate, policymakers realized that revenue growth could exceed the 3 percent projection if the economy recovered more rapidly than anticipated by the revenue forecasters. If a higher than projected growth rate was realized, a financial and structural balance could be established by the end of FY02 without additional policy actions. In other words by re-budgeting expenditures for FY02 at a 3 percent increase level (and anticipating the use of $100,000 of one-time money to financially balance its budget, if needed), the hypothetical state has one more fiscal year to period to re-establish a structural balance if a turn-around in the economy occurs and a 4 percent or greater revenue growth is realized, or if other program adjustments resulting from re-engineering or other actions can be found to permanently reduce the program expenditure base without impacting service delivery.

Now assume, that in reality, our hypothetical state did not realize the expected 3 percent revenue growth, nor the hoped for 4 percent revenue growth. Rather, revenue growth of 0% materialized in FY02 (which is more indicative of what states experienced for the period). Moreover, assume that other permanent, "service neutral" program expenditure reductions could not be achieved. Again, policy adjustments are needed to balance the budget and avoid program reductions in critical service areas such as education and human services. Assume the state manages the budget shortfall by depleting the remaining funds available in the budget reserve trust fund. Recall that the previous balance in the budget reserve trust fund had been reduced from $500,000 to $400,000 in FY01. Utilizing the remaining $400,000 to balance the FY02 budget, the budget reserve trust fund is depleted in its entirety and a structural imbalance of approximately $400,000 has been created.

The hypothetical state's FY02 policy decisions constitute a financial management strategy of "temporarily coping" with its structural imbalance, but to do so consciously with the anticipation that future policy decisions can be made to permanently increase revenues to deal with the imbalance, or that the economy will rapidly improve, permitting greater than expected revenue growth and slower expenditure growth for economic cycle driven programs such as Medicaid and Temporary Assistance to Need Families (TANF). In the absence of revenue enhancements or program expenditure demand reductions, program expenditure and service level adjustments will have to be made, but such adjustments have been delayed for two years allowing program administrators and policymakers to carefully analyze and prioritize such program adjustments.

The hypothesis stated above is supported by recent research findings of Roger E. Brinner and Joyce Brinner (Brinner and Brinner, 2002) that conclude that reasons for optimism for a forthcoming economic recovery "include an economic bias toward surpluses." The Brinners' research evaluates states' revenue systems in the aggregate and correlates the two primary sources of state revenues with changes in economic activity, such as the unemployment rate. The conclusion of their research is that the structure of state revenue systems penalizes state finances in an economic downturn, but provides for surpluses during an economic recovery.

The Brinners identify surplus as the difference between revenue growth during an economic expansion and expenditure growth. An underlying premise of their analysis is that state revenue structures are a function of (1) changes in prices and cost of services, (2) population changes, (3) productivity gains throughout the economy, and (4) the relative progressivity of state income tax structures. If the expenditures of states' governments are driven primarily by cost changes and population changes (precluding any significant change in policy initiatives), then during an economic recovery, states' revenues growth will exceed expenditure requirements, permitting a return to a structurally balanced budget.

That is, for those states who have formulated a policy decision to draw down budget reserve trust funds and to use other one-time monies as available to keep from making draconian programmatic cuts, the establishment of a structurally balanced budget can occur during the recovery phase of the budget. This is called the "Golden Rule of Thumb," according to their research, which says that states can expect a 1 percent drop in the unemployment rate to increase state revenue growth by 4 percent. Thus, the same factors that contribute to a structural imbalance in an economic downturn for a state will also help reestablish a budget surplus in periods of economic recovery. However, the surplus (which was previously a cash surplus available for tax cuts, new program initiatives, or building the budget reserve trust fund) is now required to fill the gap that has occurred as a result of the policy decision resulting in a mismatch between recurring revenues and recurring expenditures. That is, the budget surplus accumulated during an economic recovery is required to fill the gap that has resulted from achieving a balanced budget at the expense of becoming structurally imbalanced.

The Brinners conclude their analysis by noting that the expenditure of a state's budget reserve trust fund is a valid public policy consideration during periods of economic slowdown as a means of protecting programs against significant funding cuts.

Of course, this approach to a long-term structurally balanced budget management approach requires a fiscal discipline that perhaps is more rigorous than the maintenance of short-term structurally balanced budgets. Further, each state must develop and implement a carefully designed financial management program that ensures that this discipline can be achieved. The following section outlines the necessary components for such a long-term structurally balanced budget discipline.

A Management Strategy for State Governments

Components of a financial management discipline strategy required to achieve a long-term structurally balanced budget include:

1. A long-term structural budget analysis (5 to 7 years) to provide a perspective on expected revenue and expenditure patterns. Such analysis requires both an understanding of the elasticity of the state's tax struc-

ture and an understanding of the elasticity of a state's expenditure patterns, including cost and population drivers as well as exogenous expenditure influencing factors such as federal mandates, state mandates, and the like.

2. A commitment to comprehensive tax reform to ensure that the state's revenue elasticity is consistent with public policy goals and captures productivity gains in the economy.

3. An agreed upon plan for replenishment of withdrawals from the rainy day fund (budget reserve fund) that occurred during a period of economic downturn.

4. A commitment to expenditure adjustments during economic downturns. The most recent economic downturn proved that in many cases, maintaining a balanced budget through the use of rainy day funds and other one-time sources may not be sufficient to achieve the legal strictures of a balanced budget. On the other hand, expenditure cuts can often be achieved through process and management efficiencies to avoid significant programmatic impacts.

5. A communication plan for external interest groups, including the rating agencies, that provides *pro formas* which show a plan and/or strategy for regaining a structurally balanced budget during periods of economic recovery. These *pro formas* must be based on realistic projections of revenues and expenditures and should include stress tests that indicate contingency options that the state can exercise if a recovery occurs later than expected. In addition to appropriate stress tests, contingency plans must also be developed and communicated which show what will happen in the worst-case scenario. That is, a structurally imbalanced budget during a period of continued economic weakness may ultimately require significant program funding cuts that are more painful when ultimately enacted as the only option to becoming balanced, much less structurally balanced, over the long-term as opposed to more modest programmatic cuts accomplished over a short-term time frame.

Conclusion

The purpose of this chapter was to explore the structural deficit issue that has impacted financial management and budget policy of both federal and state governments in the last two decades, the origin of structural deficits, and strategies for dealing with structural imbalances once they are recognized. It also considered strategic issues involved in deciding whether it is in the interest of governments (particularly states) to take punctuated corrective actions to eliminate structural deficits in the short-term or to manage their elimination "incrementally" over a longer period if financially possible—the strategy pursued by the federal government in the 1980s and 1990s. While there are financial management risks associated with this policy (including the validity of estimates or projections of long-term revenue growth and a state's ability to manage expenditures), managing the structural balance problem over a longer period of time provides greater opportunities for maintaining program continuity and the attainment of long-term policy goals and objectives than short-term punctuated solutions.

Beyond the budget policy and management implications of the structural balance issue, the structural budget experiences of the states also shed additional light on factors that may impact budget decisions and financial management theory. For example, concern over managing and reacting to structural imbalances may restrict expenditure growth or impact state revenue or resource policy in ways that restrictions imposed by state "financially" balanced budgets may not accomplish. As a result, concern over the creation of structural imbalances may add additional credibility to the incremental theory of budget change and suggest that uncertainty may be most effectively managed by small changes in expenditures or revenues. In addition, the study of state budget imbalances suggests that unanticipated budget expenditure or revenue changes may impact budget structures and lead to unanticipated budget decisions. Such impacts are consistent with insights provided by punctuated equilibrium theorists who have attempted to fill the gap of incremental theory resulting from that theory's inability to explain change in budget patterns.

References

Advisory Commission for Intergovernmental Relations. 1987. *Fiscal Discipline in the Federal System: Experience of the States.* Washington, DC: ACIR.

Barro, Robert. 1989. "Ricardian Approach to Budget Deficits." *Journal of Economic Perspectives,* 3, no. 2 (spring): 37–54.

Boyd, Donald. 2002. *State Spending for Higher Education in the Coming Decade.* Boulder, CO: NCHEMS.

Brecher, Charles, Raymond Horton, and Dean Michael Mead. 1994. "Budget Balancing in Difficult Times." *Public Budgeting and Finance,* 14, no. 2 (summer): 79–102.

Brinner, Roger E., and Joyce Brinner. 2002. "State Revenue Prospects and Strategies: Neither as Unpredictable nor as Grim as Feared." *Business Economics* (July): 22–32.

Buchanan, James M. 1976. "Barro on the Ricardian Equivalence Theorem." *Journal of Political Economy,* 84 (April): 337–342.

Caiden, N. 1999. "The Rhetoric and Reality of Balancing Budgets." In *Handbook of Government Budgeting,* Roy Meyers, ed. San Francisco: Jossey-Bass.

Conant, James K. 2003. "Wisconsin's Budget Deficit: Size, Causes, Remedies, and Consequences." *Public Budgeting and Finance,* 23, no. 2, (summer): 5–25.

Congressional Budget Office. 1996. *The Economic and Budget Outlook: Fiscal Years 1997–2006,* Appendix A. (May): 99–108.

Doyle, Richard, and Jerry L. McCaffrey. 1993. "The Budget Enforcement Act in 1992." *Public Budgeting and Finance,* 13, no. 2 (summer): 20–37.

Hovey, Hal. "The Outlook for State and Local Finances: The Dangers of Structural Deficits to the Future of American Education." Cited in "NEA Study Predicts Looming Fiscal Crisis in Some States Could Halt Progress in Improving Education." Available online at www.nea.rog/nr/nr981118.html (accessed March 8, 1999).

Jones, Bryan D. 1994. *Reconceiving Decision-Making Democratic Policy.* Chicago: University of Chicago Press, 1994.

Jones, Dennis. 2003. "State Shortfalls Projected Throughout the Decade: Higher Education Budget Likely to Feel Squeeze." *Kentucky Long-Term Policy Research Center,* 10, no. 1.

Jordan, Meagan M. 2002. "Punctuated Equilibrium: An Agenda-Based Theory of Budgeting." In *Budget Theory in the Public Sector,* Aman Khan and W. Bartley Hildreth, eds. Westport, CT: Quorum Books.

Joyce, Philip G., and Roy T. Meyers. 2001. "Budgeting During the Clinton Presidency." *Public Budgeting and Finance,* 21, no. 1 (spring): 1–21.

Kee, James Edwin, and Scott Nystrom. 1991. "The 1990 Budget Package: Redefining the Debate." *Public Budgeting and Finance,* 10, no. 1 (spring): 3–24.

Key, V. O. 1940. "The Lack of Budgetary Theory." *American Political Science Review,* 34, (December): 1137–1144.

Kurtter, Bob. 2002. Personal comments at Office of State Budget Director, State of Kentucky, Frankfort, Kentucky, September 18.

Lauth, Thomas P. 2003. "Budgeting During a Recession Phase of the Business Cycle." *Public Budgeting and Finance,* 23 no. 2 (summer): 26–38.

Levinson, Arik. 1998. "Balanced Budgets and Business Cycles: Evidence from the States." *National Tax Journal,* 51 no. 4 (December): 715–732.

Lindblom, C. 1959. "The Science of Muddling Through." *Public Administration Review,* 19 (spring): 79–88.

McCallum, Ben T. 1984. "Are Bond-financed Deficits Inflationary? A Ricardian Analysis." *Journal of Political Economy,* 92: 123–135.

Moody's Investors Services. 2002. *Rating Changes and Refinements for the 50 States from 1973 to Date,* New York: Moody's Investors Services.

National Association of State Budget Officers. *State Expenditure Report.* Washington, DC: National Association of State Budget Officers, various issues.

National Association of State Budget Officers. 1992. *State Balanced Budget Requirements: Provisions and Practices.* Washington, DC: National Association of State Budget Officers.

National Association of State Budget Officers. 2001. *The Fiscal Survey of States.* Washington, DC: National Association of State Budget Officers, December.

National Conference of State Legislatures, Fiscal Affairs Program. *Preliminary State Budget and Tax Actions Report 2002.* Available online at http://www.ncsl.org/programs/fiscal/presbta02.htm.

National Conference of State Legislatures, Fiscal Affairs Program. "State Budget Gap Deepens to $58 Billion." Available online at http://www.ncsl.org/programs/press/2002.pr020724a.htm.

Proctor, A. J. 1992. *Structural Balance.* New York: New York State Financial Control Board.

Reschovsky, Andrew. 2002. "Wisconsin's Structural Deficit: Our Fiscal Future at the Crossroads." Robert M. La Follette School of Public Affairs, University of Wisconsin-Madison, May.

Savage, James. 1992. "California's Structural Deficit Crisis." *Public Budgeting and Finance,* 12, no. 2 (summer): 82–97.

Savage, James. 1994. "Deficits and the Economy: The Case of the Clinton Administration and Interest Rates." *Public Budgeting and Finance,* 14, no. 1 (spring): 96–112.

State Policy Research. 1998. "Identifying Structural Deficits." *State Policy Reports,* 16, no. 14: 12–19.

True, James. 1995. "Is the National Budget Controllable?" *Public Budgeting and Finance,* 15, no. 2 (summer): 18–32.

Wildavsky, A. 1964. *The Politics of the Budgetary Process.* Boston: Little, Brown.

Wildavsky, A. 1975. *Budgeting: A Comparative Theory of Budgetary Processes.* Boston: Little, Brown.

Wolkoff, Michael. 1999. "State and Local Budgeting: Coping with the Business Cycle." In *Handbook of Government Budgeting,* Roy Meyers, ed., 178–196. San Francisco: Jossey-Bass.

CHAPTER 10

E-Government Financial Management Models

Craig L. Johnson

E-government spending will constitute a significant portion of future expenditures at all levels of government. E-government investment projects involve expensive capital investments and operating expenditures on risky information technology (IT) projects and programs intended to enable government to deliver information and services in new and innovative ways. E-government investments involve electronic and information technologies that are a part of the IT hardware and software investment world–servers, routers, application packages, telecommunications infrastructure upgrades, etc.–but the potentially more enduring and transformative benefits from e-government involve much more than new hardware and software.

E-government requires government to integrate IT into program service delivery in ways that change the traditional way government does business, while saving government–and therefore taxpayers–money over the long term. E-government projects often require extensive collaboration between the public and private sectors, experts in information technology, public administration, and budgeting and finance, and across agencies and all levels of government.

Most initial e-government spending involved building Web portals to provide constituents with a common Internet gateway into government offices. Now government portals are up and running and agencies are being encouraged, often in collaboration with the central information technology office and private sector vendors, to offer a menu of information and services online. The bundle of information and services offered on-line by government can be viewed as its e-government portfolio.

The e-government portfolio must be accounted for and reported on within the new governmental accounting standards framework. The government accounting and financial reporting model changes significantly with the implementation of Governmental Accounting Standards Board (GASB) Statement No. 34.[1] Now governments must report a government-wide financial statement, which differs significantly from the traditional presentation of government operating position (Kravchuk and Voorhees, 2001). The new government-wide financial operating statement is referred to as the "statement of activities." The statement of activities focuses on net program costs by reporting program revenues and expenses before general revenues. Also, governments must now distinguish governmental activities from business-type activities, but both must be reported on the new government-wide financial statement. GASB Statement No. 34 also mandates that government-wide financial statements use the economic resources measurement focus and full accrual basis of accounting. In general, the new reporting model has significant implications for how e-government finances are managed, accounted for, and reported on.

This chapter discusses how e-government finances should be managed. We describe e-government financial management models to further the understanding of several key e-government financial decisions. As shown in Figure 10.1, government can use three basic models to manage their e-government finances: (1) traditional IT model, (2) infrastructure-finance model, and (3) vendor-finance model. Each model is described according to its revenue streams, financing methods, budgeting, and accounting and financial reporting components. E-government financial management models can be used to generate and manage a large flow of funds to support a variety of cross-agency information technology and programmatic investment projects.

Traditional Information Technology (IT) Financing Model

Traditionally, spending on IT was intended primarily to keep up with hardware and software advancements in internal business process technology, such as computer system upgrades from mainframes to personal computers. Early IT spending was mostly financed using a pay-as-you-go approach, with operating budgets funded by general fund appropriations. Occasionally, a portion of the proceeds from a general obligation

Figure 10.1
E-Government Financial Models

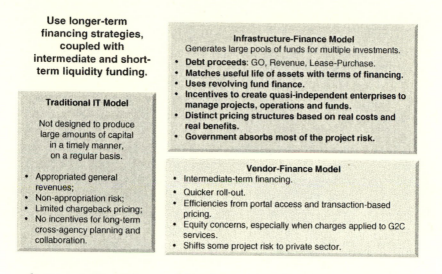

Use longer-term financing strategies, coupled with intermediate and short-term liquidity funding.

Traditional IT Model

Not designed to produce large amounts of capital in a timely manner, on a regular basis.

- Appropriated general revenues;
- Non-appropriation risk;
- Limited chargeback pricing;
- No incentives for long-term cross-agency planning and collaboration.

Infrastructure-Finance Model
Generates large pools of funds for multiple investments.
- **Debt proceeds**: GO, Revenue, Lease-Purchase.
- **Matches useful life of assets with terms of financing.**
- **Uses revolving fund finance.**
- **Incentives to create quasi-independent enterprises to manage projects, operations and funds.**
- **Distinct pricing structures based on real costs and real benefits.**
- **Government absorbs most of the project risk.**

Vendor-Finance Model
- Intermediate-term financing.
- Quicker roll-out.
- Efficiencies from portal access and transaction-based pricing.
- Equity concerns, especially when charges applied to G2C services.
- Shifts some project risk to private sector.

or lease rental bond issue sold in the municipal securities would be dedicated to IT spending.

Traditionally, most IT activities have been accounted for in internal service funds, which is consistent with the traditional role of the IT unit as a service provider within government. Internal service funds are used to report activities where an agency provides goods or services to other funds, departments, or agencies of the government on a cost-reimbursement basis. The internal service fund usually has a chargeback system where the central IT unit allocates costs to their customers–intra-government agencies–for services rendered and receives budgeted funds to cover their costs. Internal service funds do not normally charge prices; rather, they operate off of cost allocations (Davenport, 1996).

In most internal service arrangements, the physical infrastructure (e.g., telecommunications infrastructure) and hardware are often leased to the line agency by the central IT unit. While cost allocations may be sufficient to cover most of the direct costs from providing services, they are generally insufficient to cover large, project-specific investments with long payback periods. The cost allocation system used to support many IT budgets does not provide a sufficient and sustainable amount of revenue to implement full-scale e-government development in a comprehensive fashion by itself. However, a financing strategy that couples an internal service fund approach with an enterprise-based charging system that supports intermediate or long-term financing from government debt may be effective.

The traditional model is not adequate in the e-government era. It does not produce a sufficient amount of funds in a timely manner and on a regular basis. Operating funds are subject to substantial and recurring non-appropriation risk arising from political and fiscal factors outside of the control of e-government officials. Moreover, the traditional model requires e-government projects that are capital-intensive with large, upfront fixed costs and low marginal costs to compete in the annual budgeting cycle with operating programs designed meet immediate constituent needs (e.g., health care)—a competition that e-government advocates often lose. Finally, the traditional model is not conducive to the sustained, long-term cross-agency planning and collaboration that is necessary for e-government projects to realize their full potential.

The traditional model should be revised and expanded to fulfill the demands placed on government for online services and transactions. Specifically, an e-government financing model must be able to (1) generate substantial funds in a timely manner and at reasonable cost, (2) ensure that cash flows are subject to minimal non-appropriation risk, (3) shift a substantial portion of project risk from the government to private vendors, and (4) account for and report on resources in ways that create incentives for government to generate revenues to cover costs and that incorporate budgetary incentives for officials to engage in projects that produce net benefits for the government and constituents. The discussion in the next two sections on the infrastructure finance and vendor finance models provides a necessary expansion of the traditional IT financing model.

Infrastructure Finance Model

The infrastructure-financing model has proven successful at financing a wide variety of major capital improvements and can be an effective and efficient financing mechanism to support the next wave of e-government investments. Infrastructure financing models are designed to generate large pools of funds for capital investment projects. Government capital investment projects are usually financed with debt proceeds. The maturity of the debt issue should closely match the useful life of the assets being financed.[2] In general, assets with a long useful life should be financed with long-term debt, and assets with a short useful life should be financed with short-term debt. Perhaps most importantly, short-term assets should never be financed with long-term debt, which would leave the government paying debt service (principal and interest) long after the assets lose their value. For e-government investments with a short useful life, short-term notes are appropriate. For intermediate and long-term investments, bond and lease-backed financing programs are appropriate, possibly with some initial short-term financing to get the project started.

There are three basic types of debt securities: general obligation, revenue, and lease rental. General obligation (GO) bonds have been used sparingly in the past to finance traditional IT spending. GO bonds are full faith, and credit debt securities secured by the general taxing power of the issuing government. GO bond debt service is repaid from general governmental revenues. Most project-specific debt financing involves revenue bonds, which are sold to finance projects that are intended to be self-sustaining. These projects are often financed and implemented by public enterprises (authorities). The projects are designed and managed to generate enough revenue through user charges and other non-tax revenue sources to meet their debt service payments and cover operations and maintenance activities.

Prior to issuing revenue bonds, a feasibility study is usually conducted by technical experts (engineers, architects, etc.) to evaluate the project's ability to generate enough revenue to cover its expenses over the life of the outstanding debt issue. If the financial feasibility study indicates that the enterprise will not be able to cover its costs, the project may be restructured before implementation to make it more financially viable, or a political decision may be made to use general government revenues to meet any potential shortfalls, in effect placing a call option on the government's general fund. This call option, however, is designed as a back-up to protect against revenue shortfalls, and is not intended to support the full cost of the project.

A public authority is commonly established to isolate the revenue generation process from political risk. The public authority is usually fiscally and politically independent from the general government. For example, public authorities commonly have their own governing board, a separate administrative and personnel system, bonding authority, and control over their own revenue sources, including the rate-setting process. Public authorities often have independent authority to establish charges to generate annual revenue that is sufficient to cover their fixed and operating costs. For e-government services, enterprise systems can charge prices to provide an incremental revenue stream to support debt service payments, and other e-service related costs.

Governments also sell lease rental securities, particularly to support an on-going program of office equipment purchases. Lease rental securities (in some places referred to as certificates of participation (COPs)) usually include an annual appropriation requirement that is structured to cover rental payments. The rental payments are made based on the agreements in the leasing contract. Often, individual departments budget monthly fees to the centralized IT department, which pools the budgetary funds into a single appropriated lease payment to the vendor. In a lease rental financing, the rental payments are structured to cover principal and interest payments on the lease rental bonds.

Another innovative funding technique used in infrastructure finance is the revolving fund. Revolving funds are designed to be self-sustaining programs that recycle funds to finance successive generations of projects over an extended period of time. Revolving fund programs were initially developed in the mid-1980s to finance wastewater treatment projects mandated by the federal government, but implemented by state and local governments.[3] Since then the basic revolving fund concept has been extended to other areas of infrastructure finance. Revolving funds are seeded with dedicated capital from various sources, including grants, asset sales, borrowing, and equity contributions. The seed capital is then often leveraged by borrowing funds from the municipal securities market. Leveraging is used to expand the resources available to the fund. Leveraging involves using fund assets to provide additional security for debt repayment, enabling financing to be raised that is a multiple (e.g., 4 to 1) of fund assets. Revolving fund managers then lend the funds to infrastructure projects at low or zero cost. The projects are designed to generate enough revenues to repay the loans from the revolving funds. The incoming revenues are then pooled and recycled into future lending or granting activities. Revolving fund programs have been successful at providing ongoing financing programs for large-scale infrastructure improvements.

Statement No. 34 of the Governmental Accounting Standards Board

With the technological ability to deliver government services online, coupled with the implementation of Statement No. 34 of the Governmental Accounting Standards Board, government line agencies and central IT agencies should use enterprise fund accounting when appropriate, which reflects the new external, programmatic orientation of e-government activities. Enterprise funds are used to report activities for which external users are charged for goods or services. According to the Governmental Accounting Standards Board (GASB) (Governmental Accounting Standards Board, 1999), activities are required to be reported as enterprise funds if any one of the following three criteria are met: (1) debt is secured by a pledge of net revenues from fees and charges of the activity; (2) the costs of providing services, including capital costs such as depreciation or debt service, are to be recovered with fees and charges, rather than with taxes or similar revenues; and

(3) pricing policies establish fees and charges to recover costs, including capital costs. Fees and charges accounted for in enterprise funds should be derived from real costs, not a fabricated budgetary figure often used in internal service funds, where cost figures are "backed into" based on the budgetary resources of the intra-government customer.

Enterprise fund systems are especially appropriate for government-to-business (G2B) services.[4] Enterprise fund pricing systems should be based on an analysis of demand for G2B services. G2B prices may be set to cover marginal costs. Or, as a matter of public policy, G2B prices may be explicitly set to cross-subsidize government-to-citizen (G2C) services (Johnson, 2001, 2002).

The new government-wide financial operating statement, the Statement of Activities, focuses on net program costs by reporting program revenues and expenses before general revenues. Figure 10.2 provides a sample Statement of Activities that includes lines for G2C, government-to-government (G2G) and G2B services. G2C and G2G services are reported as the primary government's governmental activities with expenses and program revenues. Program revenues are shown after expenses, and are composed of charges for services, operating, and capital grants and

Figure 10.2
Government-wide Statement of Activities Including E-Government Operations

| | | Program Revenues | | | Net (Expenses) Revenue and Changes in Net Assets | | |
| | | | | | Primary Government | | |
Functions Primary government	Expenses	Charges for Services	Operating Grants and Contributions	Capital Grants and Contributions	Governmental Activities	Business-type Activities	Total
Governmental activities							
GTC	XXX	X	X	X	(XXX)	----------	(XXX)
GTG	XXX	X	X	X	(XXX)	----------	(XXX)
Other functions	XX,XXX	X,XXX	XX	XX	(XX)	----------	(XX)
Total governmental activities	XX,XXX	X,XXX	XXX	XXX	(XXX)	----------	(XXX)
Business-type activities							
GTB	XXX	X,XXX	X	X	----------	XXX	XXX
Other business-type activities	X,XXX	X,XXX	XX	XX	----------	XXXX	XXXX
Total business-type activities	XX,XXX	XX,XXX	XX	XX	----------	XXXX	XXXX
Total primary government	XXX,XXX	XX,XXX	X,XXX	X,XXX	(XXXX)	XXXX	XXX
		General revenues-detailed			XXXX	XX	XXXX
		Contributions to permanent funds			XXX	----------	XXX
		Special items			XX	----------	XX
		Transfers			XX	(XX)	----------
		Total general revenues, contributions, special items, and transfers			XXXX	XX	XXXX
		Change in net assets			XX	XXX	XXX
		Net assets-beginning			XXX,XXX	XXX,XXX	XXX,XXX
		Net assets-ending			XXX,XXX	XXX,XXX	XXX,XXX

contributions. G2G activities are also reported under governmental activities in the government-wide Statement of Activities. However, G2G activities should still be accounted for in internal service funds which have a proprietary fund type measurement focus and basis of accounting. But for government-wide reporting purposes, Statement No. 34 requires reporting internal service fund activity as a governmental activity, not a business-type activity (GASB, 1999, p. 156).

The net assets of enterprise funds can now have a direct, positive impact on the governments operating statement. G2B program revenues need not be isolated in an enterprise fund, subject to a "transfer-in" raid, but may now be passed directly through the financial statement to the Total Primary Government, Net (Expenses) Revenues column. The pass-through, unlike an actual transfer of funds from the enterprise fund to the general government, occurs only on paper and does not adversely affect the financial condition of the enterprise fund. G2B services reported as business-type activities can have a transparent, direct, and positive effect on what is the last line of the Government-wide Statement of Activities–Net assets-ending–which should become the new "bottom line" of government for informed information consumers.

E-government investments involve spending and managing capital assets. Most capital assets (e.g., expensive computer hardware and software) should be depreciated over their estimated life. Other capital assets that are long-lived and stationary in nature are considered infrastructure assets, according to GASB Statement No. 34. Infrastructure assets are not subject to depreciation as long as the government uses an asset management system to manage the infrastructure, and preserves the useful life of the asset. This is referred to as the modified approach for maintaining the life of infrastructure assets.

Capital assets will be recorded in the Statement of Net Assets, along with long-term liabilities, and reflected in the Statement of Net Activities, Net Asset lines. This should have the effect of reducing the bias against purchasing e-government capital assets in general, and against purchasing e-government capital assets with long-term financing instruments in particular. In addition, since capital assets and outstanding debt, along with funds restricted for debt service, are recorded on the Statement of Net Assets, there is also an incentive for government officials to engage in positive net present value (NPV) projects. Positive NPV projects should generate program revenues and capital asset valuations (after depreciation) that are greater than the principal and interest costs of financing.

Also, now program revenues and expenses associated with providing G2C, G2G, and G2B products and services can be readily compared. By knowing the net revenue generated by G2B services, and the net losses incurred in G2C and G2G activities, if any, officials can simultaneously develop the appropriate prices for G2B services and subsidy levels for G2C and G2G services. This should help to increase transparency and public accountability in e-government financial management.

On the Statement of Activities report, all funds will be presented using the economic resources measurement focus and accrual basis of accounting. The economic resources measurement focus, traditionally used for enterprise funds, is designed to show whether a fund is better off economically as a result of the transactions of the period. The accrual basis of accounting reports expenses rather than expenditures. Expenses account for the resources consumed during the period and not actual spending (expenditures). Inventory items show up on the balance sheet as assets until they are used (and expensed), thereby reducing the old bias against purchasing assets that would show up immediately as an expenditure, but whose asset value would not have been recorded on the governments operating statement (Statement of Revenues, Expenditures, and Changes in Fund Balance), nor recorded on the balance sheet, but rather recorded in the General Fixed Assets Group (which is eliminated by Statement No. 34).

Prior to the implementation of Statement No. 34, the measurement focus for reporting governmental activities was the "flow of current financial resources," which was designed to report whether a fund is better or worse off financially in the short term as a result of the operations of the period. Using this approach, large purchases are counted as expenditures in the year purchased, and annual principal and interest payments are also reported as expenditures, but the value of capital assets are not reported on the operating statement or balance sheet because they are not *financial* resources.

The new governmental accounting and reporting standards fit well into the infrastructure finance model, potentially reducing the bias against financing large-scale e-government capital investments. The infrastructure finance model is flexible, durable, and robust because it is able to finance a wide variety of major capital improvements, generate substantial sums of money for capital investment, and raise funds relatively quickly across the maturity spectrum. It can be an effective and efficient financing mechanism to support the next wave of e-government investments.

Vendor-Finance Model

Vendor financing involves a public-private partnership that enables the government to shift much of the risk of financing e-government projects to the private sector. Without a direct appropriation, vendors contract with governments to develop and operate the state's official Internet portal and/or create new online services. Vendor-financing is an intermediate-term financing strategy where private vendors pay for start-up costs, often using internal funds or equity proceeds. The private firm puts capital upfront in the expectation of receiving future cash flows from e-government services. The vendor makes a business decision that the discounted value of expected net cash flows from e-government services will be greater than the upfront investment. Those cash flows come from constituents—private firms and citizens. Private vendors expect to recoup their investment by generating revenue from charging users transacting government business over the Internet, and charging businesses for "enhancing" the value of basic government information. These two added-value approaches form the primary funding streams behind the *vendor-finance model.*

An example of an enduring and award-winning vendor-financed public-private partnership is provided by the state of Indiana where Indiana Interactive, Inc., a subsidiary of NIC Inc., developed and operates the state's official Web portal, *accessIndiana*, and is responsible for delivering several e-government services through the portal. According to Indiana Interactive, Inc., the portal has over 220,000 pages of information and over 175 interactive services.

Interactive government services offered to businesses (G2B) and those offered to citizens (G2C) form distinct market segments. While G2C and G2B services require the same upfront capital costs and have operating cost structures that are similar, they likely have different demand functions and different price elasticities of demand; the demand for G2C and G2B services should be distinct. Moreover, while the price elasticity of demand inevitably varies across the broad spectrum of G2B e-services, in general G2B services should be less price elastic than G2C services for several reasons.

For certain lines of business, G2B services are essential inputs into the process of making money. G2B services may be essential to a business operation because certain types of information may be available only in official government records, like property or drivers' records, and there may be few, if any, substitutes for such official information. The information is an essential business input, and the cost savings from purchasing the information online in an electronic, user-friendly format should increase the demand for the service. Moreover, the monetary value of e-services to businesses is tangible and quantifiable, since the savings from transacting business online rather than onsite or over the telephone has direct monetary value in a business environment, and businesses often purchase government information to resell at a profit. Also, business organizations have a better technological infrastructure, and business users have a more sophisticated knowledge of computer technologies than the average citizen. In addition, businesses have a greater ability and willingness to pay for services that are comparable to G2C services in terms of production costs. As a result, different pricing structures are appropriate for G2B and G2C e-commerce.

Substantial direct benefits from G2C services may not be as tangible and identifiable for individual consumers. In these early stages of e-government, Web portals may be cumbersome and online service fragmented, uncustomizable, and generally difficult to use. In addition, the demand for G2C services will likely remain elastic as long as governments maintain other channels for citizens to conduct service transactions, keeping open at least a few motor vehicle offices, for example. There is anecdotal evidence that G2C online motor vehicle registration renewals are price elastic. In Arizona, for example, adoption rates skyrocketed for online vehicle registration renewals once the $6.95 charge was eliminated in 1998. Therefore, it is reasonable to assume that for a given change in price, in general, demand changes more for G2C services than for G2B services.

For G2C services,[5] the total charge for online service (TOC) commonly consists of the statutory fee (SF) for service delivered through a traditional channel and the portal charge (PC) for online service,

TOC = SF + PC.

The G2C portal charge (PC) consists of a convenience charge (CC),[6] or a convenience discount (CD), and the electronic payment processing fee (EPP),

$$\text{PC}_{\text{G2C}} = \text{CC}_{\text{G2C}} \, (\text{-CD})_{\text{G2C}} + \text{EPP}_{\text{G2C}}.$$

The EPP fee is the cost of processing electronic payments such as debit and credit cards, which is commonly paid to a merchant bank or other financial intermediary.

Governments may provide a convenience discount (CD) where the cost to the public is lower for services transacted online. Only a few state governments use CDs. Governments appear reluctant to use CDs despite anecdotal evidence that demand is price elastic. For online services with an elastic demand, properly planned and implemented CD programs may translate into substantial long-term administrative savings and significant social benefits. CDs will substantially bolster adoption rates, and initial financial losses incurred from CDs on G2C services may be offset by increases in G2B prices.

Two-Part G2B Pricing Structure

Sometimes the pricing structure for G2B services is the same as described above for G2C services. But many governments offering added-value business services have designed a two-part G2B pricing structure:

$$PC_{G2B} = PS_{G2B} + aPT_{G2B}.$$

Firms are charged a fixed annual "premium service" (PS) subscription fee plus a per transaction fee (PT) for individual searches, downloads, reports, or other particular services or information. PS and PT can be viewed as a menu of fixed[7] and variables charges that can be changed over time to recover fixed (capital) costs and cover annual operating costs. The two-part pricing structure also provides flexibility in pricing over time, allowing the government to develop services and pricing schemes based on an understanding of demand from empirical analysis, which should ultimately generate greater customer satisfaction and more own-source revenue.

Governments can use e-service prices to increase overall consumer surplus. Consumer surplus is the net benefit produced when consumers actually paying less for a particular service than they are willing to pay. By applying different pricing structures to G2C and G2B services, officials can increase overall consumer surplus to their constituents. Based on the Ramsey rule,[8] consumer surplus is maximized when rates (prices) are set inversely proportional to their price elasticities of demand. Since most G2B services are likely to be, on average, more price elastic than G2C services, prices for G2B services can be set higher to explicitly subsidize G2C services.[9] This is a particularly prudent policy for G2C services that produce substantial social benefits. G2B pricing structures should also incorporate the potential resale value of certain information, wherein businesses can purchase certain types of information wholesale, perhaps below producer (government) costs, and sell the information for a profit at the retail level after adding some value.

One advantage the vendor model has over the other financial management models is in the nature of risk shifting. In vendor-finance models, the private firm is often responsible for developing and operating the Web portal and many e-government services, usually under the supervision of a government-sponsored governing board. The private firm absorbs many of the risks associated with an e-government investment: project completion risk, technology obsolescence risk, adoption rate risk, technology integration risk, and political appropriation risk. By shifting some risks, governments are able to reduce their overall IT risk profile without sacrificing the benefits from major, large-scale e-government projects—more information and services provided online for constituents.

An active governing board is also important to ensure that e-government projects are designed and implemented in the interest of constituents. The types of services brought online should be citizen-demand driven, not just driven by the demands of stakeholders with the greatest ability to pay. In addition, charges should be set low enough to bolster adoption rates, while still generating sufficient, but perhaps not maximum, revenue. Moreover, governing boards must understand the demand structures of their services in order to negotiate vendor contracts that protect constituent interests.

Conclusion

This chapter has analyzed three e-government financial management models. While these models are not mutually exclusive, and may be used in combination, the traditional model of IT financial management, in particular, is not adequate in the e-government era. The infrastructure- and vendor-finance models can be used individually, but may work best when used in combination.

The infrastructure-financing model is able to generate large pools of funds in a timely manner and on a regular basis, and lends itself to creative financial management arrangements. Vendor-financing models generally enable a quicker roll-out of e-government services and shift some project risk from the public sector to the private sector. In addition, they provide substantial flexibility in pricing e-services. E-government finances should be managed to take advantage of enterprise funds and the new accounting and financial reporting requirements in GASB Statement No. 34. G2B and G2C on-line services should be segmented, with G2B pricing structures designed to help subsidize G2C services that produce substantial social benefits.

Finally, decisions on e-government policies and administration should be informed by public finance and financial economic theory and analysis and implemented using proven financial management techniques. E-government should be designed and implemented in the interests of constituents, whose finances must be managed effectively, efficiently, and with an eye toward public accountability and strengthening the public trust.

Appendix

User Charges and User Fees in E-Government Finance

User fees involve the sale of licenses by government to engage in otherwise restricted or forbidden activities.[*] User charges, in contrast, are

---

[*] This section is taken from Johnson, Craig L., "Financing and Pricing E-Government Services: An Analysis of Web Portals." Report for the PricewaterhouseCoopers Endowment for the Business of Government, October 5, 2001.

prices charged for voluntarily purchased services. While user-charge based services may benefit specific individuals or businesses, they are provided to fulfill basic governmental responsibilities.

The distinction between fees and charges is important for online services provided by government, since most government services currently provided online are also provided, for a fee, through traditional mechanisms. For example, the cost to renew a vehicle registration is a user fee. Purchasing a vehicle registration is a necessary condition for operating the vehicle simply because the government requires a payment for granting someone the privilege of driving a car. The additional charge for the option of renewing a vehicle registration online is a user charge, provided there are alternative ways of renewing the registration. A critical element of a user charge is that it's voluntary, implying that consumers are not legally required to purchase the service, or if they are, that there are alternative providers. Therefore, most so-called convenience fees are user charges.

Some government officials are hesitant to impose additional charges for online services, but user charges have several benefits. First, they enable government to make people who benefit directly from the service pay for the service. This improves equity because non-users are not forced to fully subsidize users. Secondly, they help officials gauge constituent preferences and estimate demand for a service. This can enhance operational efficiency and improve internal resource allocation decisions because mandated services need only be provided for users at the level they demand, and only non-mandated services for which there is a demand need be provided. In addition, user charges make more economic sense when demand is price elastic, implying user demand is price sensitive. The more price elastic demand, the greater the potential for inefficiency if users do not face true costs.

User charges, however, may not be appropriate where the services intentionally subsidize low-income or otherwise disadvantaged households, or when the services provided generate substantial social benefits. User charges are commonly set based on both the benefit derived from usage and the cost of service provision. The basic rule for efficient economic pricing requires marginal benefit to equal marginal cost. For services that primarily benefit the direct user, the price charged should equal marginal cost. When social benefits are also generated from providing a service, then aggregate social benefits need to be considered. In cases where benefits can be separated into those enjoyed by direct users and those by society in general, prices should be divided among users (a user charge) and all of society (general revenues). Indeed, user charges make more economic sense when direct users enjoy most of the benefits.

User charges should be based on marginal benefits, not total benefits. For example, it may be argued that as more people become comfortable with using Web portals, and more services are put online, the benefits from individual online usage will spillover to all of society by reducing the digital divide and making government more constituent-centric. In such a case, direct users should only be charged their marginal benefit, not the entire social benefit. Direct users should cover marginal operating costs, but capital costs that provide societal benefits can be covered with general revenues. User charge pricing also makes sense when it can reduce congestion, which may require charging different prices at different times. There should be a difference between demand at peak times and off-peak times. This implies that Web portal charges should not be fixed, but should vary based on congestion. Higher prices are appropriate at peak times and lower prices, perhaps zero-charge, at off-peak times. Internet resources, such as bandwidth, are limited, and once the service becomes crowded additional users impose congestion costs on other users. Therefore, another role of the user charge can be to reduce overcrowding during peak hours, which should increase constituent satisfaction and overall usage.

Notes

1. The requirements of Statement No. 34 are effective for all government financial statements beginning after June 15, 2003.

2. Debt maturity and useful asset life should be closely correlated for the bulk of the financing, unless there are extraordinary exogenous circumstances, such as a substantial risk premium/discount in a maturity sector, or in the case where the debt service schedule is structured to match the expected incremental revenue from the project.

3. For a detailed discussion of revolving fund finance, see Craig L. Johnson, "Managing Financial Resources to Meet Environmental Infrastructure Needs: The Case of State Revolving Funds," *Public Productivity and Management Review*, 18, no. 3 (spring 1995).

4. G2B refers to electronic services provided by government (G) to businesses (B); similarly, G2C and G2G refer to services provided by government to citizens and governments (intra- and inter-governmental).

5. This discussion of e-government pricing is drawn from Johnson (2001).

6. The convenience charge is often referred to as a convenience fee, implying the extra charge is for the convenience of transacting business over the Internet. But if customers still have the option of using the service through a traditional venue (e.g., over-the-counter), the convenience fee is a user charge. Please see Appendix 10.1 for a discussion of the distinction between user fees and charges.

7. This fixed charge could differ across groups of customers.

8. The Ramsey Rule is a basic tax efficiency principle for optimizing tax structures. The rule states that in order to reduce total excess burden from taxation, tax rates on goods should be set inversely proportional to their price elasticities of demand. By setting high tax rates on inelastic goods and low tax rates on elastic goods, the percent reduction in the quantity demanded of each good is reduced, resulting in less excess burden from the imposition of taxes.

9. For a more detailed exposition of this argument, see Johnson (2002).

References

Davenport, Larry W. 1996. "Internal Service Fund Functions: Should They Be Required to Compete with Private Vendors?" *Government Finance Review* (October 1): 263–275.

Gant, Diana Burley, Jon P. Gant, and Craig L. Johnson. 2002. *State Web Portals: Delivering and Financing E-Service.* The PricewaterhouseCoopers Endowment for the Business of Government, E-Government Series, January.

Governmental Accounting Standards Board. 1999. Governmental Accounting Standards Series, *Statement No. 34 of the Governmental Accounting Standards Board, Basic Financial Statements—and Management's Discussion and Analysis—for State and Local Governments.* Governmental Accounting Standards Board of the Financial Accounting Foundation, June.

Johnson, Craig L. 2001. "Financing and Pricing E-Government Services: An Analysis of Web Portals." Report for the PricewaterhouseCoopers Endowment for the Business of Government, October 5.

Johnson, Craig L. 2002. "A Framework for Pricing Government E-Services." Working paper, September.

Kravchuk, Robert S., and William R. Voorhees. 2001. "The New Governmental Financial Reporting Model under GASB Statement No. 34: An Emphasis on Accountability." *Public Budgeting and Finance,* 21, no. 3 (fall).

Ramsey, Frank P. 1927. "A Contribution to the Theory of Taxation." *Economic Journal,* 37: 47–61.

CHAPTER 11

Integrating Theory and Practice
Financial Management Reform in the U.S. Federal Government

Larry R. Jones and Jerry L. McCaffery

The Government Performance and Results Act of 1993 (GPRA) has drawn great attention within the federal government and even from abroad. This is not surprising given the GPRA focus on strategic planning, customer involvement, performance and outcome measurement. Observers in New Zealand, one of the leading nations in the integration of performance and outcome measurement, have stated that the United States is a better example of reform than their nation (Scott, 2001). While this observation is subject to debate, it should not draw attention away from the fact that the core of recent U. S. government financial management reform is the Chief Financial Officers Act of 1990 (CFOA), because all improvements in financial management rest on the existence of accurate financial information. The Government Management Reform Act of 1994 (GMRA) extended the requirements of the CFOA across the federal government. If accurate financial data, reported consistent with the requirements of the CFOA, were linked to the budget planning and review process through GPRA, taxpayers and government managers would, in theory, be better able to see what they are paying for and what they are getting for their money (i.e., transparency would be vastly improved over current practice). This chapter assesses some of the requirements of these reforms and attempts to evaluate how well they are being implemented. It also addresses recent budget reform initiatives and how these are linked to financial management reform.

Why Institute Reform?

A key implementation assumption is that the information produced through these various financial management reforms will be used to make better decisions. There is reason to question this assumption given that any comprehensive reform in government is difficult to implement and manage, and that resources are not easily obtained to support implementation. These problems, combined with institutional preferences for the status quo, make successful reform very difficult to achieve, as we explain in this chapter. However, there is some evidence to suggest that real progress is underway. For example in the case of GPRA, the President's Office of Management and Budget (OMB) reported that for the first time, the Department of Veterans Affairs budget shows performance plans and resource requirements in the same alignment.[1] An OMB official saw this as a distinct improvement over previous reporting, characterized as a clutter of tiny accounts in the budget mixed with large accounts that are not homogeneous and lack systematic alignment with programs:

> [R]esources used [presently] to achieve results are not charged to the programs' budget accounts. Salaries and expenses are often entirely or partially paid centrally; there is no charge for some accruing benefits; many support services are provided free or at a subsidized price; and fixed assets may be paid centrally.[2] . . . Resources are not linked to results in budgeting, and managers have no incentive to maximize results with a resource limit.[3]

It is this potential to link data produced in compliance with CFOA standards to the performance and results measures deemed necessary by the GPRA that could lead to provision of accurate and meaningful information for decision makers in both the Executive branch and Congress. If achieved, this would represent a highly significant reform of federal budgeting, accounting and reporting.

Comprehensive Reforms Enacted

The decade of the 1980s was a turbulent period for financial management in the federal government, which culminated in the passage of the

Chief Financial Officer Act of 1990.[4] While the savings and loan rescue had drawn attention to one set of federal financial management oversight mechanisms, other problems existed that, though less apparent, were very real: GAO and the Office of Management and Budget (OMB) studies of "high risk" programs in 1989 identified as many as 78 different problems which posed potential federal liabilities reaching into the hundreds of billions of dollars.[5] Other problems identified by Congress included failure of the IRS to collect $63 billion in back taxes, an alleged $30 billion in unnecessary inventories bought by the Department of Defense, and losses at the Federal Housing Administration estimated at over $4 billion. The identification of these problems led to passage of the CFO Act and other recent financial management reforms.

In 1990 Congress passed the Chief Financial Officers Act (CFOA) to improve federal financial management.[6] Subsequently, Congress enacted the Government Performance and Results Act (GPRA, 1993), and the Government Management Reform Act (GMRA, 1994)[7] to extend the mandate for financial management reform in the federal government and accelerate its implementation. These three pieces of legislation, together with the Federal Managers' Financial Integrity Act[8] (FMFIA) and the Inspector General Act,[9] establish a framework for improved accountability and provision of better, and more timely information for Congress, the president, and the public. This structure may lead not only to improved financial management, but also to better decision making, a more responsible government and a public better informed about the actions and resource capacity of its government.

The Chief Financial Officer's Act[10] created the critical leadership and mechanisms to integrate all of these reforms and to keep the process of financial management reform moving. It established a Chief Financial Officer (CFO) for the United States in the Office of Management and Budget and 22 CFOs in the major agencies. The Chief Financial Officer (CFO) position was established to provide leadership, policy direction, and oversight of federal financial management and information systems, including productivity measurement and improvement, credit and asset management, cash management, and internal controls. While some of this structure had been created by administrative directives prior to 1990, the passage of the statute gave this reform effort a statutory basis and a life beyond the particular policies of any particular presidential administration or Congress.

The CFO of the United States is appointed by the president, with the advice and consent of the Senate. As deputy director for management, the CFO is charged to "provide overall direction and leadership to the executive branch on financial management matters by establishing financial management policies and requirements, and by monitoring the establishment and operation of federal government financial management systems" (CFO Act Sect. 202). Essentially, the CFO is tasked to provide the framework and guidelines indicating how the government should implement financial management improvements. This is to be done by specifying the type and form of information that will be produced by the government's financial management systems, identifying projects that will accomplish systems integration, and estimating the costs of the plan. The act requires that OMB submit annual reports to Congress on the status of federal financial management.

With regard to the rest of the executive branch, in accordance with the CFO Act, CFOs were appointed and confirmed by the Senate for 24 major departments and agencies. CFOs also have been appointed for major agencies within large departments. Deputy CFOs have been appointed as well, and a CFO Council was established to determine objectives and policy and to oversee implementation. Within individual agencies, CFOs report directly to the head of the agency regarding all financial management matters. CFOs oversee all financial management activities relating to programs and operations of the agency, and they develop and maintain integrated agency accounting and financial management systems, including those for reporting and financial controls. CFOs direct, manage, and provide policy guidance and oversight of financial management personnel, activities, and operations. They are also charged with monitoring the financial execution of the budget.

One CFO observed that he had not thought that there was anything wrong with federal financial management until he discovered that in many programs it was difficult to tell the results of outlays, the location and value of inventories, the wear and tear on buildings, the aging of receivables, and the souring of loan and loan guarantee portfolios. He noted that on the OMB high-risk list were some $14 billion in delinquent loans at the FHA, $13.7 billion in Department of Energy contracting that was inadequately managed, and Medicare and Medicaid misestimates of $21 billion and $9 billion, respectively. He further observed that in some cases the financial numbers were not known on an auditable basis, due diligence was not taken in extending the nation's credit and credit guarantees, and that the results of expenditures and investments often were not measured (when they were, there was little assurance that the measures were accurate and comparable across programs).[11]

In 1985, former comptroller general Charles Bowsher had recommended a number of changes in federal financial management, suggesting that "for too long" financial management in the federal government had been practiced as a rather narrow function involving mainly accountants and budget analysts, and that the idea of bringing management issues and analyses to bear upon budgeting and accounting questions had not "taken root" throughout the federal government, although some progress had been made in this direction during the previous two decades. Bowsher called for a more comprehensive and consistent budget and budgetary accounting, better data on federal agency performance, improved planning for capital investment decision making, increased accountability for costs and results, and refined fund controls. Bowsher concluded, "Action along [these] . . . lines would provide the federal government with the tools needed for practicing pro-active financial management."[12] Bowsher observed that this would not be a short-term effort.

Financial management reform takes place far from the publicity of the legislative-executive budget arena, yet the amounts that are at stake are so large that it is an effort well worth applauding, even if the attainment of an auditable financial statement for all federal agencies is not perfectly obtained.

The CFO Act is intended to knit the budget and accounting functions together and to centralize all financial management functions at the department and agency level, with a chief financial officer reporting to the head of each agency or department. The centralizing bias of this act was further revealed in the official creation of a Chief Financial Officer for the federal government as an Executive Deputy Director in the Office of Management and Budget, whose task it is to take the lead on concept creation and development of system-wide efforts to improve federal financial management. Passage of the Budget Enforcement Act compromise in the Reconciliation Act of 1990 during the same time period tended to obscure the importance of the CFO Act, but now enough time has passed to allow for the full impact of this piece of legislation to be recognized. Its goal is to dramatically change the shape of federal financial management, relying, like the Budget and Accounting Act of 1921 before it, on prominent and proven financial management practices in the private sector. Among these are the requirement for one chief financial officer responsible for all financial functions reporting to the head of the agency, an annual financial statement that is understandable in generally accepted accounting terms and which will bear the weight of an annual audit and Inspector General certification, and a reduction in the number of separate department/agency accounting systems. The act also has mechanisms for continuing modernization of financial systems.

The major initiative of the CFO Act is preparation of auditable consolidated financial statements for departments, agencies, and the federal government as a whole. Audit responsibility has been assigned to the Inspectors General (IGs) of each department and agency. IGs have performed some audits on their own. GAO has provided assistance and oversight in this effort. IGs may contract with outside private sector accounting firms to assist or to conduct audits, and GAO also has authority to outsource audits when appropriate.

Congressional oversight for implementation of the CFO Act and the other acts continues to be provided by the two oversight committees that sponsored much of this legislation—the House Government Reform and Oversight Committee and its subcommittee on Government Management, Information, and Technology, and the Senate Governmental Affairs Committee. However, substantial responsibility for oversight has been delegated to the General Accounting Office (GAO). Under the guidance of former Comptroller General Charles Bowsher and Comptroller General David Walker, the GAO has been a driving force behind much of the implementation effort[13] as is OMB.

Pursuant to the CFO Act, in the mid-1990s auditable financial statements were prepared for selected departments and agencies. The GMRA extended the audit requirement from 10 to 24 departments and agencies and for all types of accounts, required auditing within five months of the close of the fiscal year to make data available in a timely manner for the budget process, and directed an audit of the government wide financial statement for FY 1997. Departments and OMB have made substantial efforts since this time to enable preparation of these statements and to improve and consolidate agency accounting systems. Considerable investments of time, money, and energy have been made to reengineer and refine agency accounting procedures and processes. In addition, OMB has expanded the scope of initiatives to improve federal financial management under the authority of the CFO and other acts. However, initial progress was slow.

For example, in December 1996, the Department of the Navy (DON) submitted its first Annual Financial Report required by the CFO Act and the GMRA. The report was reviewed by the Office of the Secretary of Defense (OSD) Comptroller and by the Naval Audit Service prior to its publication in 1997. Information was obtained from financial and functional managers throughout the Department of Navy and from the Defense Finance and Accounting Service (DFAS) to produce the DON Principal Statements that provide the foundation for the Annual Financial Report. This report included an overview of the DON, outlined its history, mission, and programs, and included the Principal Statements and their related footnotes and a supplemental information section. This information was meant to be used by managers within the DON, Congress, and the public.[14] However, an audit of the information submitted was highly critical and found many errors. The objective of achieving a "clean" audit report (i.e., with no errors) was not met. As of this writing it still had not been met for the Navy or for the Department of Defense as a whole.

Underlying both the CFOA and GMRA was the need for a comprehensive set of federal accounting standards and principles. The Federal Accounting Standards Advisory Board (FASAB) made responsible for achieving these goals is staffed by the three principal agents concerned with overall financial management in the federal government: the Secretary of the Treasury, the Director of OMB, and the Comptroller General. The federal government has never had a body of "generally accepted accounting principles."[15] Recognizing that such standards were needed, and that compliance must be measured on a regular basis, FASAB was tasked and subsequently developed a set of financial and cost accounting principles and standards. By fiscal year 1999, auditors for 21 of the 24 CFO Act agencies reported that those agencies' financial systems did not substantially comply with FFMIA's requirements. The three agencies in compliance were the Department of Energy, the National Aeronautics and Space Administration, and the National Science Foundation.

The inability of many federal agencies to accurately record and report financial management data at the end of the year and on an ongoing basis for oversight and for decision-making purposes is a serious weakness. Without reliable data on costs, decision makers cannot control or reduce costs, effectively evaluate programs' financial performance, or direct additional resources to underprovided programs. In addition to requiring annual audited financial statements, the CFO Act sets expectations for agencies to build effective financial management organizations and systems and to routinely produce sound cost and operating performance information throughout the year. While progress seems slow, the key is to take steps to continuously improve internal controls and their underlying financial management systems. A clean audit opinion is important, but it should not be seen as the ultimate goal. The ultimate goal is a government that delivers more for less, where the outcomes of governmental action benefit its citizenry, and where the costs to achieve those outcomes can be seen, understood, and tracked. The Federal Financial Management Improvement Act helps promote this goal by creating a process for continuous improvement in financial management systems and ensuring that those systems routinely provide reliable and useful information on a timely basis: "With such information, government leaders will be better positioned to invest scarce resources, reduce costs, oversee programs, and hold agency managers accountable for the way they run government programs."[16]

Evaluating the CFO Act

The Federal Financial Management Status Report and Five Year Plan for 2000 noted that with the majority of agencies attaining a clean audit opinion, the emphasis on financial management reform would switch to improving financial management systems (OMB, 1998, p. 7). It is useful to review the size of this task. In 1997, the agencies covered by the CFO Act reported that they had 751 agency financial management systems that consisted of 1,117 applications in operation and 123 agency financial management systems under development or phased implementation.[17] In 1992, the federal government operated 878 systems with 1,306 financial management systems.[18] In the five-year period the number of systems and applications have both decreased somewhat (about 15 percent), but the federal government financial management apparatus remained large and diverse. There is no trend toward one system or just a few applications, nor should such a trend be expected. Rather, environmental complexity must by met with appropriately diverse, but effective, systems. In 1997, on average, the 24 CFO agencies operated 31 systems with over 46 applications and had 5 under development.

Agencies are also quite diverse in their financial management applications. These range from acquisition, budget, travel, payroll (several systems), inventory, property held for sale, and loans, to systems tailored to carry out the agencies own special needs built up over decades before the push to financial management reform gathered steam. Financial management systems follow the mission of the organization; thus in 1997, DOD had 16 payroll systems because it hires permanent and temporary employees and pays their salary and benefits. For temporary employees the systems differ somewhat among the services. Agriculture is complex because it is a mixture of federal employees and functions, grants and aids to various entities, and direct payments to individuals. This complex environment is not evolving toward a steady state: In September 1997, agencies indicated that they intended to planned to replace or upgrade 71 percent of their operational applications![19] This means that the environment will continue to be turbulent as new systems are developed and implemented and old systems become obsolete and are replaced. Since no perfect end state exits, this cycle of obsolescence and rebirth may continue almost forever. Moreover, the possibility exists that the rate of system development may lag behind system obsolescence. The 1998 Status Report (OMB, 1998, pp. 15–16) observed that agencies expected to upgrade 708 of their applications within 5 years, but that 891 would reach the end of their useful life span in that period. The obsolescent systems could still be operated, but inadequate financial management systems might lead to costly errors.

The departments to watch for this sort of turbulence include Defense, Transportation, OPM and the Small Business Administration. The number of systems and the applications within them indicate the size and complexity of the federal government's efforts. Those who chafe at the lack of speed with which reform is progressing must understand the tremendous complexity of the task at hand and accept that these financial management reforms do not envision applying one perfect system and/or one application to the federal government. The goal is to create systems that accurately report data in understandable ways on a timely basis according to generally accepted professional standards. This may continue to be an evolutionary and turbulent process as agency missions change, new ways of doing business are tested, and innovations in hardware/software occur. The 2000 Five-Year report states that 10 years earlier, before the passage of the CFO Act, federal agencies could not answer the most basic questions about the state of their finances, could only offer guesses at how much they had spent the previous year, did not gather financial data automatically, and consistently and could not report their finances in accordance with accepted professional standards because no such standards existed for the federal government.[20] All of this has changed. The 2000 Five-Year plan basically declared that the battle for clean audit statements had been won and the battleground would now shift to improving financial management systems.[21]

By the year 2000, all 24 agencies covered by the CFO Act issued annual audited financial statements in 2000. More than sixty percent of them received clean audit opinions. The Treasury Department issued a consolidated financial statement for the U.S. Government for the first time in 1998. A complete set of government-wide basic accounting standards was issued in 1996 by the Federal Accounting Standards Board (FASAB), itself created in 1990. In October of 1999, the Institute of Certified Public Accountants, an internationally acknowledged authority, recognized FASAB's standards as "generally accepted accounting principles (GAAP).[22] These efforts have led to visible payoffs in modernizing financial management practices and saving taxpayer dollars. For example, in 1999 the federal government made almost 1 trillion payments electronically, about 80 percent of all non-tax payments. Small-purchase bank card use had increased fourfold since 1995, saving taxpayers $450 million in administrative costs. Streamlined processes led to the reduction of delinquent debt owed the federal government from $60 billion to $53.3 billion. Agencies continued to work on modernizing and replacing their financial management systems and applications. OMB continued to help by ensuring that these efforts were carefully planned and adequately funded.[23] These are major achievements. More remains to be done, however. Fifteen of the 24 CFO agencies had clean audit opinions (62.5 percent), but nine did not. Moreover, the budget authority for these nine agencies amounted to more than 65 percent of federal government discretionary budget authority in 1999. This means more than $380 billion was spent in 1999 without the guarantee of a clean audit opinion. By any measure, this is a substantial amount of money, thus it is perhaps more accurate to suggest that the battle is being won, but it is not over.

Federal Budget Process Reform

Important developments are also occurring in the federal budget process. Under the Government Performance and Results Act of 1993, the federal government is embarked on a performance measurement experiment that may lead to performance budgeting. In this iteration, strategic planning and customer/clientele involvement have been added to activity groupings, the search for appropriate outcomes, and the effort to cost outcomes and evaluate changes in outcomes that might come from adding additional dollars. The strategic planning and customer involvement facets of this iteration are important changes. In the fifties, performance budgeting seemed to focus on costs of activities, implicitly assuming that cost-per-unit numbers would eventually lead to more centralization of the budget process and allow a few people to make good judgments about all activities by following the changes in a few key numbers. Under GPRA, this iteration of performance measurement and strategic planning in the 1990s seems more open to decentralization of goals throughout the organization and to forcing customer/client desires to percolate up into consideration at higher levels. The promise of a more useful and effective system seems tantalizingly close. This promise has attracted subordinate levels of government in the United States (Florida, Texas, Arizona) and elsewhere (New Zealand). However, the record of budget innovation suggests that one ought not be too optimistic about reform. Ultimately, object of expenditure data still remain linked to the accounting system; hence, when worst comes to worst, the data for line-item analyses can still be found. Particularly for legislators, line-item analysis seems to have an enduring appeal.

The most recent reform introduced in federal budgeting was that implemented by President George W. Bush and his Office of Management and Budget in the FY 2003 President's Budget. This budget instituted "performance-based budgeting" to link funding to performance measures and accomplishments for federal departments and agencies. In initiating performance-based budgeting for the federal government, President Bush brought the United States in line with many of the more progressive national practices around the world. Other nations including New Zealand, Australia, Canada, Switzerland, and the United Kingdom have employed performance and output or results-oriented budgeting practices over the past decade or more. Furthermore, in testimony before the Senate Armed Services Committee on February 5, 2002, OMB Director Mitchell Daniels noted that the reform interests of the Bush administration were not limited to performance budgeting. While stressing the importance in evaluating programs on the basis of achievements, Mr. Daniels also expressed approval with members of the committee who asked him about other budget reforms.

The first issue addressed was whether there was a need for new budget "caps" or spending ceilings, given that the caps previously enacted in the early 1990s and re-endorsed in the Balance Budget Act of 1997 had expired. Also mentioned was the fact that Congress often exceeded the caps even when they were in force. Mr. Daniels agreed with some members of the committee that new caps should be enacted to control congressional proclivities to spend. A second and related issue was whether new spending caps should include a ceiling for national defense spending. Mr. Daniels indicated the strong preference of the administration against a cap on national defense appropriations in a period when the nation was at war with the forces of terrorism around the globe. In rejecting the idea of a cap for defense spending, the testimony of Mr. Daniels conformed to the views expressed by Chairman of the Federal Reserve Bank Alan Greenspan in testimony to Congress with the same week. When asked directly by members of the House Budget Committee whether caps should be reinstated for the discretionary (nonentitlement) portion of the federal budget, Mr. Greenspan responded that he believed new caps were needed in all areas but national defense. Both Mr. Greenspan and Mr. Daniels reflected the priorities of the Bush administration in placing the war on terrorism as the highest priority in policy and budgeting.

However, in responding to questions from members, Director Daniels also expressed the interest of the administrations in exploring biennial budgeting and budgeting-by-results contracting. While the biennial budget initiative was not an element of the President's 2003 budget, the fact that the Bush administration expressed interest in biennial budgeting appeared to open the door to discussion of even more ambitious reform; for example, with multi-year budgets similar to the types of budget processes in use in the United Kingdom, where budgets are enacted for a three-year period and reviewed biennially, and in Australia, where three-year "running cost" budgets had been used in the 1990s with some success. Australia has, as of this writing, shifted to an even longer five-year cycle of budget enactment and review.

Budget critics have long argued the inefficiency of the annual budget cycle (McCaffery and Jones, 2002).[24] Annual budgeting satisfies congressional preferences for a cycle that provides maximum opportunity to reward constituents with spending largess. In fact, as political scientists have observed for decades, virtually all congressional politics is local politics; that is, driven by the need to satisfy the special interests of members' districts or states. And while this opportunity provides the benefits of democratic representation and responsiveness, it does not lend itself well to expenditure control, fiscal discipline, or efficiency in either spending or program performance. Rather, annual spending encourages the behavior well-known to both budget officials and academics—spend it or lose it. Further, because the problems that governments face are never constrained to periods of one year, spending demand is, given the nature of service demand, always multi-year in character. The annual budget cycle produces all kinds of perversities and strategic misrepresentation in budgeting (Jones and Euske, 1993).[25] Perhaps the best recognized is the end-of-year spend-out phenomenon, where real spending priorities often are ignored in the rush to spend or obligate every dollar available, regardless of whether the items purchased or the services provided are really needed.

Unfortunately, the annual spending cycle encourages exactly the types of behavior that Congress, the executive branch, and various audit agencies of the federal government, including the General Accounting Office, indicate is abhorrent. The incentives implicit in the "spend it or lose it" approach to budgeting push otherwise prudent budget executors to the brink of Anti-Deficiency Act violations, including spending for things not authorized or appropriated by Congress, or spending from budget accounts dedicated to one purpose for other purposes not authorized by law. And the obvious incentive from annual spend-outs is to over spend rather than under spend if what is not expended is likely to be lost in the next budget.

For these and other reasons, nations including those mentioned above have moved to multi-year budget appropriations and execution, providing programs the authority to over spend or under spend in any one particular year so long as spending conforms to totals appropriated for the longer term period of years. This provides greater opportunity for budget and program managers to execute budgets more efficiently, with greater attention to management "steering" to achieve desired results and increased flexibility to adjust short- and medium-spending plans to fit the demands of efficient budget execution.

Related to multi-year budgeting for results is the issue of contracting for results. Contracts for results written into budgets in other nations have included agreements between legislative bodies and program agencies to produce a set amount of outputs or outcomes (e.g., in New Zealand) or contracts within the Executive branch between control agencies such as OMB and departments and agencies.[26] In the United Kingdom, the Department of the Treasury engages in such contracting under the oversight of the Prime Minister and Cabinet and Parliament. However, the real work of holding service providing agencies to their contracts is held by officials of the Treasury. There are other examples of contracting in budgeting in Australia, Switzerland, Sweden, Denmark, and elsewhere. It is too early to attempt to evaluate the experience of the Bush administration with performance budgeting, but in several years there will be opportunity to assess the efforts and success of OMB with this approach, and that of Congress and the executive branch in continued implementation of the Government Performance and Results Act.

Evaluating Implementation: Where to Start?

The goals of the Government Performance and Results Act are far broader than those established in the CFO and GMRA Acts because GPRA subsumes within it the financial management reforms of the CFO Act. Ultimately, part of performance measurement will rely on financial data taken from systems created and guided by the CFO Act. GPRA expressed congressional will that performance measurement and reporting be introduced throughout the government. GPRA required federal agencies to complete a strategic plan incorporating performance measures and submit to it to OMB by September 1997.[27] Reports were submitted, although some were late. Problems with these submissions are treated in a later section of this chapter. The issues associated with implementing GPRA are highly complex, particularly because the law calls for output, outcome, and performance measurement linked to costs. This ties the purpose of GPRA to CFOA implementation. Without accurate accounting information, the types of analysis required by GPRA are impossible to perform so as to have any confidence that the data reported are valid and reliable. More on this issue is reported below.

What makes GPRA so difficult to implement effectively? In summary, (1) unspecified goals and missions, (2) agencies that do not shift their services in response to shifts in demand, and (3) the difficulty of defining and measuring outcomes. We address these issues in greater detail subsequently.[28]

CFOA and GMRA require preparation of auditable financial statements. However, with the passage of GPRA, the financial management reform mandate grew to encompass a much more ambitious set of goals. The purpose of reform, according to former Vice President Gore, was to report to American taxpayers what "bang" they were getting for their buck. He predicted unrealistically, undoubtedly influenced by his anticipation of using success as an element of his bid for the presidency, "[B]y 1998, the federal government will have its first financial statement. Americans will soon know for the first time whether they are getting what they pay for."[29] Alas, as with so many rosy political statements, Gore's politically motivated prediction was terribly optimistic. Neither act was implemented fully, and in many cases only marginally or not at all by 1998. Within six months after the elections of 2000, the Bush administration had adopted a much more realistic view of implementation—that it is needed but will require a long time and great effort to achieve.

Preparation and auditing of financial statements generally falls under the scope of responsibility of accountants and auditors. However, reengineering financial systems requires the talent and experience of seasoned financial managers, often assisted by knowledgeable external consultants. Relating costs to outcome measures in order to influence budgets requires the skills and participation not of just accountants, auditors, and financial managers; it demands the close attention of policy and budget decision makers. It is perhaps an understatement to observe that the task of improving federal financial management has become much more complicated than proponents of the CFO Act initially envisioned. Fundamentally, GPRA makes the critical and necessary connection between costs and policy and program; it recognizes the fundamental necessity to make financial data relate to program in a timely and useful manner.

Former Comptroller General Charles Bowsher stated that, "financial management is finally becoming a top priority of federal managers." Annual preparation of financial statements and the independent audit opinions required of them are "bringing greater clarity and understanding to the scope and depth of problems and needed solutions. These annual public report cards are also generating increased pressure to fix long-standing problems."[30]

In assessing the potential impact of the CFO Act, GPRA, and the other laws noted, the intent is that in the future, budget numbers will accurately relate to audited statements of government assets and liabilities. Better information should indicate to decision makers where to focus additional efforts to improve financial management. Better financial management also is intended to lead to more informed public policy decisions.

In assessing the longevity of GPRA reform, OMB Controller Joshua Gotbaum noted that those who thought GPRA would simply fade away were wrong. Moreover, said Gotbaum, "[W]e have accomplished much. Almost a hundred federal agencies developed strategic plans. They followed up with three sets of annual performance plans and this past spring (2000) completed the first-ever set of annual performance reports."[31] He claimed that many agencies did an excellent job of developing useful, informative FY 1999 performance reports and mentioned two in particular.

First, the Department of Transportation linked program decisions to results by linking its various air, rail, and highway programs to department-wide objectives such as safety, economic growth, and mobility. They then tracked performance by these measures, which Gotbaum, suggested were heavily oriented toward outcomes (i.e., reduction in transportation-related fatalities and injuries), rather than intermediate measures of program performance or output measures. Gotbaum suggested that DOT was clearly using strategic planning and performance management to steer programs and set priorities. And when it needed to redirect its efforts, or shift priorities, it did so, using these tools.

Gotbaum also praised the Department of Education for working hard to develop measures of effectiveness and for being honest about the measures' limitations. Many education programs involve grants that operate by funding the work of non-profits, states and local governments. While the Department of Education keeps track of the ultimate outcomes (e.g., nationwide literacy), they also recognize that these are affected by many factors beyond the particular grant program. Gotbaum noted that many federal agencies face this challenge.[32]

In 1996, the General Accounting Office (GAO) warned that the issues associated with implementing GPRA were highly complex. First, as noted earlier, *unclear goals and missions* have hampered the targeting of program resources and caused overlap and duplication. Secondly, agencies often do not quickly and easily *shift their focus* in response to consumer demand and congressional directives because major changes in services and processes are required. Further, *outcomes are difficult to define and measure.* However, GPRA provides a mechanism for assessing agency mission and program while downsizing and increasing efficiency, at least in theory. More federal agencies are recognizing the benefits of focusing on outcomes rather than activities or outputs to improve program efficiency and effectiveness. However, we may note that Australia has never attempted to measure outcomes because the task is too difficult from the perspective of the Department of Finance, and New Zealand, which initially led the charge to measure outcomes, began to shift back to outputs in 2001 for the same reason.

GAO also warned that strong and *sustained congressional attention* was needed to ensure GPRA success. According to GAO, Congress needed to hold periodic, comprehensive oversight hearings and to gather information on measurement of outcomes. Congressional leadership was urged to determine how GPRA performance goals and information drive daily operations, how agencies use performance information to improve their effectiveness, to review progress in improving financial and information systems and staff training and recruitment, and to pay attention to how agencies are aligning their core business processes to support mission-related outcomes.[33]

In summary, beyond CFOA and GMRA, with the passage of GPRA the financial management reform mandate has grown to encompass a much more ambitious set of goals. As Congressman Dick Armey put it in July 2000:

> The Results Act we passed eight years ago recognizes that government must be held accountable. Used properly, the Results Act is a powerful tool by which agencies can measure their performance and root out the waste, fraud, and abuse of taxpayers' money. . . . [O]ur federal government exists for the people. Federal agencies are and should be expected to spend tax dollars efficiently and to implement the laws Congress passes as they are intended—to achieve results. [However] The most brilliant laws can fail to make America a better place when the execution is mishandled.[34]

How well is execution being managed? To this question we turn to subsequent sections of this chapter.

Executive Branch Implementation Dynamics

OMB has responded with a number of initiatives to the challenge posed by simultaneous implementation of these ambitious pieces of legislation. To understand the priorities for change, it is useful to review the OMB eight-point program for improving financial management.

1. Financial Management Organization: To establish a government-wide and agency level organization structure to support financial management improvements and foster communication and cooperation among financial management personnel.
2. Financial Management Personnel: To improve financial management education, training, and career development programs for federal financial management employees.
3. Accounting Standards: To establish clear and comprehensive accounting standards and performance measures.
4. Financial Systems: To develop and operate agency-level systems that process, track, and provide accurate, timely information on financial activity in the most cost-effective manner.
5. Internal Controls: To design and operate management structures that ensure accountability for achieving results, complying with laws and regulations and safeguarding assets.
6. Asset Management: To design loan programs, collect taxes and other debts owed to the federal government, and to manage federal cash.

7. Federal Assistant Management: To provide management guidance for grants to state and local governments, colleges and universities, and not-for-profit organizations.

8. Audited Financial Statements: To create and maintain a systematic means for disclosing information that enables decision makers to understand the financial implications of budgetary, policy, and program issues and for strengthening agency accountability for sound management performance. [35]

In issuing five-year plans for improving federal financial management, OMB has attempted to integrate the tasks required by each of the individual acts in a consistent manner. Former Director Alice Rivlin asked departments and agencies to prepare financial statements and develop performance standards and measures that could be reported both in financial statements and in budget proposals submitted to OMB. Spring reviews of strategic and performance plans, including performance measures developed by departments, were conducted by OMB as early as 1995 and 1996.

In September 1995, OMB issued two important documents, a memorandum on strategic planning and a new addition to the budget guidance circular A-11. In the strategic planning memo, the director stated that the A-11 revision was to be the first step in a larger effort to link various GPRA requirements to the budget process. The addendum to A-11 provided instructions for preparation and submission of strategic plans.[36] OMB intended that performance measures be used in budget review. As former OMB Director Alice Rivlin observed, "Given today's questioning of government, we must work harder: GPRA gives us a set of tools, an excuse to do what we should be doing anyway.[37] This supports the OMB stewardship role to ensure that departments and agencies prepare both auditable financial statements as stipulated by the CFO Act and performance measures as demanded by the GPRA. Budget examiners in the five Resource Management Offices in OMB were designated as the principal points of contact responsible for analysis of agency budget submissions.

OMB reviews agency strategic plans, performance plans and measures, and where possible attempts to use audited financial statement information to improve the integrity of budgets examined. Performance measures were required from agencies for FY 1999, but they were included in some budget submissions for FY98. Pursuant to a new part of OMB Circular A-11, OMB staff has assisted agencies in developing measures and comprehensive plans for improving their financial systems and management practices. Strategic plans prepared by departments and agencies are intended to indicate what initiatives need to be taken and in what order of priority.[38] Department and agency strategic plans are not identical, in that each organization has its own definitions of mission, performance plans and measures, and priorities.

In his testimony in the summer of 2000, Joshua Gotbaum emphasized that GPRA had been a high priority for the Clinton administration: "The administration created a set of priority management objectives: After Y2K, GPRA was ranked the next most important objective for the first several years. Now the administration's number one priority management objective is to "use performance information to improve program management and make better budget decisions." Gotbaum noted that OMB's work implementing GPRA had been intensive and long-standing. He pointed out that OMB staff helped draft the original legislation, and each year OMB has worked to improve and use agency performance information in its internal discussions on agency funding levels. He said that at the same time OMB had worked actively with agencies to improve their performance plans and to increase their own use of GPRA information. Within OMB, he observed that the same analysts who work on a particular agency's budget and management issues every day also reviewed the agency's performance reports and worked with the agency on GPRA implementation. This was certainly one of the major goals of GPRA, and one that some who were skeptical of GPRA implementation felt might not be achieved. Gotbaum added that each year in developing the president's budget, OMB employed more performance information and made better use of it. He said that for the FY 2001 process, OMB asked the agencies to provide performance information as part of their budget submissions and, using that information, OMB was better able to analyze what performance could be achieved at different levels of investment. Relevant performance information was used for every agency budget review.

In looking ahead, Gotbaum observed that one ideal OMB was pursuing was to help agencies realign their budget accounts to follow programmatic lines. He noted that the budget structure is in most cases distinctively different from the groupings of program performance goals set out in individual plans. While historical and logistical reasons explain why this happens, the fact is that this divergence makes it harder to compare program results accurately with program costs. One of OMB's goals is to examine how better alignment would contribute to better integration of performance plans and budgets, and how OMB could better account for the cost of individual programs and activities. Gotbaum noted that another ideal would be to use performance measures more actively as an incentive to better management. He said, "rewards could increasingly be tied to program performance goals and their achievement. Similarly, distribution of grants could consistently be tied to past performance and promised performance. Rewards for contractors could also be tied to performance targets. Good information and appropriate incentives are powerful drivers toward achievement of performance targets. . . ."[39]

In the absence of strong support from the president, OMB and Congress would retard the effort to implement the CFOA, GPRA, and the new federal financial management structure supported by this and other financial management reform legislation. However, Presidents Clinton and Bush have supported implementation of these reforms. OMB has been steadfast in its determination to move ahead with these reforms. Shawn O'Keefe, then Deputy Director, OMB, in a letter on May 11, 2001, reviewed the GAO report on a survey of federal managers regarding results-oriented agency climates, measurement of program performance, and use of performance information to make decisions in high performance organizations. O'Keefe said, "It is encouraging that significantly more managers overall reported having performance measure (both outputs and outcomes) for their programs. But it is disappointing that you found a significant decrease in the reported use of performance information from your last report" (in 1997). O'Keefe continued that these findings were "consistent with our view that while many agencies have made substantial progress implementing the Government Performance and Results Act (GPRA), many others are still simply going through the motions. While all are in full compliance with the law—preparing strategic and annual plans and finalizing performance reports—most are not yet at a stage where they are truly 'managing for results.'" O'Keefe added that systematic inclusion of performance into budget decisions had yet to occur, and that GPRA "has not been fully harnessed to improve management and program performance."[40] He then promised that OMB was going to formally integrate performance with budget decisions and that program managers would be help accountable for managing to targets. His letter indicates that these plans would come to fruition in the FY04 budget, where detailed performance and budget data will establish a strong public link between agency budget requests and performance measurement in the president's budget.

Grappling with Implementation

Due to the budget squeeze on discretionary spending resulting from efforts to reduce the deficit and an executive and Congressional decision in 1994 to further downsize the federal workforce by 272,900 employees by 1999, reform has had to proceed in an environment of staff reductions.[41] The size of the 1994 personnel reduction was based on the logic that half of the 700,000 federal financial management and related positions estimated to be engaged in "overseeing" work (managers, supervisors, and specialists in personnel, procurement, budget, and audit) could be eliminated if up-to-date information systems were put in place. It also was estimated that 100,000 new positions would need to be created and filled by new people with new skills, or by retrained employees, thus leaving a net reduction of 250,000 equivalent full time employees. This number was increased as the bill passed through Congress.[42] By 1999, federal full-time equivalent employees had been reduced from 3.017 million in 1992 to 2.686 million, a reduction of 331,000. In the narrower category of civilians civil service employees, the federal government was reduced from 2.174 million employees in 1990 to 1.778 employees in 1999, a reduction of 396,000 employees. The year 1990 was chosen as the base year because the CFO Act was passed then, and because it allows for benchmarking of the "peace dividend" from the end of the cold war. Most civilian personnel reductions came from defense, which was downsized from 1.006 million civilian employees in 1990 to 681,000 in 1999, a reduction of 325,000, or 82 percent of the total federal reduction. (Military personnel were reduced from a high of 2.213 million in 1987 to 1.386 million in 1999, for a total 827,000 positions or more than 37 percent).[43] As these reductions were made, departments and agencies faced a dilemma in that they were asked to do more and to perform more efficiently while also developing and implementing major financial systems improvements with fewer people. Moreover, the new systems demanded skills the current employee cohort did not have. In the mid-1990s this tension was clearly apparent. Scott Fosler commented:

> The problem is that the position reductions have begun, but in very few instances have the new systems been developed or the new employees and skills put into place. Consequently, throughout the government one finds fewer employees attempting to operate cumbersome old systems, while simultaneously designing and implementing new systems, but without the training or access to skills required to do either.[44]

To help remedy this situation, Fosler advocated a larger investment in training. He observed that top-rated businesses commonly invest as much as 10 percent of their payroll in training and development, while the federal government, by contrast, spends less than 1 percent of payroll costs for these purposes.[45]

Ron Young, Executive Director of the FASAB, observed that while agencies were actively pursuing changes needed in their financial management systems, progress is not as rapid as envisioned under the CFO Act and by some members of Congress. Young concluded that, "much of the slowness is due to the significant cutbacks in funding of government financial management and the resulting inability to attract and retain highly regarded financial management specialists."[46]

Meanwhile the pace of reform confronts a new problem. By 2010, some 70 percent of the personnel now working in financial management positions in the federal government will be eligible for retirement. The wave of retirements may begin as early as 2004. Accounting, auditing, budgeting, purchasing, contracting, disbursing—all the personnel specialties that comprise federal financial management will face a severe and prolonged diminution of expertise. The challenge of the next decade in federal financial management will be replacing these experts while keeping current systems functional. Reform may be subordinated to form. We assume that these retirements will slow, but not stop, reform efforts. In the meantime, there are other impediments to reform to consider.

GPRA Revisited

Review of CFO and GPRA and their associated vehicles as of 2002 suggests that steady progress is being made, albeit slowly. GPRA seemed to have attained a higher level of visibility with its broad bipartisan support, its emphasis on government accountability and performance, and its focus on the actual results of government actions, measuring outcomes rather than outputs. Its insistence on the requirement that agency results be integrated into the budget process makes it rare among governmental reforms, as does the fact that much of it has been carried out in a climate of downsizing, reinvention, and privatization of government functions.

Criticism of GPRA has focused on the complexity of its mission, credibility of the data produced, and its focus.[47] GAO has pointed out that performance measures chosen by agencies do not meet Congressional needs for oversight data and that agencies have problems producing credible performance data. These two points were eminently predictable from the start of GPRA. What was perhaps not as easily foreseen was the complexity of government and the grandiosity of the GPRA intent. GAO has noted that virtually *all government results are produced by two or more agencies,* and, as a consequence, mission fragmentation and overlap are widespread and cross-cutting programs are poorly coordinated, resulting in wasted dollars, customers who are confused and frustrated, and the undermining of overall effectiveness. In 2001, a best features list

drawn from department performance plans illustrated the attention paid
to cross-cutting goal identification, both those that exist within departments but between or among agencies, and between and among departments. Unfortunately, identifying cross-cutting goals does not mean that
problems of coordination and focus and unity of effort are solved. GAO
further notes that many state goals are outside the control of agencies,
departments, and even government. For example, those agencies that
would improve the economy, the environment, or an ecosystem do not
really have the capability to do so. They may have some impact on those
targets, but events totally unrelated and outside the control of the agencies may dilute, reverse, or overturn their efforts. The attempt to specify
outcomes—the move to some desirable end state—may always risk setting
up a goal that is not realistically attainable solely through government
action. Yet to stop at output measures is inherently self-defeating. GPRA
may be used as a cost-cutting measure as it encourages government to
operate more efficiently, but it is inherently very optimistic in its specification of outcomes that improve government and the life of the governed. Perhaps the bottom-line is that outcomes must be plausibly seen
to be impacted favorably by government action. In this sense a carefully
crafted statement is far superior to an exaggerated statement of what
might happen; that is, to reduce the effect of evil is plausible, when rid-
ding the world of evil is not plausible and only calls into question the
amount of resources used to pursue an unobtainable goal.

The structure of American government also poses a problem for
GPRA. Very few public service provision functions are performed by
the federal government alone. Even defense relies on state level components like the National Guard or cooperation from private sector contractors to produce weapons systems at acceptable prices. For agencies
who pass money through to states and local governments in grants and
aids or who pay non-profit corporations for health or welfare delivery
services, the problem of cross-cutting complexity and goal specification
and attainment are equally difficulty. Block grant agencies who pass
money to states have problems specifying outcomes because they can
not bind states to pursuing those outcomes; states may have other items
on their agenda than federal goals.

Ellen Taylor of OMBwatch, a public advocacy and oversight organization, observed that the non-profit community was only dimly aware
of GPRA and that federal agencies whose money ultimately went to
non-profits were similarly unaware of non-profits. OMBwatch warned
that this would be a problem for goal setting and for goal achievement,
as measures that are not correctly chosen can end promoting outcomes
that are undesirable.[48] OMBwatch advocated more non-profit interest
and involvement in GPRA by non-profits and a reaching out to all

stakeholders by those implementing the law at the federal level, including both Congress and the executive branch agencies. Taylor observed that GPRA success still depends on government's commitment to it, and that there was considerable uncertainty about whether GPRA was working.

Taylor urged that public access to information used to develop performance measures be improved and suggested that public knowledge in itself may lead to corrective measures.[49] As a case in point, she observed, "Although EPA never identified specific amounts of reduction in emission of toxic chemicals, the public accessibility of the Toxics Release Inventory helped create a 45 percent decline in the release of those chemicals."[50] This again suggests the great optimism with which some reformers view GPRA efforts.

Cross-Cutting Programs and Congress

Cross-cutting programs pose a special problem for Congress because it is not set up to review, fund, or exercise oversight of cross-cutting programs. Chris Mihm of GAO re-enforces this point:

> Unfocused and uncoordinated crosscutting programs waste scarce resources, confuse and frustrate taxpayers and program beneficiaries, and limit overall program effectiveness. Our work in over 40 program areas across the government has repeatedly shown that mission fragmentation and program overlap are widespread, and that crosscutting federal program efforts are not well-coordinated. For example, we have reported on 50 programs for the homeless that were administered by 8 federal agencies. Housing services were provided under 23 programs operated by 4 agencies, and food and nutrition services were under 26 programs administered by 6 agencies.[51]

Mihm argued that the government-wide performance plan and the agencies' annual performance plans and subsequent performance reports should provide Congress with information on agencies and programs addressing similar results. Once these programs have been identified, then Congress can consider the associated policy, management, and performance implications of crosscutting programs as part of its oversight over the executive branch. Mihm notes that this will present challenges to the traditional committee structures and processes, and observes that Congress has no direct mechanism to use in providing a congressional perspective to the president's government-wide performance plan or to agency goals, missions, and alternatives, particularly for mission areas and programs that cut across committee jurisdictions. It seems that the logical outcome of oversight of GPRA efforts will have to change the structure of Congress itself—an effort not lightly undertaken or easily accomplished.

Barriers to Implementation

In a *Counterpoint* essay in 1993, it was argued that the Chief Financial Officers (CFOA) and other financial management reforms might not achieve their objectives due to a number of barriers to implementation.[52]

1. Accounting system weaknesses
2. Congress passed the act for the wrong reasons
3. Inability of Congress to use financial statement data for decision making
4. Executive branch incentives to avoid scrutiny
5. Incapability within the management component of the President's Office of Management and Budget
6. Weaknesses of financial statements
7. Inability to successfully implement performance measurement in budgeting
8. Budgetary incentives to avoid identification of full program costs
9. Unachievable requirements for agency cooperation and compromise in implementation

It is useful to review some of these arguments to conclude this discussion.

Unachievable Requirements for Agency Cooperation and Compromise in Implementation

Counterpoint[53] observed that implementation of the CFO Act (and GPRA) requires extensive cooperation and coordination between OMB, the Department of the Treasury, GAO, 24 departments and agencies, two oversight committees of Congress, authorization and appropriations committees, the CFO Council, the Federal Accounting Standards Advisory Board, and other entities. It was noted that the track record for cooperation, coordination, and compromise of this magnitude between and among federal government entities in attempting broad scale reform was mixed at best.

However, GPRA is law; unlike other reforms that were the whim of one administration or another (Carter and zero-based budgeting; Nixon and management by objectives), GPRA has statutory underpinnings for its performance measurement requirements.[54] Consequently,

GPRA has been marked by steady deployment of more complex tasks; for example, the Strategic Plans of September of 1997 and Performance Plans in 1998 (and submitted with each budget since, revised to reflect actions in the president's budget) and the Performance Reports first submitted in March 2000, to be revised annually.

What was not recognized so clearly in the first evaluations of these reforms was the extent that government programs cut across departmental jurisdictions, over governmental boundaries, and through the public and private sectors, as Chris Mihm suggests above. Coordination problems are even more fundamental than supposed. This appears clearly when departments attempt to define performance goals that they have no chance of realizing because many of the factors that would produce success are outside their control. For example, a critique of the 1999 department performance plans criticized the Department of Education plan because it did not discuss coordination of specific programs with similar programs in other agencies, and the Department of Commerce was criticized for the absence of complementary performance goals and measures for the many crosscutting programs and activities in which Commerce shared responsibility with other federal agencies. This was seen as particularly serious in view of the fact that Commerce was essentially a "holding company" composed of numerous disparate missions, programs, and activities. In sum, it was clear that significant improvements had been made, but it was also clear that significant problems remained for all agencies as they attempted to envision concrete ways to affect outcomes, and particularly for those agencies with complex missions cutting across departmental lines, across governmental jurisdictions, and between the public and private sector.

Accounting System Weaknesses

Accurate and reliable accounting systems are critical to successful production of auditable financial statements. *Counterpoint*[55] suggested that departments and agencies might not invest sufficient effort to improve accounting systems to produce accurate data upon which financial statements would be based. This absence of investment was not predicted because departments would not want to make such an investment, but because they would lack the money. It appears that departments and agencies have invested considerably in improving their accounting systems. In some instances, they have also provided detailed estimates of the costs of substantial improvement and consolidation. The president and Congress initially made an effort to address these funding demands. For example, the president's budget for 1992 requested $647 million for funding financial systems upgrades, and

Congress appropriated $628 million.[56] But since this time, no significant amounts have been appropriated specifically for improving accounting systems, with the exception of funding for the Internal Revenue Service and the Department of Defense.[57]

Weaknesses in accounting systems still abound, and some cases cause large-scale problems. For example, current statutes dictate that excise taxes be earmarked for certain purposes, but according to GAO the IRS accounting system does not have the capability to segregate these funds by type. Consequently it is possible that the Superfund Trust Fund and the Highway Trust Fund may be receiving more or less than is due them. Another example is the inability of the IRS to match social security wage information and actual tax payments. The Social Security Administration receives payments based on wage information reported to IRS, even if the taxes are ultimately not paid. This results in amounts going to the Social Security Fund from other tax sources, and while the IRS knows there is a discrepancy, it could not identify the amount in 1995.[58] Testimony in 2002 by Dov Zakheim, the DOD Comptroller, about DOD accounting and financial management system problems was so compelling in its description of DOD's problems that it seemed that the reform efforts of the 1990s might not have happened. Insufficient funding to make improvements to accounting and related systems is still a significant problem.[59] It is clear that much work remains to be done and a significant investment in modernizing systems, upgrading procedures (e.g., data entry), and training people has to be made. Initial estimates were that the cost of financial management reforms covered by the CFO Act would be about $7.5 billion per year.[60] For 2000 it was estimated at approximately $7.6 billion.[61] In a decade of fiscal pressure, students of these reforms were correct in worrying where the money was going to come from and if it would be sufficient, but Congress and the executive branch thus far have found the funds to carry out the reforms. Whether or not that money found its way to the most appropriate places is still not clear. OMB's Report for 2000 states that the past decade had seen the downsizing of administrative financial management functions in government, along with a marked increase in the number of employees eligible to retire, and a highly competitive job environment for people with pertinent skills.[62] Thus substantial achievements have been made under difficult conditions, but more remains to be done.

Inability of Congress to Use Financial Statement Data for Decision Making

Counterpoint[63] speculated that even if Congress wished to implement the CFO Act for the "right" reasons (i.e. to stimulate needed financial reform), *and* even if financial statement data were accurate, Congress is institutionally incapable of making long-range financial decisions based upon information in financial statements. The same observation may be made with respect to the use of performance measures and strategic plans mandated by GPRA. It was argued that financial statements would not replace the annual budget as the primary methodology for resource decision making in the nation's capitol because the budget provides the money that keeps the wheels of politics rolling, and financial reports do not provide budget justification. What members of Congress and their staffs care most about in budgeting is winning and losing battles over programs and money to operate them. Further, it was argued that despite the work of some committees and some individuals, Congress as an institution appears not to have much interest in costs.

It is still not clear exactly how OMB staff and congressional oversight staff are going to use financial statement and performance data. OMB is still moving GPRA forward, but neither the president nor OMB can force Congress to use data as they wish. Congress will have to be persuaded that it is in its interest to do so before any significant change in congressional practice will occur.

Budgetary Incentives to Avoid Identification of Full Program Costs

Counterpoint[64] concluded that the CFO Act may fail to meet its goal of causing the full costs of programs to be considered from a financial management perspective at the point of decision because some agency budget analyst and decision makers might not be skilled enough to apply net present value to determine appropriate discount rates, or to carefully weigh benefit-cost ratios of alternatives from a long-range financial perspective.

The point of this criticism was that decision makers and program advocates in some instances do not want the full costs of decisions to be assessed in budgeting. Alteration of this incentive structure through implementation of CFOA, GMRA, and GPRA is unlikely. There remain very real incentives for departments and agencies to hide the full costs of comprehensive social welfare, national defense, public land management, transportation, energy, and other programs in the federal budget decision process. This tactic that rewards full cost concealment in the budget process was identified long ago by Aaron Wildavsky as the "camel's nose" strategy.[65]

The manner in which Congress makes decisions in the annual budget cycle at times stimulates the concealing of full costs. However, in considering the budget from a long-term perspective to achieve balance, and in attempting to insure the financial stability of entitlement programs, including Social Security, Medicare, and Medicaid, both Congress and the executive branch demonstrate an increasing ability to use more sophisticated analytical methods in budgeting. Appropriations committees now deal with some budget requests based on present value estimates, especially in credit programs and for major capital acquisitions. Appropriators are also particularly sensitive to full cost disclosure in this era of capped domestic discretionary spending. Congressional staff suggest that appropriators do not seek to hide full program costs, but rather have led the fight against "coercive deficiencies." They also note that appropriators are not so much resistant to using financial statement data, but rather have never been given clear examples of how and why such broadly aggregated and dated information ("quite dated" in the words of one staffer) should be used in the appropriations process. Moreover, congressional staff support our previous assertion that aggregated data is generally inconsistent with the congressional appropriation budget structure and cycle.[66]

Philosophically, some members of Congress and staff are likely to resist performance-based budgeting as a mechanistic approach to resource allocation because it assumes certain linear cause and effect relationships, while "very little of the federal government is so innocently linear."[67] However, whatever the virtues of the appropriators, congressional resource allocation decisions in the 1990s have typically involved "end games" of continuing resolutions, government shutdowns, omnibus appropriation acts, and reconciliation bills where pursuit of macro goals often requires dysfunctional side payments that confound logical approaches to resource allocation, such as performance indicators tied to costs.

Still the attraction of reform remains persistent: Speaking of GPRA, Congressman Dick Armey noted:

> This tool gives Congress the ability to identify what's working, what's not, what's wasted, what's duplicative, and to end wasteful and unnecessary spending. These laws are not ends in themselves; rather they are a means to obtain systematic, credible information about the operations of the federal government, while holding government accountable to the taxpayers. The core tenet of the Results Act is "you get what you measure."

Armey observed that the "urgent" too often crowds out the time for issues that are merely "important"–that too much time is spent on fighting fires and not enough on preventing them. Said Armey, "GPRA forces us to take the long view: to consider our goals and measure our results."[68] These are indeed worthy efforts.

Conclusion

Our overall conclusion is that while GPRA and the CFO Act are worthy reform initiatives, less will be accomplished in their implementation than was desired by those who drafted, supported, and passed these laws. For example, CFO Act accrual accounting requirements for the federal government are not likely to be implemented due to cost and absence of funding, and also because of strong objections from Congress. Likewise, GPRA implementation is less than sought because performance measurement is difficult and expensive. Many federal government department and agency financial management and other executives do not see the value of GPRA when neither OMB nor Congress is clear about how performance data will be used. Finally, in terms of the integration of theory and practice, we observe that Aaron Wildavsky's thesis about the incremental nature of budgetary change is supported with respect to financial management, as well by evidence on implementation of the CFO Act, GPRA, and other federal government reform initiatives.

Notes

1. See Justine Rodriquez, "Connecting Resources with Results," *Public Budgeting and Finance* (winter 1996): 2–4.

2. Rodriquez, 3.

3. Rodriquez, 3.

4. For example, other legislation designed to improve financial management at the federal level included the Federal Managers Financial Integrity Act, the Inspector General Act, the Debt Collection Act, the Prompt Payment Act, the Single Audit Act, the Federal Grant and Cooperative Agreement Act, the Competition in Contracting Act, the Debt Collection Act and the Intergovernmental Cooperation Act. (Statement of John L. Lordan. *Hearings on Improving Federal Financial Management*, House of Representatives, Committee on Government Operations, Sub-Committee on Legislation and National Security. 100th Congress, 2nd Session, September 22, 1988. Washington: USGPO, 1989.)

5. House of Representatives Report no. 101-818, 101st Congress, 2d Session, pt. 1., *Chief Financial Officer Act of 1990,* 14.

6. Previous research has reported on the objectives and initial steps taken to implement this act. See L. R. Jones and Jerry L. McCaffery, "A Symposium: Federal Financial Management Reform," *Public Budgeting and Finance,* 12, no. 4 (winter 1992): 70–106. Also see *Public Budgeting and Finance* 13, no. 1 (spring 1993): 59–94.

7. PL 103-356 1994, also referred to as the *Federal Financial Management Act of 1994.*

8. This act requires each agency to establish internal controls that provide reasonable assurance that obligations and costs are in compliance with applicable law; that fund, property, and other assets are safeguarded against waste loss or abuse; and that revenues and expenditures are properly recorded. See Allen Schick, Robert Keith, and Edward Davis, *Manual on the*

Federal Budget Process (Washington, DC: Library of Congress, Congressional Research Service, 1991), 187.

9. P.L. 95-452, Oct. 12, 1978. The *Inspector General Act of 1978* is the legal foundation of the IG Community. It has created more than 60 IGs in federal agencies and given them wide authority to conduct audits, investigations, and inspections in their agencies. The purpose of the IGs is to promote economy, efficiency, and effectiveness, and to prevent and detect fraud and abuse. The act gives the IGs independence of action by providing for separate administrative authority, direct reporting to Congress, and protection against removal. Another major reform not addressed in this article is the *Information Technology Management Reform Act of 1996* (P. L. 104-106, February 10,1996).

10. L. R. Jones and J. McCaffery, "Implementation of the CFO Act," *Public Budgeting and Finance,* 13, no. 1 (spring 1993): 68–76. See also L. R. Jones and J. McCaffery, "Federal Financial Management Reform and the Chief Financial Officer's Act," *Public Budgeting and Finance,* 12, no. 4 (winter 1992): 75–86.

11. Frank Hodsoll, "Facing the Facts of the CFO Act," *Public Budgeting and Finance,* 12, no. 4 (winter 1992): 72–74.

12. Charles Bowsher, "Government Financial Management at the Crossroads: The Choice is Between Reactive and Productive Financial Management," *Public Budgeting and Finance,* 3, no. 2 (1985): 21.

13. Researchers interested in this area are directed to the following sources: the *Federal Financial Management Status Report and Five Year Plan* produced each July by the Office of Management and Budget; annual JFMIP reports, e.g., *Report on Financial Management Improvements,* 1993; records of Hearings held by the Senate Governmental Affairs Committee and the House Committee on Government Reform and Oversight and its subcommittee on Government Management, Information and Technology; and various GAO publications and reports. For example: *Executive Guide: Effectively Implementing the Government Performance and Results Act.* Washington, DC: GAO/GGD-96-118, June, 1996; *Managing for Results: Achieving GPRA's Objectives Requires Strong Congressional Role.* Washington, DC: GAO/T-GGD-96-79; see also GAO reports GAO/T-GGD-AIMD-95-187, GAO/GGD-95-20, GAO/GGD-95-22, GAO/T-GGD-95-187, GAO/T-GGD/AIMD-95-158, and GAO/AFMD-93-4. See also reports issued by OMB; for example, OMB Circular A-11, OMB Memoranda 95-05, 95-19, 96-18, and 96-22. See also OMB *Primer on Performance Measurement,* February 28, 1995. The CFO Council issues reports from time to time, as do JFMIP and FASAB. Financenet on the Internet is an excellent clearinghouse for citations to many of these vehicles; it also has reports, testimony, and briefs that may be downloaded. There are also subscription lists that will distribute electronic mail on various topics and to which one may post questions. Lastly, the federal budget carries various summary schedules, including the list of federal financial high risk entities and financial management reports OMB recommends

be discontinued; in the FY 1997 budget, there is a carefully written explanation describing the development of a framework for evaluating the stewardship of resources, somewhat similar to a business balance sheet. This framework requires three charts and five tables to explain what would normally be presented in a business balance sheet. See "Stewardship: Toward a Federal Balance Sheet," 15–31, *Analytical Perspectives, Budget of the U.S. FY97.* See also Al Gore, *Reaching Public Goals: Managing Government for Results,* Resource Guide, National Performance Review, October 1996.

14. See "DON CFO Statements Issued," *DC Connection,* 15, (January 1997): 3.

15. See "FASAB Standards Completed and Signed by Principals," *JFMIP News,* 8, no. 2 (summer 1996): 2. The FASAB June newsletter notes that the new standards signal the beginning of the creation of a reliable and meaningful database to better report on the financial condition of federal government entities and mark the first time cost accounting requirements will be imposed to help measure the cost of outputs as called for under GPRA. Developing the standards took about five years. Former standards were not accepted because they were based on private sector standards and the "for profit" reporting model. The new accounting standards have been "uniquely designed" to provide useful information for those interested in analyzing the financial condition and cost of government programs. See the June 1996 FASAB Newsletter: 1.

16. Testimony of J. Christopher Mihm, Associate Director, Federal Management and Workforce Issues of the General Government Division of the U.S. General Accounting Office, before the House Committee on Government Reform, Subcommittee on Government Management, Information and Technology, July 20, 2000.

17. Federal Financial Management Status Report and Five Year Plan prepared by the CFO Council and OMB, October 1998. This series of reports is referred to hereafter as the OMB Five Year Plan.

18. OMB Five Year Plan, 1995, table 2.

19. OMB Five Year Plan, October 1998: 5.

20. OMB Five Year Plan, November, 20, 2000: 1.

21. OMB Five Year Plan, November, 20, 2000: 7.

22. OMB Five Year Plan, November, 20, 2000: 1.

23. Ibid.

24. Jerry L. McCaffery and L. R. Jones, *Budgeting and Financial Management in the Federal Government* (Greenwich, CT: Information Age Press, 2002).

25. L. R. Jones and Kenneth Euske, "Strategic Misrepresentation in Budgeting," *Journal of Public Administration Research and Theory,* 3, no. 3 (1991): 37–52.

26. L. R. Jones, et al. *Learning from International Public Management Reform* (New York: JAI-Elsevier Press, 2002).

27. See the Committee Report accompanying GPRA, Senate Report 103-58, especially pp. 18–19. See also Genevieve J. Knezo, *Government Performance and Results Act, P. L. 103-62: Interim Status Report: Revised*. CRS Report for Congress. 95-713 SPR. June 15, 1995.

28. "Managing for Results: Achieving GPRA's Objectives Requires Strong Congressional Role." Testimony, March 6, 1996, GAO/T-GGD-96-79: 5.

29. Al Gore, *Common Sense Government: Works Better and Costs Less*. Third report of the National Performance Review, Washington, DC: USGPO, 1995: 5.

30. Charles Bowsher, Comptroller General of the United States, statement before the Committee on Governmental Affairs of the U.S. Senate, December 14, 1995.

31. Joshua Gotbaum, Executive Associate Director and Controller, Acting Deputy Director for Management, U.S. Office of Management and Budget, in testimony before the House Committee on Government Reform, Subcommittee on Government Management, Information and Technology, July 20, 2000.

32. Ibid.

33. "Managing for Results: Achieving GPRA's Objectives Requires Strong Congressional Role," testimony, March 6, 1996, GAO/T-GGD-96-79: 5.

34. Rep. Dick Armey in testimony before the House Committee on Government Reform, Subcommittee on Government Management, Information and Technology, July 20, 2000.

35. Harold I. Steinberg, "The CFO Act: A Look at Federal Accountability," *Government Accounting* (March 1996): 57.

36. See part 2, OMB Circular A-11 *Preparation and Submission of Annual Budget Estimates* and the memorandum from the Director, Alice Rivlin entitled *Strategic Plans, Budget Formulation and Execution*, Washington, DC: OMB, 1995.

37. Alice M. Rivlin, "Linking Resources to Results: Management and Budgeting in a Time of Resource Constraints," *Public Manager* (summer 1995): 3.

38. GMRA accelerated the adoption of auditable financial statements, increased the number of CFOs, required a government-wide financial statement by 1998. See Al Gore, *Common Sense Government: Works Better and Costs Less, Third Report of the National Performance Review*, Washington, DC: USGPO, 1996.

39. Gotbaum, testimony.

40. Sean O'Keefe, letter, May 11, 2001.

41. See the Federal Workforce Restructuring Act (FWRA) of 1994 (P. L. 103-226) that made these cuts was enacted March 30, 1994. See also P.L.103-130, 1994. (Congressional Quarterly 1994: 2872); see also statement by Alice Rivlin, Director of OMB before the Senate Committee on Governmental Affairs. May 17, 1995: 4.

42. See statement of R. Scott Fosler, President of the National Academy of Public Administration before the Senate Committee on Governmental Affairs, May 17, 1995. Federal News Service (FNS):193. By the end of 1994, federal employment had already been cut by 100,000 positions. (Rivlin statement, May 17, 1995. FNS: 176.)

43. From *Historical Statistics of the U.S. Budget,* FY2002. Table 17.5, 284

44. Fosler, statement, May 17, 1995. FNS: 93. Fosler also adds that there is some evidence that the most experienced and capable people are leaving government, sometimes enticed by buyouts, just at the time their special knowledge is needed.

45. Ibid.

46. See "FASAB Standards Completed and Signed by Principals," *FASAB Newsletter,* 35, no. 2 (June 1996): 2.

47. Recent GAO reports evaluating GPRA include: *Managing for Results: Barriers to Interagency Coordination,* GGD-00-106, Mar. 29, 2000 (23 pages); *Managing for Results: Challenges Agencies Face in Producing Credible Performance Information,* GGD-00-52, Feb. 4, 2000 (19 pages); *Managing for Results: Views on Ensuring the Usefulness of Agency Performance Information to Congress,* GGD-00-35, Jan. 26,2000 (35 pages); *Managing for Results: Measuring Program Results that are Under Limited Federal Control,* GGD-99-16, Dec. 11, 1998 (24 pages); *Managing for Results: Opportunities for Continued Improvements in Agencies' Performance Plans,* GGD/AIMD-99-215, July 20, 1999 (124 pages); *Managing for Results: Analytic Challenges in Measuring Performance,* HEHS/GGD-97-138, May 30, 1997 (44 pages).

48. OMBWATCH GPRA Study, 1999

49. Ellen Taylor, "Seven Years of GPRA: Has the Results Act Provided Results?" Testimony before the House Committee on Government Reform, Subcommittee on Government Management, Information and Technology, July 20, 2000.

50. Ibid. The data is taken from the EPA "1998 Toxics Release Inventory Data Summary," EPA-745-00-001, May 2000, p.4, but the data is so carefully qualified that it is difficult to judge what the real outcome is.

51. Christopher Mihm, Associate Director, Federal Management and Workforce Issues, General Government Division, GAO. Testimony before the House Committee on Government Reform, Subcommittee on Government Management, Information and Technology, July 20, 2000.

52. L. R. Jones, "Counterpoint Essay: Nine Reasons Why the CFO Act May Not Achieve Its Objective," *Public Budgeting and Finance,* 13, no. 1 (spring 1993): 87–94.

53. Ibid, 93.

54. OMBWATCH, GPRA Basic Information. GPRA 2000.

55. Jones, "Counterpoint," 88.

56. *Federal Financial Management Status Report and Five Year Plan,* July, 1992.Washington, DC:USGPO, 1992.

57. The IRS has been criticized by the GAO for its poor performance in redesigning and reengineering portions of its accounting systems. See GAO,

IRS Compliance Initiative, AIMD/GDD-95-220, August 1995; and GAO, *Financial Audit: Examination of IRS FY94 Financial Statements*, AIMD-95-141, August 1995. See also GAO financial audits of IRS for FY92, FY93, and FY95 (AIMD-93-2, 94-120, 96-101). The Department of Defense also has experienced difficulty in consolidating and redesigning its mammoth accounting system, partly due to the large number of individual systems operated by the Office of the Secretary and the three Military Departments. Responsibility for DOD system redesign and consolidation rests with the Defense Financial and Accounting System.

58. Bowsher, testimony, Committee on Governmental Affairs of the U.S. Senate, December 14, 1995.

59. *Five Year Plan*, 1995: 5.

60. "Foreword," *Five Year Plan*, 1995: iii. This estimate is required each year.

61. *Federal Financial Management Status Report and Five Year Plan*, November, 2000: 16.

62. *Federal Financial Management Status Report and Five Year Plan*, November, 2000: 6.

63. Jones, "Counterpoint," 89.

64. Jones, "Counterpoint," 92.

65. Aaron Wildavsky, *The Politics of the Budgetary Process* (Boston: Little, Brown and Co, 1964):111-113.

66. Review of earlier draft of this paper by Congressional staff, March 1996.

67. Ibid.

68. Armey, testimony, July 20, 2000.

Selected
Bibliography

Adler, Terry B. et al. "An Empirical Test of Transaction Cost Theory: Validating Control Typology." *Journal of Applied Management Studies,* 7 (1998): 185–200.

Ang, James S. "Agency Costs and Ownership Structure." *The Journal of Finance,* 55 (February 2000): 81–106.

Aronson, Richard J., and Eli Schwartz. *Management Policies in Local Government Finance.* 4th edition. Washington, DC: International City Management Association, 1996.

Ashley, Graham W. "Administrative Science as a Socially Constructed Truth." *Administrative Science Quarterly,* 30 (December 1985): 497–513.

Bajari, Patrick, and Steven Tadelis. "Incentives versus Transaction Costs: A Theory of Procurement Contracts." *Rand Journal of Economics,* 32 (autumn 2001): 387–407.

Barro, Robert J. "Ricardian Approach to Budget Deficits." *Journal of Economic Perspectives,* 3 (spring 1989): 37–54.

Bebczuk, Robert R. *Asymmetric Information in Financial Markets: Introduction and Applications.* Cambridge: Cambridge University Press, 2003.

Bennet, Robert J. *Decentralizational: Local Government and Markets.* London: Clarendon Press, 1990.

Break, George F. *Financing Governments in a Federal System.* Washington, DC: Brookings Institution, 1980.

Breton, Albert. *The Economic Theory of Representative Government.* Chicago: Aldine, 1974.

Buchanan, James M. *The Demand and Supply of Public Goods.* Chicago: Rand McNally, 1968.

Buchanan, James M. "Why Does Government Grow?" In *Budgets and Bureaucrats: The Sources of Government Growth,* ed. T. E. Borcherding. Durham, NC: Duke University Press, 1977: 3–18.

Buchanan, James M., and Gordon Tullock. *The Calculus of Consent.* Ann Arbor, MI: University of Michigan Press, 1962.

Capeci, John. "Credit Risk, Credit Ratings, and Municipal Bond Yields: A Panel Study." *National Tax Journal,* 44 (December 1991): 41–56.

Chandler, Alfred. "Organizational Capacities and the Theory of the Firm." *Journal of Economic Perspectives,* 6 (1992): 79–100.

Coe, Charles K. *Public Financial Management.* Englewood Cliffs, NJ: Prentice Hall, 1989.

Coombs, Hugh M., and D. E. Jenkins. *Public Sector Financial Management.* London: Chapman and Hall, 1991.

Crawford, Sue E., and Elinor Ostrom. "A Grammar of Institutions." *American Political Science Review,* 89 (September 1995): 582–600.

Drucker, Peter F. *The Practice of Management.* New York: Harper and Row, 1986.

Easton, David. *The Political System.* New York: Knopf, 1953.

Einhorn, Hillel J., and Robin M. Hogarth. "Decision Making Under Ambiguity." *Journal of Business,* 59 (October 1986): S225–S250.

Fisher, Lawrence. "Determinants of Risk Premiums on Corporate Bonds." *Journal of Political Economy,* 67 (June 1959): 217–237.

Fogarty, Timothy J. "Organizational Socialization in Accounting Firms: A Theoretical Framework and Agenda for Future Research." *Accounting, Organizations, and Society,* 17 (February 1992): 129–149.

Freeman, Robert J., and Craig D. Shoulders. *Governmental and Nonprofit Accounting: Theory and Practice.* 6th edition. Englewood Cliffs, NJ: Prentice Hall, 2000.

Friedman, Lee. S. *The Microeconomics of Public Policy Analysis.* Princeton, NJ: Princeton University Press, 2002.

Friedman, Milton. "The Methodology of Positive Economics." In *The Philosophy of Economics: An Anthology,* 2nd edition, ed. Daniel M. Hausman. Cambridge: Cambridge University Press, 1994: 180–213.

Gist, Hohn R. "Decision Making in Public Administration," in *Handbook of Public Administration,* 2nd edition, eds. Jack Rabin, W. Bartley Hildreth, and Gerald J. Miller. New York: Marcel Dekker, 1998: 265–291.

Golembiewski, Robert T. "Shortfalls of Public Administration as Empirical Science." *Public Administration Quarterly,* 23 (spring 1999): 3–17.

Golembiewski, Robert T., and Jack Rabin, eds. *Public Budgeting and Finance: Theory and Practice.* New York: Marcel Dekker, 1997.

Gul, Faruk. "A Theory of Disappointment Aversion." *Econometrica,* 59 (May 1991): 661–686.

Habermas, Jurgen. *Theory and Praxis.* Boston: Beacon Press, 1973.

Happenstall, Talbot C. Jr., and Roger G. Hayes. "The Path to Bond Market Efficiency: How Increased Retail Distribution Can Lower Borrowing Costs." *Government Finance Review,* 19 (June 2003): 25–28.

Harless, David W., and Colin F. Camerer. "The Predictive Utility of Generalized Expected Utility Theories." *Econometrica,* 62 (November 1994): 1251–1289.

Hasbrouck, Joel. "Assessing the Quality of a Security Market: A New Approach to Transaction-Cost Measurement." *Review of Financial Studies,* 6, no. 1, (1993): 191–212.

Hillier, Brian. *The Economics of Asymmetric Information.* New York: Palgrave MacMillan, 1997.

Hodgson, Geoffrey M. "The Approach to Institutional Economics." *Journal of Economic Literature,* 36 (March 1998): 166–192.

Johnson, Carig L. *Financing and Pricing E-Government Services: An Analysis of Web Portals.* Report for the Pricewaterhouse-Coopers Endowment for the Business of Government, October, 2001.

Kahneman, Daniel, and Amos Tversky. "Prospect Theory: An Analysis of Decision under Risk." *Econometrica,* 47 (March 1979): 263–292.

Kettl, Donald. *Sharing Power: Public Governance and Private Markets.* Washington, DC: Brookings Institution, 1993.

Key, V. O. Jr. "The Lack of a Budgetary Theory." *American Political Science Review,* 34 (December 1940): 1137–1140.

Khan, Aman, and W. Bartley Hildreth, eds. *Budget Theory in the Public Sector.* Westport, CT: Quorum Books, 2001.

Kiser, Edgar. "Comparing Varieties of Agency Theory in Economics, Political Science, and Sociology: An Illustration from State Policy Implementation." *Sociological Theory,* 7 (1999): 146–170.

Lamb, Robert, and Stephen P. Rappaport. *Municipal Bonds: The Comprehensive Review of Tax-Exempt Securities and Public Finance.* New York: McGraw-Hill, 1980.

Lerner, Josh. "The Government as Venture Capitalist: The Long-Run Impact of the SBIR Program," *Journal of Business,* 72 (July 1999): 285–318.

Lindblom, Charles. "The Science of Muddling Through." *Public Administration Review,* 19 (spring 1959): 79–88.

Livingston, Miles. "The Pricing of Municipal Bonds." *Journal of Financial and Quantitative Analysis,* 17 (June 1982): 179–193.

Loomes, Graham. "Regret Theory: An Alternative to Rational Choice under Uncertainty." *The Economic Journal,* 92 (December 1982): 805–824.

March, James G. *A Primer on Decision Making: How Decisions Happen.* New York: Free Press, 1994.

March, James G., and J. P. Olsen. *Ambiguity and Choice in Organizations.* Bergen, Norway: Universitetsforlaget, 1976.

Marlin, George J., and Joe Mysak. *The Guide to Municipal Bonds: The History, the Industry, the Mechanics.* New York: American Banker/BondBuiyer, 1991.

Maxwell, James, and J. R. Aronsosn. *Financing State and Local Governments.* Washington, DC: Brookings Institution, 1977.

McCaffery, Jerry L., and L. R. Jones. *Budgeting and Financial Management in the Federal Government.* Greenwich, CT: Information Age Press, 2002.

Melicher, Ronald W., and Edgar A. Norton. *Introduction to Institutions, Investments, and Management.* New York: John Wiley and Sons, 2003.

Milgrom, Paul, and John Roberts. "Information Asymmetries, Strategic Behavior, and Industrial Organization." *American Economic Review,* 77 (May 1987): 184–193.

Miller, Gerald J. *Government Financial Management Theory.* New York: Marcel Dekker, 1991.

Miller, Girard, and M. Corrine Larson. *Investing Public Funds.* Chicago: Government Finance Officers Association, 1998.

Myagkov, Mikhail, and Charles R. Plott. "Exchange Economics and Loss Exposure: Experiments Exploring Prospect Theory and Competitive Equilibria in Market Environments." *The American Economic Review,* 87 (December 1997): 801–828.

National Performance Review. *Improving Financial Management.* Accompanying report of the National Performance Review, ffice of the Vice President. Washington, DC: The Review, 1993.

Niskanen, William. *Bureaucracy and Representative Government.* Chicago: Aldine, 1971.

North, Douglas C. "A Transaction Cost Theory of Politics." *Journal of Theoretical Politics,* 2 (1990): 355–367.

Oates, Wallace E. "An Essay on Fiscal Federalism." *Journal of Economic Literature,* 37 (September 1999): 1120–1149.

Olson, Mancur. *The Logic of Collective Action.* Cambridge, MA: Harvard University Press, 1965.

Osborne, David, and Ted Gaebler. *Reinventing Government: How the Entrepreneurial Spirit Is Transforming the Public Sector.* Reading, MS: Addison-Wesley, 1992.

Ostrom, Elinor. *Governing the Commons: The Evolution of Institutions for Collective Action.* Cambridge: Cambridge University Press, 1990.

Ostrom, Elinor, Roy Gardner, and James Walker. *Rules, Games, and Common-Pool Resources.* Ann Arbor, MI: University of Michigan Press, 1994.

Pagano, Michael A., and Richard J. T. Moore. *Cities and Fiscal Choices: A New Model of Urban Public Investment.* Durham, NC: Duke University Press, 1985.

Petersen, John E., and Dennis R. Strachota, eds. *Local Government Finance: Concepts and Practices.* Chicago: Government Finance Officers Association, 1991.

Reed, B. J., and J. W. Swain. *Public Finance Administration.* Thousand Oaks, CA: Sage Publications, 1997.

Rose, Peter. "Financial Reporting." In *Handbook of Public Finance,* eds. Fred Thompson and Mark T. Green. New York: Marcel Dekker, 1998.

Rosen, Harvey S. *Public Finance.* Boston: McGraw-Hill, 2002.

Ross, Stephen A. "The Economic Theory of Agency: The Principal's Problem." *American Economic Review,* 63 (May 1973): 134–139.

Rubin, Irene S. *The Politics of Public Budgeting.* New York: Chatham House Publishers, 4th edition, 2000.

Saddler, Michelle R. B. "GFOA's New Model Investment Policy." *Government Finance Review,* 19 (December 2004): 41–45.

Shannon, John, and James E. Kee. "The Rise of Competitive Federalism." *Public Budgeting and Finance,* 9 (winter 1989): 5–20.

Simonsen, William and Larry Hill. "Municipal Bond Issuance: Is There Evidence of a Principal-Agent Problem?" *Public Budgeting and Finance,* 18 (winter 1998): 71–100.

Starmer, Chris. "Developments in Non-Expected Utility Theory: The Hunt for a Descriptive Theory of Choice under Risk." *Journal of Economic Literature,* 38 (June 2000): 332–382.

Tiebout, Charles M. "A Pure Theory of Local Expenditures." *Journal of Political Economy,* 64 (October 1956): 416–424.

Tullock, Gordon. *Private Wants, Public Means: An Economic Analysis of the Desirable Scope of Government.* New York: Basic Books, 1970.

Tversky, Amos, and Daniel Kahneman. "Rational Choice and the Framing of Decisions." *Journal of Business,* 59 (October 1986): S251-S278.

Tversky, Amos and Peter Wakker. "Risk Attitudes and Decision Weights." *Econometrica,* 63 (November 1995): 1255–1280.

Wildavsky, Aaron. *The Politics of the Budgetary Process.* Boston: Little, Brown and Company, 1964.

Williamson, Oliver E. *Markets and Hierarchies: Analysis and Antitrust Implications.* New York: Free Press, 1975.

Wu, Chunchi. "A Certainty Equivalent Approach to Municipal Bond Default Risk Estimation." *Journal of Financial Research,* 14 (fall 1991): 241–247.

Index

About the Editors and Contributors

WILLIAM G. ALBRECHT is assistant professor of political science and public administration at the University of North Carolina at Pembroke. Professor Albrecht received his BS in business administration from Ferrum College, his MBA from Western Carolina University, and his PhD in public policy with a concentration in public finance from Nelson Mandela School of Public Policy and Urban Affairs at Southern University. His current interests include public policy, budgeting and financial management, managerial economics, municipal administration, and investment practices of state and local government pension funds.

JOHN R. BARTLE is professor in the School of Public Administration, University of Nebraska at Omaha. His research and teaching interests are in the areas of public finance, budgeting and financial management, applied economics, and transportation. He has published work in numerous professional journals, including Public Budgeting and Finance, Public Administration Quarterly, Public Budgeting, Accounting and Financial Management, International Review of Public Administration, and State and Local Government Review. He is the editor of *Evolving Theories of Public Budgeting* (2001).

CURTIS E. BAYNES, CIA, is a certified internal auditor and senior legislative analyst with the Florida legislature's Office of Program Policy Analysis and Government Accountability.

BRIAN K. COLLINS is assistant professor and director of the graduate program in public administration at Texas Tech University. He has published academic research involving corporate tax policy and, as an employee for the National Council of State Governments, has published numerous reports regarding local government investment pools and cooperative state purchasing. He has directed several projects recently for state and federal agencies, including the National Highway Traffic Safety Administration and the Texas Office of Rural Community Affairs.

Professor Collins received his PhD in political science from Indiana University.

MERL HACKBART is professor of finance and public administration at the University of Kentucky. He previously served as budget director of the state of Kentucky, director of the Martin School of Public Administration at the University of Kentucky, and associate dean of the College of Business and Economics at the University of Kentucky. Professor Hackbart is also a senior fellow at the Council of State Governments and served as an appointed member of the Kentucky Council of Postsecondary education. His research has focused on public budgeting and financial management.

W. BARTLEY HILDRETH is the Regents Distinguished Professor of public finance in the Hugo Wall School of Urban and Public Affairs and the W. Frank Barton School of Business at Wichita State University. Professor Hildreth has authored many articles, books, and chapters, in addition to serving as a city finance director and a member of the National Advisory Council on State and Local Budgeting.

IRYNA ILLIASH is a PhD candidate with the Department of Public Administration, Rutgers University, Newark.

CRAIG L. JOHNSON is associate professor of public finance and policy analysis at the School of Public and Environmental Affairs, Indiana University–Bloomington. Professor Johnson received his MPA and PhD degrees from the State University of New York at Albany with specialization in public finance. He has authored numerous articles and research reports in the area of public financial management and financial markets, and has recently co-edited a volume on *Tax Increment Financing and Economic Development: Uses, Structures, and Impact.* His current research interest focus is in e-government involving pricing, financing, development, and evaluation of e-government services and investments.

LARRY R. JONES is a professor at the Naval Postgraduate School in Monterey, California, where he teaches public budgeting in the defense-focused MBA program. He has written extensively on budgeting and budget execution at federal and state levels. He is the author (with Professor Jerry McCaffery) of the recently published book, *Budgeting and Financial Management for National Defense* (2004). His current research interest is defense acquisition reform.

JONATHAN B. JUSTICE is assistant professor in the School of Urban Affairs and Public Policy and an associate policy scientist in the Institute for Public Administration of the College of Human Services, Education and Public Policy at the University of Delaware. His professional experience, research, and teaching activities include public budgeting and finance, local economic development, accountability and decision making, institutional analysis and development, and nongovernmental and collaborative public administration.

JAMES EDWIN KEE is professor of public policy and administration at the George Washington University. Professor Kee has had an extensive career in state government administration in New York and Utah. He was counsel to the New York State Legislature and served under two Utah governors as state planning coordinator, state budget director, and executive director of the Department of Administrative Services. His publications include, among others, *Out of Balance* (with Scott Matheson), "The Crisis and the Anticrisis Dynamic: Reshaping the American Federal System" in *Public Administration Review*, and "Benefit-Cost Analysis" in *Handbook of Practical Program Evaluation.*

AMAN KHAN is associate professor of political science and public administration at Texas Tech University, where he teaches public budgeting, financial management, and quantitative methods. He has previously served as director of the graduate program in public administration at Texas Tech University and currently serves on the editorial boards of several professional administration journals. Author and coauthor of several books, Professor Khan has contributed work to various edited and professional journals.

WILLIAM EARLE KLAY, CGFM, is professor and former director of the Reubin Askew School of Public Administration and Policy at Florida State University, where he teaches public budgeting and financial management. A former senior governmental associate in Florida's Executive Office of the Governor, Professor Klay served as a policy analyst for the Georgia General Assembly, and a faculty member at Mississippi State University and the University of Georgia. He also served as a logistics systems specialist for the U.S. Department of Defense and a captain in the U.S. Army.

KENNETH A. KRIZ is assistant professor of public financial management and policy at the School of Public Administration, University of Nebraska at Omaha. His research focuses on municipal debt management, financial risk management, economic development policy, and transportation finance. Professor Kriz has worked in the public sector as a U.S. Navy supply officer, in private sector financial services firms, and has consulted with several public and nonprofit organizations on financial and economic issues. He is a frequent presenter at budgeting and financial management conferences and has published papers in the areas of municipal bond issuance, revenue limitation initiatives, and tax increment financing. Professor Kriz received his PhD in public affairs from Indiana University.

Rev. THOMAS D. LYNCH is professor of public administration at Louisiana State University. He has published numerous articles in various professional journals and is the author of twelve books, including *Public Budgeting in America,* which has been in print for 30 years and is in its 5th edition. Conceptually, his major contribution was developing and applying systems theory to public budgeting.

JUN MA is associate professor in the Center for Public Administration, College of Politics and Public Affairs at Zhongshan University in People's Republic of China. His current interests include public budgeting and financial management, new institutional economics, public management, and administrative history. His publications have appeared in the *Journal of Administrative Theory and Praxis* and in several Chinese journals, including *Economic Studies.*

LAWRENCE L. MARTIN is professor of public affairs and director of the Center for Community Partnership at the University of Central Florida in Orlando. Prior to becoming an academic, Professor Martin worked for some 15 years as a state and local government administrator. His research interests include public budgeting and financial management, social services administration, privatization, contracting out, public-private competition, performance measurement, and, most recently, outcome budgeting.

JERRY L. MCCAFFERY is professor of budgeting and finance at the Naval Postgraduate School in Monterey, California, where he teaches public budgeting in the defense-focused MBA program. He has written extensively on budgeting and budget execution at federal and state levels. He is the author (with Professor L. R. Jones) of the recently published book, *Budgeting and Financial Management for National Defense* (2004). His current research interest is defense acquisition reform.

SAM M. MCCALL, CPA, CIA, CGFM, is the auditor of the city of Tallahassee and formerly deputy auditor general of Florida. He was the 1997 recipient of the AICPA's outstanding CPA in Governmental Award.

GERALD J. MILLER is professor of public budgeting and finance in the graduate department of Public Administration at Rutgers University, the State University of New Jersey, Newark. Author of over 50 research articles and 18 books, his work includes *Government Financial Management Theory* and *Handbook of Debt Management.* Professor Miller received his BS in economics and MPA from Auburn University, and his PhD in political science from the University of Georgia.

JAMES R. RAMSEY is president and professor of economics at the University of Louisville. He previously served as Kentucky's state budget director and held positions at Western Kentucky University and the University of North Carolina. He also served as chief economist for the state of Kentucky and as member of the Kentucky Consensus Revenue Forecasting Group. Professor Ramsey's research has emphasized public budgeting and financial management, debt finance, and related topics.